THE HOLOCAUST

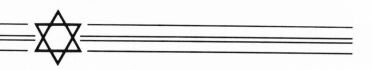

Selected Documents in Eighteen Volumes

John Mendelsohn
EDITOR

Donald S. Detwiler
ADVISORY EDITOR

A GARLAND SERIES

CONTENTS OF THE SERIES

THE HOLOCAUST

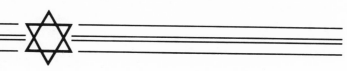

18. Punishing the Perpetrators of the Holocaust
The Ohlendorf and Von Weizsaecker Cases

Introduction by
John Mendelsohn

GARLAND PUBLISHING, INC.
NEW YORK • LONDON
1982

These documents have been reproduced from copies in
the National Archives. Dr. Mendelsohn's work was carried out entirely on his own time and without endorse-
ment or official participation by the National Archives as
an agency.

Library of Congress Cataloging in Publication Data
Main entry under title:

Punishing the perpetrators of the Holocaust.

(The Holocaust ; 18)
Contents: The Ohlendorf and Von Weizsaecker cases.
1. Holocaust, Jewish (1939–1945)—Sources.
2. Nuremberg War Crime Trials, 1946–1949.
I. Mendelsohn, John, 1928–   . II. Series.
D810.J4H655 vol. 18   940.53'15'03924s   81-80326
ISBN 0-8240-4892-X   [364.1'38]   AACR2

Design by Jonathan Billing

The volumes in this series have been printed on acid-free,
250-year-life paper.

Printed in the United States of America

ACKNOWLEDGMENTS

I owe a debt of gratitude to many people who aided me during various stages of preparing these eighteen volumes. Of these I would like to mention by name a few without whose generous efforts this publication would have been impossible. I would like to thank Donald B. Schewe of the Franklin D. Roosevelt Library in Hyde Park, New York, for his speedy and effective help. Sally Marcks and Richard Gould of the Diplomatic Branch of the National Archives in Washington, D.C., extended help beyond their normal archival duties, as did Timothy Mulligan and George Wagner from the Modern Military Branch. Edward J. McCarter in the Still Picture Branch helped a great deal. I would also like to thank my wife, Tish, for letting me spend my evenings during the past few years with these volumes rather than with her and our children, Michael and Lisa.

J. M.

INTRODUCTION

Perhaps the most visible trials of the perpetrators of the Holocaust were those held at Nuernberg. The indictments of each of the thirteen cases against the major war criminals included charges of crimes against Jews. The trials were complicated legal proceedings. The prosecution of the Nuernberg trials, including those of Otto Ohlendorf *et al.* (the *Einsatzgruppen* case) and of Ernst von Weizsaecker *et al.* (the *Wilhelmstrasse* or ministries case), relied largely on documentary evidence rather than on the testimony of witnesses in court, despite the willingness of many thousands of Europeans to testify to their suffering or witnessing Nazi atrocities. The prosecution thought that such evidence would presumably be more incontestable than affidavits and direct testimony of witnesses who might easily be brought by defense lawyers to waver in their statements during cross-examination. In the Ohlendorf case the prosecution presented 252 documentary exhibits and in the von Weizsaecker case nearly 4400 to the tribunals. In the course of the various Nuernberg trials the prosecution chose from the millions of records available to them about eighteen thousand to be presented as evidence to the tribunals. Only twenty-five hundred of these were depositions, although thousands of additional pretrial interrogation transcripts were available. The exhibits were generally presented to the tribunals in the form of document books. Actually the name document book is somewhat misleading, since the contents of the book consisted of mimeographed copies of documents either in their original language or translated into English, fastened or loosely placed inside manilla folders. Hundreds of these document books were in use in the Palace of Justice in Nuernberg from 1945 to 1949. They were the most frequently used court documents and represented a convenient means to conduct multilingual proceedings with massive documentary evidence.

The prosecution briefs often included summaries of the background and criminal involvement of the defendants. In the *Einsatzgruppen* case, for example, they included detailed summaries of the backgrounds of the twenty-two defendants convicted of murdering over a million people in the Soviet Union. Four *Einsatzgruppen* followed the German Army Groups invading the Soviet Union in June 1941 in order to provide security for the conquered territory and to murder Jews as well as other groups such as communists and gypsies. *Einsatzgruppe* A was assigned mainly to the Baltic region, *Einsatzgruppe* B to Smolensk and the surrounding area, *Einsatzgruppe* C to the region around Kiev, including the site of the Babi Yar massacre, and *Einsatzgruppe* D to

Judges of the United States military tribunals at Nuernberg

Standing from left to right: Victor B. Swearingen, Johnson T. Crawford, Michael A. Musmanno, Justin W. Harding, Carrington T. Marshall, William C. Christianson, Richard D. Dixon, George J. Burke, Paul M. Herbert, Clarence F. Merrell; *seated from left to right:* Walter B. Beals, John J. Speight, Harold L. Sebring, Mallory B. Blair, Robert M. Toms, Lee B. Wyatt, James T. Brand, Charles F. Wennerstrom, Curtis G. Shake, Frank N. Richman, Edward F. Carter, Daniel T. O'Connor

National Archives Still Picture Collection, Record Group 238

southern Russia, including the Crimean. Otto Ohlendorf, the chief of *Einsatzgruppe* D, admitted before the International Military Tribunal at Nuernberg that his unit killed over ninety thousand, mostly Jews, during the period of roughly one year when he was in command.

The primary evidence against these mass murderers was the Operational Situation Reports USSR, which were produced in Berlin from the reports of the mobile killing units. The chiefs and commanders of these units, subdivided into *Einsatzkommandos*, *Sonderkommandos*, and *Vorkommandos*, were generally educated persons. Nearly half of them had studied law or economics; one held a chair of political science at the University of Berlin; and an opera singer, an architect, a historian, a dentist, and even a Protestant minister were included among them. Yet together they carried out the most ruthless and massive murder in recorded history.

In the Ernst von Weizsaecker case the officials of several governmental agencies were convicted of complicity in the mass murder of Jews. These included members of the Foreign Ministry who participated in making deportations possible from a diplomatic aspect, leaders of the Finance Ministry who were found guilty of storing and utilizing the concentration camp loot including melted dental gold taken from the victims, and two high-ranking SS generals who were found guilty of facilitating deportations and killings. Executives of the Food and Agriculture Ministry and agencies dealing with industry were held responsible for discriminating against Jews, as were bureaucrats in the Ministry of the Interior and the Reich chancellery. Also responsible for anti-Semitic propaganda was the Reich press chief.

The documents selected for reproduction in this volume are trial briefs, closing briefs, and final briefs against defendants tried in the Ohlendorf and von Weizsaecker cases. They were all taken from the Nuernberg Trials record collection in the National Archives. These documents include briefs against the three *Einsatzgruppen* leaders who were tried by the United States Military Tribunal 2A at Nuernberg: Otto Ohlendorf, Heinz Jost, and Erich Naumann. They were unable to convince the tribunal that their actions were necessitated by military requirements and were consequently convicted. Ohlendorf and Naumann were sentenced to death and executed in Landsberg Prison on June 7, 1951. Jost was sentenced to life imprisonment, but his sentence was commuted to a ten-year term, and he was released in 1951. Also included are briefs against four men convicted of killing many thousand Jews: Werner Braune, who carried out the Christmas Massacre at Simferopol; Walter Haensch; Erwin Schulz; and Franz Six, who commanded *Vorkommando* Moscow, which never reached its assigned destination. Braune was executed with Ohlendorf and Naumann on June 7, 1951. Haensch was sentenced to death, but his sentence was commuted to a term of fifteen years and he was released from Landsberg Prison in 1955. Also released in 1955 was Erwin Schulz, who had originally been sentenced to twenty years. His sentence was commuted to a term of fifteen years by High Commissioner John J. McCloy in 1951. Six was sentenced to twenty years also, but his sentence was commuted to ten years and he was released from prison in 1952.

This volume also contains briefs against four men convicted in the von Weizsaecker case, partly for crimes against Jews. Gottlob Berger, known in the upper echelons of the SS as "the almighty Gottlob," was convicted for his complicity in the killing of Jews in Minsk and deportations from various countries; Reich Finance Minister von Krosigk for his part in dealing with the belongings taken from Jews; Lammers, the chief of the Reich chancellery, for aiding in providing a legal basis for the persecution of the Jews; and Ambassador Ritter from the German Foreign Office for facilitating the deportation of Jews. Berger was sentenced to a prison term of twenty-five years, which was commuted to ten years; he was released in the early fifties. Lammers's original term of twenty years was commuted to ten, and he was released in 1951. Von Krosigk was sentenced to ten years imprisonment, and he was released in 1951. Ritter was released in 1950 after receiving a seven-year term.

The punishment of the perpetrators of the Holocaust varied considerably. Some were punished and killed without any judicial proceedings immediately following the end of the Second World War. Others were tried in more than one country and received widely differing sentences. Often the worst offenders were tried first when the brutality of their crimes was still fresh in the memories of judges and counsels. Hence sentences tended to be stiff at first, but became more lenient as time progressed. Most *Einsatzgruppen* personnel were tried in West Germany. Those tried by United States Military Tribunal IIA at Nuernberg received severe punishment, including fourteen death sentences. Only four were executed, however, and the sentences of the remaining convicts were commuted, ensuring their release from prison by 1958. United States Army courts trying concentration camp personnel meted out heavier sentences with less drastic reductions. Many more death sentences were carried out in these cases than in the United States military cases at Nuernberg, but as with the Nuernberg cases all Army war crimes prisoners were released by the end of June 1958. Today the only perpetrators of the Holocaust jailed in the Federal Republic of Germany are a few sentenced by West German courts.

The briefs reproduced in this volume often include references to documentary prosecution exhibits or pages in the English language version of the transcripts of the proceedings. In the closing brief against Colonel Werner Braune (Document 1), for example, Prosecution Exhibit 52 is the Operational Situation Report USSR No. 165, and Prosecution Exhibit 163 is an affidavit by Braune taken September 30, 1947. The letter R followed by a numeral refers to a page in the English language version of the transcript of the proceedings. Thus R-3010 is page 3010 in that transcript, where Braune was examined by his counsel, Erich Mayer, before the U.S. Military Tribunal trying him. *Special List No. 42. Nuernberg War Crimes Trials. Records of Case 9. United States of America v. Otto Ohlendorf et al. September 15, 1947–April 10, 1948*, comp. John Mendelsohn (Washington, D.C.: National Archives and Records Service, 1978), is a guide to all the references of the Ohlendorf case. Microfilm Publication M895 for the Ohlendorf case and M897 for the von Weizsaecker case with its descriptive pamphlet, which may be consulted in the National Archives in Washington or obtained from that institution, contain further information on these references.

John Mendelsohn

SOURCE ABBREVIATIONS
AND DESCRIPTIONS

Nuernberg Document Records from five of the twenty-five Nuernberg Trials prosecution document series: the NG (Nuernberg Government) series, the NI (Nuernberg Industrialist) series, the NO (Nuernberg Organizations) series, the NOKW (Nuernberg Armed Forces High Command) series, and the PS (Paris-Storey) series. Also included are such Nuernberg Trials prosecution records as interviews, interrogations, and affidavits, excerpts from the transcripts of the proceedings, briefs, judgments, and sentences. These records were used by the prosecution staff of the International Military Tribunal at Nuernberg or the twelve United States military tribunals there, and they are part of National Archives Record Group 238, National Archives Collection of World War II War Crimes Records.

OSS Reports by the Office of Strategic Services in National Archives Record Group 226.

SEA Staff Evidence Analysis: a description of documents used by the Nuernberg prosecution staff. Although the SEA's tended to describe only the evidentiary parts of the documents in the summaries, they describe the document title, date, and sources quite accurately.

State CDF Central Decimal File: records of the Department of State in National Archives Record Group 59, General Records of the Department of State.

T 120 Microfilm Publication T 120: records of the German foreign office received from the Department of State in Record Group 242, National Archives Collection of Foreign Records Seized, 1941–. The following citation system is used for National Archives

Microfilm Publications: The Microfilm Publication number followed by a slash, the roll number followed by a slash, and the frame number(s). For example, Document 1 in Volume I: T 120/4638/K325518— K325538.

T 175

Microfilm Publication T 175: records of the Reich leader of the SS and of the chief of the German police in Record Group 242.

U.S. Army and U.S. Air Force

Records relating to the attempts to cause the U.S. Army Air Force to bomb the extermination facilities at Auschwitz and the railroad center at Kaschau leading to Auschwitz, which are part of a variety of records groups and collections in the National Archives. Included are records of the United States Strategic Bombing Survey (Record Group 243), records of the War Refugee Board (Record Group 220), records of the Joint Chiefs of Staff, and other Army record collections.

War Refugee Board

Records of the War Refugee Board, located at the Franklin D. Roosevelt Library in Hyde Park, New York. They are part of National Archives Record Group 220, Records of Temporary Committees, Commissions and Boards. Included in this category are the papers of Myron C. Taylor and Ira Hirschmann.

CONTENTS

M I L I T A R Y _ T R I B U N A L _ N O. _ II

Case No. IX

CLOSING BRIEF FOR

THE UNITED STATES OF AMERICA

AGAINST

WERNER BRAUNE

BENJAMIN B. FERENCZ
        Chief Prosecutor
PETER W. WALTON
ARNOST HORLIK-HOCHWALD
JOHN E. GLANCY

For:

TELFORD TAYLOR
Brigadier General, U.S.A.,
Chief of Counsel for War Crimes

Doc. 1

1

and

JAMES M. McHANEY
Deputy Chief of Counsel
        for War Crimes

Alfred Schwarz
Nancy H. Fenstermacher
    Research Assistants

Nurnberg, Germany
    January 1948

INTRODUCTION

Count One of the Indictment charges that between May 1941 and July 1943 Dr. Werner BRAUNE was the commanding officer of Einsatzkommando 11b, one of the component parts of Einsatzgruppe D. As did all other sub-units of the Gruppe, it did its proportionate part in virtually removing all existing and potential threats to the security of the German Armed Forces in the occupied territories of Russia. Count One further charges that the defendant committed crimes against Humanity in that he was a principal in, accessory to, ordered, abetted, took a consenting part in and was connected with plans and enterprises involving the commission of such crimes. The crimes set forth in the bill of particulars under this Count of the Indictment were part and parcel of the over-all plan and policy of the National Socialist State to destroy foreign races and ethnic groups by murder.

It is further charged in this Count of the Indictment that Dr. Werner BRAUNE, by his connection to the plans for commission of these crimes and in acting as an Einsatzkommando leader, organizer, instigator, and accomplice in these stated crimes, became individually responsible for the acts of others performed in the execution of the aforesaid plans and enterprises (Paragraph 9 of Count One). It is also charged that within the period covered by the Indictment, Einsatzkommando 11b murdered over 700 persons in the Simferopol area.

Count Two charges that the crimes committed by the defendant Dr. Werner BRAUNE were committed between 22 June 1941 and July 1943 against the persons and property of inhabitants of occupied territories, non-citizens of Germany and such acts were not justified for reasons of military necessity.

Count Three charges that Dr. Werner BRAUNE was, after 1 September 1939 a member of the SS, the SD, and the Gestapo, organizations declared to be criminal by the International Military Tribunal.

The acts recognized as Crimes against Humanity and War Crimes, are set out in Paragraph 1 (b) and (c) of Article II of Control Council Law No. 10. Membership in organizations declared criminal by the International Military Tribunal is defined as a crime in Paragraph 1 (d) of the same Article.

Criteria of criminality are established by Paragraph 2 of Article II of Control Council Law No. 10.

POSITIONS OF RESPONSIBILITY

The defendant Dr. Werner BRAUNE was born on 11 April 1909 in the village of Meerstadt, Thuringia. He was educated in the schools in Meerstadt and in Sondershausen and attended the Universities of Bonn, Munich, and Jena. In the University of Jena he took his law degree in July 1932. He became a Doctor of Juridical Science from Jena in January 1933. For three years he took practical training in the law in various localities; finally in May 1936, in Berlin, he successfully completed his "Assessor" examination. (Doc. Bk. III D, p. 54, Doc. NO-4234, Pros. Ex. 163).

On 15 May 1931, defendant joined the NSDAP because he was desirous of taking part in political events (R-3008). Since there was a surplus of governmental attorneys, this defendant was unable to find suitable employment, and through the intercession of friends he joined the SD in November 1934 (R-3010). On cross-examination, however, BRAUNE admitted that he joined the SD voluntarily on

18 November 1934 and that he knew when he volunteered
for service with the SD he would also become a member
of the SS. (R-3132). From his direct testimony it can
be seen that he was one of the founders of the SD organization (R-3013). In the fall of 1937 the defendant was
transferred to the Gestapo (R-3134) in which organization
he rose in rank until he became Chief of the Gestapo
office located in Halle der Salle, by May 1941 (Doc.
NO-4234 cited supra). He remained a member of all three
organizations until the capitulation of Germany on 8 May
1945.

The defendant in October 1941 was transferred to
Einsatzgruppe D (R-3031), arriving in Nikolajew about
the 21st that same month. (R-3032). He was shortly
thereafter assigned as Chief of Kommando 11b by his
co-defendant Otto OHLENDORF (R-3033) and formally took
over the Kommando during the first days of November 1941
(R-3039). He led this unit of Einsatzgruppe D into the
Crimean Peninsula and saw service as its leader until he
returned to his former position in the Gestapo in August
or September 1942 (Doc. NO-4234) cited supra.

At the beginning of the year 1943 he became Chief
of the German Academic Exchange Service in Berlin and in
December 1944 he was appointed Commander of the Security
Police and SD in Oslo, Norway, where he remained until
the end of the War. (Doc. NO-4234, cited supra).

ACTIVITY IN EINSATZKOMMANDO 11-B

Some time during the first part of the month of
October 1941, BRAUNE received an order from Berlin to
report to Einsatzgruppe D. On 18 October 1941 he left
Berlin in the company of his Chief, Otto OHLENDORF and

arrived in Nikolajew some three or four days later
(R-3031 and 3032). A few days afterwards he was assigned
to Einsatzkommando 11-B but he did not immediately report
to that sub-unit. He spent the intervening time
acquainting himself with his duties of a kommando leader
by means of discussions with staff members of the
Einsatzgruppe and with other kommando leaders, and by
reading the office files and reports (R-3033). Before he
left he discussed his duties and missions with his Chief,
who confirmed the Hitler Order for the liquidation of all
Jews in the conquered territories of the East (R-3034).

He arrived in Odessa, where Kommando 11-B was then
located, and formally took over his command during the
first days of November 1941 (R-3039). BRAUNE stated that
some ten days after he assumed command, his Kommando was
ordered to move to the Crimea and that he left shortly
after 20 November, but he denies that his Kommando ever
carried out any executions in Odessa (R-3077). In the
last days of November 1941, he, with the forward units of
his command, arrived at Simferopol in the Crimea and set
up the Kommando headquarters in the same building with the
headquarters of Einsatzgruppe D. (R-3078-79). By the
middle of December he had units of his command operating
in the Russian towns of Karasubasar, Aluschta and Eupatoria
as well as Simferopol (R-3079, R-3105, R-3106). He was
continuously active as Commander of Einsatzkommando 11-B
until sometime during the "first half of March 1942", when
he went on leave. He was absent until 26 April 1942
when he returned to his command (R-3115). He was again
active in command until the end of July 1942 when he was
relieved and left the Crimea. During this latter period
the Kommando was attached to the First Armored Army and
moved with it from Rostov to Maikop, in the Northern part
of the Caucasus (R-3124). On his return to Germany,
after another period of leave, he resumed his Gestapo
office in Halle. (R-3125).

5

Should the statements made by BRAUNE from the witness stand be accepted in their entirety and his explanations as gospel, then there are even yet some points of the Prosecution's case in chief totally unexplained, and a close examination of the documents reveal that he has confirmed the charge of murder laid against him. He admits that his teil kommandos were present in Aluschta and Karasubasar from the beginning of December and in Eupatoria from the 10th of December 1941 (R-3089). He further admitted that his Kommando had a sub-kommando in Aluschta until the end of July 1942. (See answer to first question. R-3169).

In a report dated 6 February 1942 which is in Document Book IIA, p. 115, Document NO-3401, Pros. Ex. 52, it is stated:

> "As a result of the search for communists and other untrustworthy elements in the area Simferopol, Karasubasar, Aluschta, and Eupatoria, and especially as a result of the use of a network of special confidential agents, it was possible during the period covered by this report, to apprehend and shoot, for instance alone in Simferopol besides Jews, more than 100 Communist NKWD agents and saboteurs." (Emphasis supplied).

The language of the report shows that it covered the latter part of January and the first part of February 1942. BRAUNE was in this area with his kommando at this time. His headquarters was in Simferopol at least until April 26, 1942. (R-3115 cited supra).

In another report which specifically mentions the activities of Kommandos 10b, 11a and 11b in the Crimea from 16 to 28 February 1942, it is stated that 1515 persons were shot, 729 of them Jews, 271 communists, 421 gypsies

and 74 saboteurs. (Document Book IIA, pp. 122-123,
Doc. NO-3241, Pros. Ex. 83). Certainly BRAUNE must
assume responsibility for his proportionate share of
these killings.

The third report on which BRAUNE carefully avoided
comment, showing the date of 25 March 1942, is contained
in Document Book II-A, p. 126, Doc. NO-3235, Pros. Ex. 54.
This is a report of events during the month of March 1942
and under the activities of Einsatzgruppe D it says in
part:

> "The_territory_south_of_Karasubasar,_
> investigations for the preparation of
> extensive actions on the part of the
> Wehrmacht were carried out by_the_kommando
> stationed there.
> "The removal of asocial elements led to
> the fact that 800 gypsies and insane
> people were rendered harmless." (Emphasis supplied).

If all of these people were slaughtered by the Wehrmacht,
as the defense would have the Tribunal believe, then the
Kommando 11-B is particeps criminis for rounding up
these people and turning them over for slaughter to the
Wehrmacht. If, however, as can be reasonably assumed
from reading this report, that the Kommando at Karasubasar
was performing its normal function in accordance with its
basic mission of securing the rear areas while the Wehrmacht
engaged in "extensive actions" on the fighting front, then
Kommando 11-B is reporting on the investigations and
the results, i.e., the slaughter of 800 gypsies and
insane people to insure the security of the fighting
forces.

Should the defendant have, and/or offer an explanation
to the above cited documents which could be reasonably

7

accepted by an impartial Tribunal, he has stated under
oath that he is responsible for the execution of hundreds
of Jews, gypsies and Krimtchakes in Simferopol during
the first half of December 1941. (R-3091).   While
BRAUNE attempts to show that this execution was carried
out under the auspices of the 11th German Army, the
fact is clear that the only interest the 11th Army had in
the matter was, that should the Kommando in Simferopol
have Russians marked for slaughter, it should execute them
prior to the beginning of the Christmas season. (See
BRAUNE statement Doc. Book III-D, pp. 54, 55, Doc. NO-4234,
Pros. Ex. 163).   (R- pp. 3091 to 3093, inclusive).   He
testified that he turned over the details of the execution
to his sub-Kommando leader, one SCHULZ, who obtained the
necessary forces for the task.   When asked by his own
counsel if he supervised the execution he stated:

> "Yes, I did.   It took place under my
> responsibility.   Once I was at the place
> of execution with Mr. Ohlendorf and there
> we, convinced ourselves that the executions
> took place according to the directives laid
> down by Ohlendorf at the beginning of the
> assignment.   I personally was there
> several times more and I supervised.....
> Furthermore my subkommando leader Schulz
> was always present, the company commander
> of the police Company and, I think, another
> Captain." (R-3094).

On cross-examination the defendant stated in regard
to this same execution in Simferopol that he was "certain
that there were more than 1,000" and they included women
and a "few children", (R-3147) and that their outer
clothing was taken from them before execution and turned
over to the National Welfare Organization. (R-3152).

When asked concerning the reasons why the 11th German
Army wanted these executions performed prior to the
Christmas Season 1941 he gave a very illuminating answer
when he stated:

> "Mr. Prosecutor, the Fuehrer Order was there
> and now the Army said 'We want it finished
> before Christmas'. I wasn't able at the
> time to find out all the reasons. Maybe reasons
> were strategic reasons, military reasons,
> which caused the Army to issue that order.
> Maybe they were territorial questions. Maybe
> they were questions of food. The Army was
> afraid at that time that hundreds of thousands
> of people might have to starve to death during
> that winter because of the food situation...."
> (R-3148).

To kill people because they would starve to death
anyway is, to say the least, a novel and fantastic motive
for murder!

The defendant then confirmed what the Prosecution has
contended in Document NO-3401, contained in Document Book
III-D, p. 115 (cited supra) when in reply to the question
asked whether or not executions were carried out in
Simferopol after Christmas 1941 he answered in the
affirmative. (R-3149). He further admitted the
possibility that elements of his command carried out
executions in Aluschta and Karasubasar in January 1942.
(R-3167).

The responsibility for the execution of 1184 suspects
of partisan activity in Eupatoria is contained in Document
Book III-D, pp. 58 to 61, Doc. NOKW-1863, Pros. Ex. 164.
This document is an operational order for the purpose which
it states in paragraph 1 thereof:

9

"in order to apprehend unreliable elements
(partisans, saboteurs, possibly enemy troops,
parachutists in civilian clothes, Jews,
leading Communists, etc.)."

BRAUNE admitted that he issued the order (R-3175). He
gives as justification for this action that he was obliged
to carry it out because he was ordered to do so by the
Wehrmacht (Idem). He further states that   auxiliary
troops were furnished him by other agencies, but, after
close questioning, he does admit that in each of the
tactical divisions of the city, members of his kommando were
in charge of the various phases of the rounding up of the
suspects (R-3178), that if Jews were found among these
suspects "they were shot just as the other Jews" and
without trial of any kind (R-3180). He claims that he
saved the lives of some 300 suspects simply because they
had worked with the German Forces. (R-3190). He denies
that he gave any orders to fire to the execution squad,
but in the same Document Book III-D, p. 62, Doc. NOKW-584,
Pros. Ex. 165, in an official report of the results of
the action ordered by BRAUNE himself, it is clearly shown
that "Dr. BRAUNE gave orders on the place of execution
for the carrying out of the shootings". (R-3191). In
his attempt to explain this, he states that the report was
in error and that the Wehrmacht Major made it out long
after the events took place. (Idem). Furthermore he
admitted that he accompanied the march of the suspects
to the place of execution (R-3194-3195). When asked
whether innocent people could have been executed as a
result of the Eupatoria action, he stated that eight to
ten hours after his arrival in this area for purposes of
commanding this action (R-3192) he was convinced that "the
whole lot of them had engaged in illegal activities....."
Just after this statement he further admitted that there
was a possibility that some of these 1184 executed people

were innocent of any crime (R-3193).

The Prosecution in this brief does not intend to treat exhaustively of BRAUNE's responsibility for the use of gas vans in performing executions. It is, however, incumbent upon the Prosecution to point out to the Tribunal that although he denies that his Kommando ever used one, OHLENDORF in his cross-examination stated that to the best of his recollection, Einsatzkommando 11-B used one. (R-698). There is no point also in the Prosecution urging other and further incidents of executions accomplished by kommando 11-B as to do so would only be cumulative to this defendant's guilt so clearly shown and which in at least one instance he admits. (Executions in Simferopol in December 1941 cited supra). Before this section of this brief is closed, however, it is pointed out that in all BRAUNE's career as an Einsatzkommando leader, he admits that he never once showed mercy to a single Jew who was subjected to the tender mercies of his hand of cut-throats. (R-3074).

CONCLUSION

To the charges in the Indictment, the defendant has entered a plea of "Not guilty in the sense of the Indictment" which is treated under the procedure of this Tribunal as a plea of "Not guilty". His defense in effect is that while he admits that executions were performed by the unit under his command, they were done only in obedience to the expressed order of Adolf Hitler as the head of the German State and the Supreme Commander of the Armed Forces of the Third Reich, or that such orders for executions came from the Commanding General of the Eleventh German Army, which was the agency primarily responsible for the security of the area in which this defendant's command operated. Finally, the membership of this defendant

in organizations declared criminal by the International
Military Tribunal is defended on the grounds that he had
no choice in the matter but was "drafted" for service
in Einsatzgruppe D.

The question of superior orders as a defense is
treated in a separate brief filed by the Prosecution, which
is incorporated in this closing brief against Dr. Werner
BRAUNE by reference. Reference is also made in like
manner to the brief of the Prosecution on the question
of membership in criminal organizations. The treatment
of either of these questions therefore becomes unnecessary
for purposes of this brief.

BRAUNE admits that executions were performed by
elements of his command in the Russian cities of
Simferopol, Aluschta, Karasubasar, and Eupatoria. While
he was not personally present and giving the necessary
orders each time, it is apparent from his statements that
each time an officer belonging to his kommando was present
as his representative. He admits that he did supervise
at least one execution that occurred in Simferopol
before Christmas 1941 and states that an officer of his
command made all necessary arrangements. He states that
he "inspected" various phases at several different times.

BRAUNE further admits that he and some 47-50 of his
Kommando personnel were in charge of and directed a
reprisal action against 1184 male inhabitants of Eupatoria,
that he carried this through to the logical conclusion
by marching with these condemned to the place of execution
and the documents show that he, as the commander of the
operation, gave the orders for the actual shooting of
these men. His admissions show beyond a doubt that
since the round-up and executions together consumed eight

to ten hours time, none of the victims were allowed any sort of a trial nor could he produce any evidence in his own defense.

The admissions of the defendant become more credible when one considers his additional admission that all the time he was in the East in service with the Security Police and SD he never showed mercy to a single Jew over whom he had the power of life and death.

BRAUNE early in his career volunteered for service in the SD, helping to establish this organization. He knew when he volunteered for this service he would become a member of the SS. When he was transferred to the Gestapo he performed his duties in this organization with such efficiency and skill that he rose steadily in rank and position. He was aware of the criminal nature of these organizations, having participated in the crimes committed by himself and other members in the German Occupied Territories of the East against nationals of foreign nations.

The Prosecution, therefore, respectfully submits that Werner BRAUNE ordered, aided, abetted, and took a consenting part in the crimes of murder and persecution of racial or religious groups composed of non-German peoples. He voluntarily joined the SD and SS and was a member of these organizations subsequent to 1 September 1939. He was, until less than a year before the end of the late World War, a member of the Gestapo.

The Prosecution respectfully submits that this defendant should be found guilty as charged in the Indictment.

Respectfully submitted
on behalf of Chief of Counsel
for War Crimes

PETER W. WALTON

Nurnberg, Germany
January 1948   -12 -

13

MILITARY TRIBUNAL II

Case No. 9

TRIAL BRIEF OF THE PROSECUTION AGAINST

WALTER HAENSCH

Benjamin B. Ferencz
Chief Prosecutor
Peter W. Walton
Arnost Horlik-Hochwald
John E. Glancy
      of Counsel

FOR :

TELFORD TAYLOR
Brigadier General, USA
Chief of Counsel for War Crimes

and

James M. McHaney
Deputy Chief of Counsel
      for War Crimes
Director, Military and SS
      Division

Doc. 2

14

Alfred Schwarz
Nancy Fenstermacher
Research Assistants

Nuernberg, Germany
5 February 1948

INTRODUCTION

It is alleged in essence under Counts I and II (Crimes Against Humanity and War Crimes respectively) that Walter HAENSCH was a principal in, accessory to, ordered, abetted, took a consenting part in, was connected with plans and enterprises involving, and was a member of organizations or groups connected with: atrocities and offenses including but not limited to, persecution on political, racial and religious grounds: murder, extermination, imprisonment and other inhumane acts committed against civilian populations including German Nationals and Nationals of other countries. It is further alleged that these acts, conducts, plans and enterprises were carried out as part of a systematic program of genocide aimed at the destruction of foreign nations and ethnic groups by murderous etermination. It is alleged under Count III of the indictment that HAENSCH was a member after 1 September 1939 of the SS and the SD, organizations declared to be criminal by the International Military Tribunal.

The acts recognized as War Crimes and Crimes against Humanity are set forth in Paragraphs I (b) and (c) of Article II of Control Council Law No. 10. Membership in organizations declared criminal by the International Military Tribunal is defined as a crime in Paragraph I (d) of the same Article. The criteria of criminality are set forth in Paragraph 2 of Article II of Control Council Law No. 10, which reads in part as follows:

"2. Any person without regard to nationality or the capacity in which he acted, is deemed to have committed a crime as defined in Paragraph 1 of this Article, if he was (a) a principal or (b) was an accessory to the commission of any such crime or ordered or abetted the same or (c) took a consenting part therein or

- 1 -

(d) was connected with plans or enterprises involving
its commission or (e) was a member of any organization
or group connected with the commission of any such
crime......"

I. POSITIONS OF RESPONSIBILITY

The defendant HAENSCH was born on 3 May 1904. He studied
Law and Political Science and passed his state-examination in 1934
(R-3226). HAENSCH joined the NSDAP. in 1931 (R-3231).

In May or June 1935, Haensch started his activities as confidential agent of the SD and from the first of August of this year,
became a full-time employee of the SD-Regional Headquarters Elbe. On
the same day, Haensch joined the SS (Doc.Bk. III C, page 53, NO-3261,
Pros.Ex. 141 compare R-3238-3240). Haensch testified that he "made
continuous attempts" to leave the SD (R-3241). From his own testimony, however, it is clear what consideration compelled him to
remain in this organization. Haensch stated :

> "I could not leave because I saw no possibility
> to find a position which would have been in
> accordance with my professional inclinations,
> that is, to join the Administrative service."
> (R-3242).

And when examined by the Tribunal:

> "Because I had no possibility to find a position
> which would have been in accordance with the aim
> I had set for myself." (R-3243).

In the SS, Haensch rose to the rank of Lt-Colonel (Doc.Bk. III C,
page 53 , NO - 3261, Pros.Ex. 141). In the SD, he served from 1936
on in the SD Main Office and when the RSHA was formed in the latter
(R-3240).

In the middle of January of 1942, HAENSCH was appointed commander of Sonderkommando 4 b of Einsatzgruppe C (R-3245),

- 2 -

and remained in this position until the middle of June of the same year (R-3287). At that time, Haensch returned to his work in the RSHA (R-3288). In September of 1943, he was assigned to the Office of the Reichs Plenipotentiary in Denmark and remained in this position until the collapse of Germany (Doc. Bk. III C, page 49, NO - 4567, Pros.Ex. 140).

II. PARTICIPATION IN CRIMINAL ORGANIZATIONS

Haensch admitted having been assigned commander of Sonderkommando 4 b in the middle or end of January of 1942 (R-3245). He maintained, however, that he did not physically take over this command earlier than the middle of March (R-3253). Haensch has tried to prove that until the end of February, he had been in Berlin. The witness, SCHREYER, testified that, according to her cash book, appointment pads and the photographic negatives which she had preserved in her studio, she herself had taken a photographic picture of Haensch on 21 February 1942 in Berlin. This testimony is corroborated by the court-witness REICH. The witness WEINMANN, the wife of one SS-Lt-Colonel WEINMANN, testified that Haensch left Berlin together with her husband, for an assignment in the East, at the end of February. A record, allegedly taken from the files of the dentist Dr. MAENNLE, was introduced in order to prove that Haensch had been treated by MAENNLE on the 14th of January and the 7th of February in Berlin. For an analysis of this evidence reference is made to Part III of this brief.

Several independent documents prove that Haensch physically took over the command of Sonderkommando 4 b before or on the 16th of January 1942. Operational Situation Report No. 156, which is dated 16 January, shows that, by that time, Haensch had replaced BRAUNE and WEINMANN had replaced the defendant BLOBEL (Doc.Bk. II A, page 60, NO - 3405, Pros.Ex. 42).

- 3 -

It is of special significance that the names of BRAUNE and BLOBEL, which originally appeared in this report, are crossed out and replaced in handwriting with the names of Haensch (as commander of Sonderkommando 4 b) and Weinmann (as commander of Sonderkommando 4 a) respectively. The Defense Counsel for Haensch had admitted in open-court that two more Operational Situation Reports, dated 25 February (Doc.Bk. I, page 86, NO-3340, Pros.Ex. 22) and 6 March 1942 (Doc.Bk. II C, page 59, NO-3240, Pros.Ex. 80) refer to Haensch as "Fuehrer of Sonderkommando 4 b" (R-3255). In both reports it is stated that the "location" of the independent units, mentioned in previous reports, remained unchanged.

Moreover evidence, which is entirely independent from the RSHA reports, proves clearly that Haensch actually and physically took over the command of Sonderkommando 4 b in January of 1942. Haensch testified that he went to the East together with WEINMANN (R-3254). According to his service record, WEINMANN had been assigned with the Security Police since 13 January 1942 (Doc.Bk. V C, page 29, NO-3251, Pros.Ex. 207). That this date is correct is not only proved by the report of 16 January, which shows that BLOBEL had been replaced by Weinmann before that date (NO-3405 supra), but by two pre-trial affidavits of the defendant BLOBEL stating in both documents that he had been replaced in January of 1942 (Doc. Bk. I, pages 129, 132, NO-3824, Pros.Ex. 31, Doc.Bk. III C, page 15, NO-3947, Pros.Ex. 133). This excludes the possibility that Haensch had physically taken command of Sonderkommando 4 b later than in the middle of January of 1942.

The evidence proves that, during the time when Haensch was in command of this unit, Sonderkommando 4 b participated

- 4 -

18

in the general extermination program in the same way as all other units of the Einsatzgruppen. During the period between 14 January and 12 February 1942, Sonderkommando 4 b executed 861 persons — 649 of them were political officials, 52 saboteurs and partisans, and 139 Jews. (Doc.Bk. I, page 87, NO-3340, Pros. Ex. 22). A report of 6 March 1942 reveals that :

> "The Sonderkommando 4 b executed a number of 1317 persons (among them 63 political agitators, 30 saboteurs and partisans and 1224 Jews). By this measure the locality Artemowsk was also freed of Jewish components."
> (Doc.Bk. II C, page 60, NO - 3240, Pros.Ex. 80).

There is further evidence in the record that large-scale executions had been carried out by Sonderkommando 4 b during the time between 15 March and 15 June 1942 when Haensch admittedly was commander of this unit.

Operational Situation Report No. 188 proves that on the 1 April 1942, Sonderkommando 4 b was located in Shitomir. Another report, which is dated only two days later, states that the location of the kommandos of Einsatzgruppe C remained the same as those in the report of 1 April. This report reveals under the heading "Einsatzgruppe C" that 50 hostages were arrested and half of them shot in Shitomir. Between the 28 and 31 of March, 434 persons were killed (NO-3238, NO-5941, Pros.Exs . 186 a and 186 b, R-3398-9). That Shitomir was within the area of Sonder-kommando 4 b is further proved by other evidence in the record (Doc.Bk. II D, page 4, NO-3359, Pros.Ex. 84).

A report of 5 June 1942, which lists Sonderkommando 4 b under the command of Haensch with location at Gorlovka, proves that in the district of the Gorlovka Command in late April and early May, 727 out of 1,038 arrested persons were given "special treatment". Among the victims of Sonderkommando 4 b (the Gorlovka Command) were 461 partisans; members of destruction battalions, saboteurs, looters, communists and NKWD agents (NO-5187, Pros.Ex. 185, R-3394). When asked how many of the victims had been communists or NKWD agents, the defendant was unable or unwilling to give any details. He admitted, however, that he had been informed of the action and alleged that he learned about it only after the executions had been carried out (R-3393). Haensch further had to admit that officials of Sonderkommando 4 b, i. e., officers who were actually under his command, had participated in this action (R-3392-3).

While denying responsibility for the numerous executions mentioned in the reports (supra), Haensch admitted that during his tenure of office, four executions had been carried out in which approximately 60 persons were killed (R-3377). These executions were carried out by sub-commanders who were subordinated to Haensch (R-3378). Haensch further admitted that he would have been in a position to reverse the decisions of these sub-commanders (R-3379). The execution of 25 persons in Gorlovka in April and six or seven persons in May in the same place (R-3377), Haensch admittedly had ordered himself (R-3383). He finally admitted that all 60 persons were killed under his orders (R-3384), and that he received reports in cases where the victims were executed by sub-kommandos (R-3385).

III. GENERAL DEFENSES

With the exception of the execution of 60 persons, who according to Haensch's testimony had committed offenses which merited death (R-3385), allegedly no executions were carried out by Sonderkommando 4 b under his command (R-3377)

20

Haensch has tried to substantiate his alibi with the witnesses WEINMANN, SCHREYER, REICH, MAENNLE, and MAENNLE's secretary and has submitted evedence which is supposed to support the testimony of these witnesses.

Assuming arguendo that Haensch could prove his alibi, this fact would not serve as a valid defense as there is ample evidence in the record that Sonderkommando 4 b killed numerous persons in pursuance of the extermination policy even after the 15th of March 1942 when Haensch was admittedly in command of this unit (supra). Nevertheless, a careful analysis of the evidence which is supposed to support Haensch's alibi seems to be appropriate.

In this analysis the testimony of Dr. MAENNLE can be disregarded as it is patently clear from the statements of this witness that he has no knowledge of facts which would shed any light on the matter in issue. As his secretary and the expert witness of the Prosecution, who is to testify on the handwriting of the record of Dr. MAENNLE's office, have not appeared as yet before the Tribunal. The Prosecution reserves the right to file a supplementary brief concerning the evidence acquired from the testimony of these two witnesses.

The witness, WEINMANN, declared that Haensch went with her husband to the East at the end of February of 1942 (R-3056). She, however, fixed the date of the departure, not according to her memory, but testified that she remembered as he told her mother-in-law "Well the child is just three weeks old and father already has to leave". As her child had been born on 6 February 1942, the witness deducted that the departure of Haensch and her husband must have taken place at the end of February (R-3056). It does not need to be argued that so weak a recollection cannot destroy the evidence which, in four entirely independent documents, establishes the date of WEINMANN's (and consequently Haensch's) arrival in the East as the middle of January (Doc.Bk. II A, page 60, NO - 3405, Pros.Ex. 42; Doc.Bk. I,

page 129, 132, NO-3824, Pros.Ex. 31; Doc.Bk. III C, page 15,
NO - 3947, Pros.Ex. 133, Doc.Bk. V C, page 29, NO-3251, Pros.Ex.207).
It should be noted that among these documents the SS-Personnel Record of WEINMANN proves that he took over his assignment in the East
on the 13th of January (NO-3251 supra). The only conclusion that can
be drawn from the testimony of the witness WEINMANN is that she either
was mistaken in the date of the departure, or went too far in her wish
to assist a fellow-officer of her husband.

The witness SCHREYER testified that she herself took the
photographic picture of Haensch on 21 February 1942 in her studio
in Berlin (R-3324). She declared that she, being a photographer, has
a very good memory for people and when she saw the negative of the
picture, she immediately knew that she took the picture herself (R-
3330). She further alleged that she remembered Haensch personally
(R-3331), and went on to say, "As a photographer every face is im-
printed on my memory" (R-3332). Nevertheless, she could not remember Haensch's rank (Ibid). When examined by the Tribunal, SCHREYER
changed her testimony and said that the only reason for her knowledge was that nobody else could have taken the picture (R-3348),
and that she could not remember the faces of the many persons
whose pictures she had taken independent of the negatives of the
pictures themselves (R-3353).

From this testimony, it is clear that the contention of
the witness goes only to the fact that (a) she took a picture
of HAENSCH, and (b) a picture of a Dr. HAENSCH (of the same address
as the defendant's) was taken on 21 February 1941. However, it was
not apparent from the witness' testimony that the picture which was
taken on the 21st of February was, in reality, a picture of the defendant. The pictures themselves were sent to HAENSCH's parents (R-
3361, compare R-4511, R-3413). The customer's first name is not mentioned either in the appointment pad (HAENSCH Ex. 1, R-3423) or the

cash book (HAENSCH Exh. 3, R-3423). There is a strong presumption that, on the 21st of February 1942, not the picture of the defendant, but one of the male relative, presumably his father, was taken, and this presumption is strengthened by the fact that, in both documents, appointment pad and cash book, the title Dr. and not the rank of the defendant is used. HAENSCH's father was a doctor (R-3225). It is proved in other entries in the cash book (HAENSCH Exh. 3) that the military rank of the customer was noted (R-3333). There was sufficient time and possibility to exchange the negatives of the picture of HAENSCH's with other negatives, and SCHREYER testified that Mrs. HAENSCH visited her studio in her absence and that a potographic copy of the page of the appointment pad had been made by SCHREYER's employee, without her previous knowledge (R-3358). It goes without saying that the negatives could also have been exchanged without SCHREYER knowing of it.

Moreover, it should be noted that there are many discrepancies between the witness' statements and the actual facts. SCHREYER declared under oath that all appointment pads kept by her during the entire time when she had her studio were in her possession (R-3346). When, however, the Prosecution approached her with the permission of the Tribunal, in order to obtain one of these pads which would have served as evidence for the impeachment of the Witness REICH, SCHREYER declared in a sworn affidavit that the pads had been destroyed by Russian soldiers (Doc.Bk. V C, page 34, NO-5808, Pros.Ex. 209). SCHREYER stated further under oath "I live alone, I have been separated from my husband for ten years" (R-3327) The police records, however, prove that Mrs. SCHREYER and her husband live together at the same address (Berlin-Zehlendorf, Teltower Damm) (Doc.Bk. V c, pages 30, 33, NO-5700, Pros.Ex. 208). SCHREYER's motive for this incorrect statement on the witness stand might well have been that she desired to disassociate herself from her husband who had been a member of the NSDAP, SA and the Waffen-SS (Doc.Bk. V c, page 32, NO-5700, Pros.Ex. 208) . Be that as it may, the two strikingly incorrect statements of SCHREYER's under oath destroy the credibility of her entire testimony.

The court-witness REICH who was supposed to clarify the question as to whether HAENSCH had been in the studio of SCHREYER on 21 February 1942 was in no position to do so. After she executed an affidavit in which she declared that she considered it highly improbable that HAENSCH had been there (R-4507-8) she changed her testimony on the witness stand. REICH, however, did not testify that she had seen HAENSCH (R-4505) and only stated that she made the entries in the appointment and cash books (R-4507, R-4509). Moreover, she declared that she worked for Mrs. SCHREYER only in the afternoon and evening hours (R-4515). SCHREYER testified under oath that she took HAENSCH's picture in the forenoon of 21 February (R-3349). REICH testified that she made the entries in the appointment pad (R-4509), and the expert opinion establishes that the entries in the appointment pad and the cash book were both made by REICH. It is clear that the entry in the appointment pad was not made at the time the picture was taken. REICH declared she was married on 27 December 1942 and, consequently, was not in the office on this day (R-4526). In the check book, however, entries appear in REICH's hand-writing for this date (Ibid.). She tried to explain that she made these entries on a later date, on the basis of the appointment pads which had been filled out by SCHREYER but that just these appointment pads had been "destroyed by the Russians", according to the affidavit of SCHREYER (Doc.Bk. V C, page 34, NO-5808, Pros.Ex. 209).

The testimony of these two witnesses, when viewed together, makes it patently clear that the story that HAENSCH had his picture taken on 21 February is fabricated.

Assuming arguendo that HAENSCH was in Berlin on the 21st of February, it can hardly be understood how this could serve him as a defense. It is proved by documentary evidence that HAENSCH actually took over the command in the middle of January (supra). The fact that he eventually had been in Berlin for a few days in February on leave, cannot change his responsibility for the activities of the unit of which he physically took command in the middle of January. In addition, it shold be noted that HAENSCH admitted having received the assignment in January (R-3245, compare Doc. Bk. III C, page 36, NO-4567, Pros.Exh. 140), and his testimony proves that he had knowledge of this assignment as early as December of 1941 (R-3248). It cannot be assumed that HAENSCH would have been in a position to postpone, in war time, such an assignment for approximately two months.

The other lines of HAENSCH's defense are equally fabricated and untrue. HAENSCH contended that only four executions in which, all in all, approximately 60 persons were killed had been carried out by Sonderkommando 4 b under his command (R-3377). His own hand-written and sworn affidavit, however, proves that many more executions were carried out by Sonderkommando 4 b under his command. This affidavit reads in part :

> "If the investigations established that arrested persons,
> according to the current orders or decrees whose contra-
> vention carried with it the death penalty, were guilty and
> had to be executed, such executions were carried out in
> accordance with those orders and decrees and in agreement
> with the Army High Command and the competent military
> authorities, respectively.
>
> Where such executions had to be carried out, strict at-
> tention was paid to ensuring that the severity of this
> measure which had become necessary would not be increas-
> ed by inadequate preparation or irresponsible handling.
>
> I declare :

25

Upon my appropriate inquiries, the liaison officers told me quite clearly, already immediately after my assumption of office, that I need not worry on that score. It was recognized, that the kommando carried out the executions in a correct manner.

Despite the increasing massacre of German soldiers of which the troops were warned again and again by descriptions in orders of the day and which were calculated only to aggravate the severity and bitterness of the war in the East, I never, not even subsequently, observed any excesses on the part of the kommando members, even at executions.

The supervision of each execution was always in the hands of a leader or authorized person, responsible for the preparation, and the carrying out of the execution, including the issue of the certificate of death by a medical orderly.

The executions were effected by shooting from the nearest sure-aim distance. That distance, as I recall it, was not more than 8 to 10 paces. The assumption that the shootings were effected 'by revolver' does not correspond with the facts." (Doc.Bk. III C, page 41-42, NO-4567, Pros.Exh. 140, emphasis supplied).

"Moral sufferings for the victims as well as for the members of the execution command were to be avoided as far as possible. Thus, great care was to be taken that a person waiting to be executed, would not be eye-witness to a preceding shooting and that the corpses of people shot would be removed before a further execution took place.

I am convinced that none of these considerations were disregarded during my time with the kommando. I have a right to be convinced of this also for the following reasons:

26

1) I, myself, never tired in my constant efforts for discipline and good conduct in the kommando, in accordance with my assignment, to point out over and over again these considerations to the leaders, subleaders and men. This would be confirmed at any time by the men of the Army with whom I discussed the matters pertaining to the kommando during official and also personal conversations.

2) I, myself, watched a few executions. Where possible, this was done in a manner so as to surprise the execution command by my sudden appearance. During this, I saw nothing which indicated that the considerations enumerated were being disregarded.

3) The executions were not carried out under the cover of "secrecy". Place and time of the executions had to be arranged previously between the leader of the execution command and the competent military authorities.

4) Occasionally, officers or authorized persons also attended the executions as representatives or deputies of their appropriate officers.

5) During the many discussions with the liaison officers and the leaders of the competent military authorities responsible for the Teilkommandos, it was the sincerity, sense of responsibility and inherent decency of the leaders, subleaders and men of the kommando that were stressed to me. I still remember that the absolutely necessary insuring of instantaneous death without previous mere wounding was brought up during these discussions and that it was emphasized to aim at the head as a sure guarantee for instantaneous death.

I, myself, watched three or four executions. The places of execution
were situated in the area around Gorlovka and the remaining area of
operations of the Army in hilly territory." (Ibid., page 42-43,
emphasis supplied).

"As to the composition of the execution command, the rule
existed that, under no circumstances, so-called 'shooting
kommandos' were formed, that is to say, that for the different executions, not always the same men were to be used.
The leader of each execution command varied his choice of
men according to these directives and assigned them on the
day before the execution." (Ibid., page 43, emphasis
supplied).

This language makes it clear that executions were daily
occurrences in Sonderkommando 4 b under HAENSCH's command. Moreover, it is clear from the affidavit itself that the number of
60 victims which was given by HAENSCH in his testimony is an in-
vented one. He stated further in his affidavit:

"I was requested to make statements concerning the number of executions which, in my estimation, were carried
out by the kommando, according to orders during my time
as leader of the Sonderkommando 4 b. To this, I must
state the following: In the absence of records, I am
no longer able to give such information. An estimated
number would lack any basis of fact. For this reason
and those reasons stated above, I cannot give such an
estimate." (Ibid., page 44, emphasis supplied).

It should be noted that the entire affidavit was written
by HAENSCH in his own hand and that its language was not in-
fluenced by a representative of the Prosecution.

That HAENSCH's testimony as a whole cannot be viewed as

credible is proved further by his statement that he did not know about the Hitler-Order (R-3260-3261) or about the extermination policy against the Jews (R-3259). HAENSCH maintains that he heard about the Fuehrer-Order for the first time in Nuremberg when he was interrogated on 23 July 1947 (R-3262), yet he spoke to STRECKEN-BACH who had handed down this order, before he went to the East (R-3249). HAENSCH testified in this connection:

> "STRECKENBACH also drew my attention to the fact that
> in particular, in cases of executive decisions, I was
> to rely on the investigations of the experts who had
> the necessary experience in the East. In connection
> with my work as to desciplinary matters, STRECKENBACH
> also pointed out to me that, in the East, in the fight
> against the illegal elements and to fight against the
> saboteurs and obstructionist, formal court proceedings,
> such as we were accustomed to carrying out in the Home-
> land, in the Police Courts, or another court, didn't
> exist in the East, but that a decree by the highest
> neutral authority, that is, by the OKA, that, by that
> decree, matters in the East had been settled in a dif-
> ferent way; that the chiefs or chief of the executive
> department of kommandos and the Armies proceed in ac-
> cordance with these decrees, or, rather the decrees by
> the highest political authorities." (R-3250).

HAENSCH also spoke to HEYDRICH and the latter, according to HAENSCH's own testimony, "essentially" told him the same as STRECKENBACH (R-3252), but, in the conversations with STRECKENBACH and HEYDRICH, the word "Jew" or "Gypsy" allegedly was never men-tioned, (R-3259-60). HAENSCH also spoke to the Chief of the Ge-stapo, MUELLER, before he left for the East (R-3253).

When HAENSCH arrived at Einsatzgruppe C he reported to his commander, THOMAS (R-3262). He spoke to his predecessor BRAUNE and to the leaders of the sub-commandos (R-3263). All of these men instructed him about executions, yet HAENSCH states that none of them told him whom he was supposed to execute (R-3249-50, R-3252-3, R-3259-3266).

There is ample evidence in the record that Sonderkommando 4 b carried out the Hitler-Order (See Part II supra). HAENSCH maintained that he was ordered that the executive activities of Sonderkommando 4 b should remain unchanged and that he carried out this order (R-3372). Nevertheless, he stated that, from the moment he arrived at the kommando, only "guilty" persons were executed. When asked, in cross-examination, why the general policy of Sonderkommando 4 b, to kill Jews and communists, was suddenly abondoned, after his arrival at the kommando, he was unable to give a satisfactory explanation (R-3374). Viewed in the light of all these contradictions, the entire defense of HAENSCH cannot be considered credible.

Finally, the question should be considered as to whether the defendant HAENSCH can plead the Doctrine of Superior Orders in mitigation of his crimes. The Prosecution contends that no such mitigation is justified in this case.

HAENSCH's immediate superior was the commander of Einsatzgruppe C, THOMAS. By the testimony of the witness HARTL it is proved that THOMAS did not compel any of the officers under his command to participate in executions or to order such measures. HARTL stated :

"THOMAS, at the time, passed on an order that all those people who could not reconcile with their conscience to carry out such orders, that is, people who were too soft, as he said, to carry out these orders, should be sent back to Germany or should be assigned to other tasks. Thus, at the time, a number of people, also commanders, just because they were too soft to carry out orders, were sent back by THOMAS to the Reich." (R-2932).

and

"A. Obersturmbannfuehrer RATZESBERGER who said that he could not do it was immediately sent back. He was released and came to Vienna.

. . . .

Q. If THOMAS would have known, he would have sent a commander home, is that correct?

A. He would have sent him home, saying that he was too soft. In a number of cases, this happened, that THOMAS actually sent these people back to Germany." (R-2933).

From HARTL's testimony, it is apparent that HAENSCH need not have feared any repercussions. If there is no fear of reprisal for disobedience, obedience constitutes a completely voluntary participation in the crime.

HAENSCH did not serve in the field of battle. His activities did not take place in the front lines. He did not act in the spontaneous heat of passion. He had full time to consider and reflect on his course of action. Moreover, the Doctrine of Superior Orders cannot be considered when such malignant crimes have been consciously and ruthlessly committed, as the killing of defenseless men, women and children.

- 17 -

CONCLUSION

The defendant HAENSCH was a member of the SS and the SD from 1935 until the collapse of Germany. He rose in the SS to the rank of Lieutenant Colonel and was active in the SD offices of the RSHA. In January of 1942, HAENSCH took over the command of Sonderkommando 4 b and remained in this position until the middle of June of the same year. Under his command, Sonderkommando 4 b participated in the indiscriminate killing of racial and political undesirables. Approximately 3,000 persons were killed by Sonderkommando 4 b under HAENSCH's command. There is nothing to be said in mitigation of the guilt of the defendant HAENSCH. The plea of superior orders does not apply to him.

The Prosecution contends that the evidence proves that HAENSCH was a principal in, accessory to, ordered, abetted, took a consenting part in, was connected with plans and enterprises involving, and was a member of organizations or groups connected with: atrocities and offenses included but not limited to; murder, extermination, imprisonment, and other inhumane acts committed against non-German nationals; and that these acts, conducts, plans and enterprises were carried out as part of a systematic program of genocide, aimed at the destruction of foreign nationals and ethnic groups, by murderous extermination. The Prosecution further contends that the evidence proves that HAENSCH was a member, after 1 September 1939, of the criminal organizations, the SS and the SD. His guilt has been established on Counts I, II and III of the Indictment.

Respectfully submitted
on behalf of Chief of Counsel for
War Crimes

ARNOST HORLIK-HOCHWALD

Nuremberg, Germany
February 1948

5

M I L I T A R Y   T R I B U N A L   II

CASE NO. 9

TRIAL BRIEF OF THE PROSECUTION AGAINST

HEINZ JOST

Benjamin B. FERENCZ
  Chief Prosecutor,
Peter W. WALTON
Arnost HORLIK-HOCHWALD
John E. GLANCY
  of Counsel

For:

Telford TAYLOR
Brigadier General, USA
Chief of Counsel for War Crimes

and

James M. McHANEY
Deputy Chief of Counsel
for War Crimes
Director, Military & SS Division

Doc. 3

33

Alfred Schwarz
Nancy H. Fenstermacher
  Research Assistants

17 January 1948

34

I. THE CHARGES

In Counts One and Two of the Indictment it is charged that the defendant HEINZ JOST was a principal in, accessory to, ordered, abetted, took a consenting part in, was connected with plans and enterprises involving and was a member of organizations or groups connected with certain atrocities and offenses, constituting crimes against humanity and war crimes. These offenses included persecutions on political, racial and religious grounds, murder, extermination, imprisonment and other inhumane acts committed against civilian populations, in violation of the law of Nations, general principles of Criminal Law and the Laws and Customs of War as defined in Control Council Law No. 10.

The defendant Jost is further charged with membership in the SS and SD, organizations declared to be criminal by the International Military Tribunal and Control Council Law No. 10.

II. INTRODUCTION

The defendant Jost was born of middle-class parents on 9 July 1904 in Holzhausen in the district of Marburg. He studied at the universities of Giessen and Munich, majoring in Law and Economics. (R-1129). In 1927 he completed his studies and passed the required bar examinations. In order to meet the German pre-practice requirement prescribed, he worked in the District Court in Darmstadt until 1930. (Supra).

He joined the Nazi Party in February 1928, when the Party was in its infancy, and did his utmost to further its growth and to add impetus to its movement by disseminating Party propaganda and by speaking at Party rallies, exhorting the populace to join the Party which would once more give Germany a place in the sun. (R-1132). Although Jost has stated on direct examination that he did not join the SA until 1931 because it would have interfered with his professional development (R-1133), the Prosecution, in contradiction thereof, has shown that he actually joined this Hitlerian strong-arm group in March 1929 (IIIA, page 5, NO-2896, Pros. Ex. 98). Despite the fact that he disclaims any knowledge of or experience in police work (R-1142), Jost was directly engaged in pursuits of this nature from March 1933 until March 1934. During this time he acted in the capacity of Chief of Police in Worms and Giessen (R-1133). It is interesting to note that these were critical times and marked the inception of concentration camps. In 1934, as a continuance of his activity in the SA, he became a member of the SS (IIIA, page 7, NO-2896, Pros. Ex. 98) and in the same year became a full-time member of the SD. (Supra). Here he was connected with counter-intelligence affairs. In 1939, having attained the rank of a Brigadier General in the SS and Major General of the Police (R-1133) (IIIA, page 7, NO-2896, Pros. Ex. 98), he accompanied the Third Army into Poland as an SS officer on the staff thereof.

III. DETERMINATION OF JOST'S COMMAND AUTHORITY AS LEADER OF
     EINSATZGRUPPE A AND AS THE COMMANDER-IN-CHIEF OF THE
     SECURITY POLICE AND THE SD FOR THE EAST.

The defendant Jost, in his affidavit of 27 July 1947, admitted that he was the Commanding Officer of Einsatzgruppe A and also the Commander-in-Chief of the Security Police and the SD for the Eastland (Bds Ostland). (IIIA, page 2, NO-4151, Pros. Ex. 99). However, on direct examination, he attempted to becloud the issue by stating that HEYDRICH had assured him that while he should be the Commanding Officer of Einsatzgruppe A and the Bds Ostland, he would be concerned only with the administrative tasks. (R-1156). In view of Heydrich's reputation for ruthlessness, his slave-like devotion to duty, and his rabid demand for blind obedience, such a contention as Jost's is, at best, implausible. Such a contention that he placed Jost in command in one breath and allowed him, albeit reluctantly, to divorce himself from the task which would naturally follow this appointment, in another breath, is not worthy of belief.

Through the use of a peculiar type of circumlocution, his own idea of a verbal "Nacht und Nebel", Jost has continuously evaded delineating in concise and succinct form his actual position as the Commanding Officer of Einsatzgruppe A and as the Commander-in-Chief of the Security Police and the SD. However, if we cut a swath through the fields of verbiage, we are finally rewarded by the facts as they actually existed. In his affidavit of 27 July 1947 Jost states:

"During my activity as Chief of the Einsatzgruppe A, I was also Commander-in-Chief of the Security Police and SD in Eastland (Bds Ostland). Headquarters for the Einsatzgruppe A was located in KRASNOWARDEISK, whilst headquarters for the Commander-in-Chief for the Security Police and SD Eastland was located in Riga. On the whole, the duties of a Commander-in-Chief of the Security Police and SD were the same as those of a Chief of an Einsatzgruppe, and the duties of a Commander of the Security Police and SD (Kds) the same as those of a Chief of a Sonderkommando or Einsatzkommando respectively. The difference in these names can be explained by the fact that a Commander-in-Chief or a Commander of the Security Police and SD was subject to civilian adminis- tration and received his orders from the Higher SS and Police Leader of SS and Police Leader respectively, whilst the Einsatzgruppen and Kommandos received their orders from the Chief of the Security Police and SD on the one hand or from locally superior Wehrmacht offices on the other hand. After this district had been declared an area of civilian administration all Einsatz units were changed into units of the Commander-in-Chief or Commander of the Security Police and SD. There was no basic change of duties." (Emphasis supplied). (IIIA, page 2, NO-4151, Pros. Ex. 99).

-3-

From the above we see that rather than any reduction in troops, change of duties, or limitation or curtailment of authority, the only change which took place when the area fell under civilian administration was that it was re-designated, its titles were changed to conform with the extension of the chain of command. Its tasks were the same. In order to confuse the issue Jost attempted to draw a herring across the factual trail leading to the truth by grossly overemphasizing the importance of this mere change in name. Jost had two titles, in order that his authority would be all-encompassing so as to allow his position to correspond to changing conditions effected by the Army's moving forward and the civilian administration assuming command of the area. As the area was gradually taken over by the civilian administration, the troop designations changed from Sonderkommando 1a in Esthonia, commanded by Sandberger with headquarters in Reval, Sonderkommando 1b in Lithuania, commanded by Ehrlinger with headquarters in Tossno, Einsatzkommando 2 in Latvia, commanded by Batz with headquarters in Riga, Einsatzkommando 3 in White Ruthenia, commanded by Jaeger with headquarters in Minsk, (I, page 27, NO-4134, Pros. Ex. 7) to KdS Esthonia, commanded by Sandberger with headquarters in Reval, KdS Lithuania, commanded by Jaeger with headquarters in Tossno, KdS Latvia, commanded by Lange with headquarters in Riga, and the KdS White Ruthenia, commanded by Strauch with headquarters in Minsk, (IIIA, page 53, NO-3256, Pros. Ex. 100). One thing must be continually borne in mind, that is, although designations changed, the mission, purpose and duties did not change. Studying the reports we see that when the titles changed, the commanders remained the same; the troops remained the same and the headquarters remained the same. Despite Jost's evasions and denials, the evidence introduced by the Prosecution on cross-examination clearly shows that he was, in fact, the leader of Einsatzgruppe A and the BdS Ostland, charged with responsibility for all the duties which this position involved. (NO-5156, Pros. Ex. 178, R-1252).

- 4 -

In order to further clarify Jost's position we may examine the record of his direct examination, cross-examination and the documentary evidence. As the Commanding Officer of Einsatzgruppe A he could receive orders from Himmler, who transmitted them to Heydrich, to the Chief of the Einsatzgruppe (Jost) who was in a commanding position over the Einsatz and Sonderkommandos. The Chief of the Army group, through an agreement with OKH and OKW, was also authorized to issue orders to the Chief of the Einsatzgruppe. When asked by counsel:

Q. " Witness, what were the channels of command in the Einsatzgruppen?"

Jost replied:

A. "The Einsatzgruppe could receive orders from the Reichsfuehrer SS, the Chief of Police (Himmler), the Chief of the Security Police (Heydrich), the Chief of the Army Group (Wehrmacht) and from the commander of the rear Army area."

When the area was declared to be under the direction of the Civil authorities, the chain of command was, accordingly, extended so as to include the General Kommissar, the representative of the Ministry for Eastern Affairs. This was eventually clearly stated by Jost, after much bandying of words. Upon questioning by Defense Counsel:

Q. "Witness, who could give you your commands and orders as the Chief of the SD (BdS) in the Einsatzkommandos?"

A. "As the Commander-in-Chief of the territory under the civilian administration (BdS) I had to obey the orders of the Chief of the German Police and the Security Police (Himmler) and of the Chief of the Security Police and SD (Heydrich), and of the Higher SS and Police Leader (Jeckeln); that is, the local commander and the Reichs Kommissar for the Eastland. (Identification added) (R-1156).

From the above is is patent that the only change which occurred when the civilian administration assumed control was that the unit and designation changed and the chain of command was extended to include the General

- 5 -

Kommissar. The mission remained the same, as can readily be seen by searching the record for Jost's own utterances:

"The civilian administration was headed by the Reichs Kommissariat, as supreme official of the Reich. Subordinated to him personally was the Higher SS and Police Leader (Jeckeln), who dealt with all Police and SS matters. Under him, in turn, there was the Commander of the Regular Police and the Commander of the Security Police who, in this case, was myself." (R-1156)

Again, in answer to a question posed by Defense Counsel:

Q. "What were the differences in the tasks and assignments of the Einsatzgruppen within the Army territory and the office of the Security Police and SD (BdS) in the territory of the civilian administration?"

A. "The basic assignments of the Einsatzgruppen and the Einsatzkommandos to rule the Army rear area are known. I am not speaking of the special orders. The same applied to the territory under the civilian administration. Here, also, our task consisted of detecting communist activities in any shape whatsoever. In that respect one could speak of an identical task for both." (R-1159)

In the occupied territories the formal relationship between local units of the Gestapo, Criminal Police, and SD was slightly closer. They were organized into local units of the Security Police and SD and were under the control of both the RSHA and of the Higher SS and Police Leader who was appointed by Himmler to serve on the staff of the occupying authority. The offices of the Security Police and SD in the occupied territories were composed of departments corresponding to the various Amts of the RSHA. In occupied territories which were still considered to be operational military areas, or where German control had not been formally established, the organization of the Security Police and SD was only slightly changed. Members of the Gestapo, Kripo, and SD were joined together into military type organizations known as Einsatzkommandos and Einsatzgruppen in which the key positions were held by members of the Order Police, the Waffen SS, and even the Wehrmacht, were used as auxiliaries. These organizations were under the over-all control of the RSHA, but in front line areas were under the operational control of the appropriate army commander. (Judgment of the International Military Tribunal, pages 92, 93).

Thus the IMT has concisely explained the slight changes which took place when the Civilian Administration entered upon the scene.

To recapitulate, it is readily seen that Jost retained the same position; that is, as the Commanding Officer of the Security Police and the SD under the civilian administration, as he had under the Army as the Chief of the Einsatzgruppe. The same function, the same forces, the same mission — murder.

IV. PERIOD OF COMMAND

In his affidavit of 27 July 1947 Jost stated that he was in a position of command from the end of March 1942 until the end of August 1942. On direct examination, however, he was more specific. Here it was stated:

> Q. "Witness, we now come to another set of questions; that is, your activity in Einsatzgruppe A, as the Commander of a SIPO and the SD, Ostland, (BdS). When and where did the order reach you to take over the leadership of Einsatzkommando A?"

> A. "On the occasion of this information tour which I have just mentioned, which began in the beginning of March 1942 during my stay in Smolensk - in fact, approximately on the 24th or 25th of March 1942 - an order reached me. This order was to the effect that I was to get in touch with the Chief of Einsatzgruppe A, that I was to become Chief of Einsatzgruppe North (A) and the Security Police

41

and SD (BdS), Eastern territories, and that any regula-

tions in accordance with this would be made later." (R-1143)

and

Q. "Now, what did you do when you received this order?"

A. "I had to comply with the order and I went to Riga.

There I arrived at the earliest on the 26th of March

1942. I think it must have been a Sunday. On Monday,

which was the 29th of March, I took over the office...."

(R-1145)

It is, of course, Jost's intention to convey the impression that al-

though he was appointed as the Commanding Officer of Einsatzgruppe A and

as Commander of the Security Police and SD (BdS) on the 24th of March

1942, he is not to be charged with responsibility for acts committed

within the boundaries of Esthonia, Latvia, Lithuania and White Ruthenia

until the 29th of March 1942. The distance from Smolensk to Riga is

approximately 400 miles and is situated on a main line railroad. It is

ridiculous to assume that an SS officer with the rank of Major General

(IIIA, page 4, NO-2896, Pros. Ex. 98) would travel in such a slow manner

that it would consume four days to travel less than 400 miles. Jost,

according to his own admission, was appointed on the 24th and we must

assume that he was actually physically present in Riga, his headquarters,

by the 26th or 27th of March 1942. According to his own statement he

remained in this position of command until relieved on or about the

second of September 1942.(R-1177). Therefore, his period of command

responsibility extends from the 27th of March to the 2nd of

September 1942.

V. CRIMES AND ATROCITIES COMMITTED DURING JOST'S PERIOD OF COMMAND

In his affidavit of 27 July 1947 Jost, although attempting to evade

the responsibility which is rightfully his, does not deny the possibility

that execution of Jews, gypsies, communists and other "asocial" elements

took place:

"While I was Chief of Einsatzgruppe A I did not give

orders to execute Jews, racially inferior persons, criminals

- 8 -

or mental deficients or other persons. I instructed my kommando leaders not to carry out any executions. However, there is a possibility that one leader or another did not obey my orders." (IIIA, page 1, NO-4151, Pros. Ex. 99). (Emphasis supplied).

Here, again, we see Jost's tactics coming to the fore. They are three in number: (1) Prevarication (2) Forgetfulness (3) Evasion. While admitting that executions could have taken place "because one leader or another did not obey my orders", he asserts that in flagrant contradiction of a Fuehrer order, he issued countermanding orders to the effect that no executions should take place.

On cross examination Jost seeks to defend himself by a convenient loss of memory and by the typical Nazi tactics of trying to mitigate his crimes by distinguishing between the murder of thousands and the murder of hundreds. In reluctant response to questions he states:

Q. "How many people were killed by units under your command during that time?" (Period of Command)

A. "In any case there can't have been many."

Q. "But there were some people, at least, killed by units under your command during the time you were in command. Is that correct?" (R-1270)

Jost shrugs off the answer as if it were a long-forgotten bridge score rather than a tally of human lives. Being pressed by further questions and having been admonished by the President, he stated:

Q. "The question is, were some people killed by units under your command...?"

A. "I presume that individual cases occurred but I have already explained during my examination that this could only have been small numbers. All that concerned me was that the order given to me was kept back as far as possible." (R-1271)

Here, again, in slightly stronger language, Jost admits that killings took place during the time in which he was responsible for atrocities carried out by troops subordinate to him. Here, of course, he is speaking in generalities but in response to a more particular question:

> Q. "Do you recall ever having received a report that
> Jews were killed by units under your command?"
>
> A. "At the moment I cannot remember that. Certainly I do
> not remember any reports about mass executions during
> my time." (R-1271)

His typically callous demeanor is clearly evidenced by his mental shrug of the shoulders. Instead of remembering these "few murders" which horror itself should have written indelibly on his mind with sufficient clarity to deny all attempts at forgetfulness, he merely says:

> "At the moment I cannot remember".

Perhaps his own memory conveniently fails him at this time but his own reports and the reports of others have not yet failed.

On the 7th of April 1942, 22 persons were shot in Kauen, among them 14 Jews who had spread communist propaganda. (IIA, page 128, NO-3381, Pros. Ex. 55). The section of this report in which this information is contained is headed "Lithuania". This territory was subordinate to Jost, as may be seen from his own statements:

> "Q. "Were you the highest officer in the organization
> consisting of the BdS or the Commander-in-Chief of
> the Security Police and SD for Esthonia, Latvia,
> Lithuania, and White Ruthenia?"
>
> A. "In those areas I was the highest officer of the
> Security Police and SD." (R-1276)

Further, the Prosecution offered Document NO-5156, which clearly shows Jost's position of command and which delineates the areas and commanders which were subordinate to him. Among those is the territory of Lithuania with Jaeger noted as the KdS Lithuania, subordinate to Jost as the BdS Ostland. (NO-5156, Pros. Ex. 178). (R-1252). Jost, because of his position, is clearly responsible for the killings cited above.

In the same manner Jost is responsible not only for the murder of defenseless people but also for their enslavement, which very often meant death - death by torture, abuse, humiliation and starvation. In the document which reported the deaths of 22 persons, it is further noted that under the heading of White Ruthenia, also subordinate to Jost (NO-5156, supra):

> "On orders by the new plenipotentiary for mobilization
> of labor, Gauleiter SAUCKEL, the Commissariate General
> 'White Ruthenia' has to muster 100,000 workers but until
> now only 17,000 have been shipped. In order to make
> available the manpower requested, the principle of
> voluntary recruiting is abandoned and compulsory
> measures will be adopted."

It must be borne in mind that White Ruthenia was a part of the territory under Jost's command and that it was Jost's duty to inform himself of the measures here adopted. (IIA, page 129, NO-3281, Pros. Ex. 55).

In another report dated 24 April 1942, almost an entire month after Jost admits he assumed command, the following is reported - ironically enough under the heading of "Miscellaneous":

45

> "Within the period of the report a total of 1,272
> persons were executed, 983 of them Jews who had
> infectious diseases or were so old and infirm that they
> could not be any more used for work, 71 gypsies, 204
> communists and 14 more Jews who had been guilty of different
> offenses and crimes." (IIA, page 133, NO-3277, Pros. Ex. 56).

To paraphrase Jost's comment on these occurrences, there is the all-too-familiar weak and plaintive cry of the accused: "That was before my time." (R-1199).

In still another document there is a digest prepared by the Russian Extraordinary State Investigating Commission which certifies that a captured document contained a report by Sturmbannfuehrer Kirste in which he certifies to the deaths of 243 mental patients on the 28th of May 1942, and 98 mental patients on the 14th of April 1942. The reports were signed by Kirste, who was a member of the KdS Latvia, (as is evidenced by the heading of the model letter) with headquarters in Riga, and who was subordinate to Jost as the BdS Ostland. (IIIA, page 3, USSR 41, Pros. Ex. 10). Confronted with this document on direct examination, Jost made the following statement:

A. "As this document concerns an event which happened in Riga, it is outside my field of command of my Einsatz-gruppe and these units could not have taken part in this event. The document itself is a letter of the Commander of the Security Police of Latvia and it is adiressed to the inhabitants Registration Office in Riga and that although it is addressed to this authority, this document was not found at that place but it was found in the office of the sender. If it is to be regarded as an original document it should have arrived at the addressee and not only the sender should have held it. So far as the content matter of the letter is concerned, I must say that it has not been known to me and was not known to me afterwards. If it had, I would have prevented the carrying out of those measures. If I had known of this measure, I would have prevented the carrying out of it in Krasnowardeisk. The document, however, is no proof of any kind that the shooting was actually carried out by the authority concerned. That was an order of which it is absolutely possible that it was issued by another agency or it was carried out by whoever gave the commander the order to make out the document." (R-1197, 1198).

These orders are date-lined "Riga, Latvia", the office of the Com-mander of the Security Police and SD for Latvia (KdS, Latvia). It should be noted that Jost's headquarters, as the Commander-in-Chief of the Security Police and SD (BdS), was also in Riga. (IIIA, page 2, paragraph 6, NO-4151, Pros. Ex. 99). Jost, in stating that these measures would have been outside his field of command as Chief of Einsatzgruppe A, scrupulously avoids mentioning the fact that it was within the scope of his authority as the Commander-in-Chief of the Security Police and SD and, as these measures were carried out by his subordinate, the Commander of the Security Police and SD for Latvia, he is responsible therefor. As to his contention that the letter to be considered as authentic should have been found in the office of the addressee and not in the office of the sender, we might comment on the fact that while Jost was an excellent officer, he is obviously quite ignorant of the customary office procedure of retaining a file copy. Jost has stated that he had no knowledge of these "measures", as he phrases it, but it, but it must be pointed out that his headquarters were in the same city and that he received reports from his subordinates. (R-1248). Regarding his statement that had he been aware of these actions he would have prevented them, the document them and, as a result, 341 mental deficients met their deaths at the hands of his subordinates.

In almost every instance Jost, when confronted with incriminating evidence, has shown an affinity for a frightened ostrich, hiding his head in the sand, seeking refuge against all onslaughts by the monotonous use of "I do not remember". But in one instance here cited, these tactics failed, as the evidence prepared originated in his own office. Here we refer to two letters addressed to the Reichs Security Main Office in Berlin. The body of the letter is as follows:

> "A transport of Jews, which has to be treated in a special
> way, arrives weekly at the office of the Commandant of the
> Security Police and the Security Service of White Ruthenia.
> The three S-Vans, which are there, are not sufficient for
> that purpose. I request assignment of another S-Van (5-tons).
> At the same time I request the shipment of 20 gas hoses for
> the 3 gas vans on hand, (2 Diamond, 1 Sauer) since the ones
> on hand are leaky already.
>   (signature) The Commandant of the security police
>   and the Security Service
>   'Ostland'
>   Roem IT-126/43 GRS
>   (signed)   TRUEHE-SS Hptstf.
(I, pages 136, 137, 501-PS, Pros. Ex. 32)

This letter is dated 15 June 1942, during which time Jost was admittedly the Commandant of the Security Police and SD for the East, with headquarters in Riga. (Supra). He denies knowledge of the letter, as is to be expected, (R-1286) but he does admit knowledge of the identity of the signer of the letter (TRUEHE), who was the person requesting these murder cars. (R-1288). He identifies this person as his subordinate, his administration chief, vested with authority to order "normal" items of equipment as needed. (R-1288, 1289). The defendant Jost states that he exercised the functions of a commanding officer by inspecting his vehicles but denies that he was ever aware of the existence of these lethal vehicles. It is ridiculous to assume that in inspections of less than 100 vehicles (R-1301) over a protracted period of 5 months, an officer would not become aware, would not notice, 4 vehicles so singular in character, appearance and purpose as these gas vans. Jost attempts to evade responsibility for and denies knowledge of these vehicles by pointing out the statement in the letter that these massacre machines were intended for use in White Ruthenia. Furthermore, employing his old tactics of attempting to create confusion where none actually exists, he states that White Ruthenia is outside the territory of the Einsatzgruppe, ignoring his position as Commander-in-Chief of the Security Police and SD, with a subordinate commander in White Ruthenia. However, in response to pertinent questions asked by the President, he admits that he had command of that area.(R-1304). In the face of evidence of this nature, the dulled edge of Jost's prevarications is of no avail in sundering the snare that truth has formed about him.

As the Commander-in-Chief of the Security Police and the SD and as the leader of Einsatzgruppe A (actually interchangeable positions devised to meet changing conditions) Jost is, of course, responsible for the acts of his subordinate commanders and the execution of their duties in the furtherance of their plan to rid the world of Jewry and communists. Admittedly, White Ruthenia was under the command of Jost and he is chargeable and responsible for atrocities which occurred there under the direction of his subordinates. The defendant STRAUCH was Jost's representative and

- 14 -

subordinate in White Ruthenia. He occupied the position of the Commander of the Security Police and SD for White Ruthenia (KdS) (R-1280). Jost has frequently expressed an alleged lack of knowledge about mass executions which took place in the areas under his command. However, if we examine the letter dated 31 July 1942, at which time Jost was in command, we see that such a profession of ignorance is an idiotic assertion, at best. One sentence of this letter reads as follows:

> "During detailed consultations with the SS-Brigadefuehrer
> ZEHNER and the extremely capable Chief of the SD, SS-
> Obersturmbannfuehrer Dr. Jr. STRAUCH, we found that we
> had liquidated approximately 55,000 Jews in White
> Ruthenia during the last 10 weeks."
>
> (IIIA, page 32, 3428-PS, Pros. Ex. 111)

It is apparent from this excerpt that approximately from 15 May 1942 until 31 July 1942 forces under the command of Jost murdered 55,000 defenseless persons in White Ruthenia alone. Unless he claims that he lived in a veritable vacuum, Jost could not have remained unaware of these mass slaughters. Perusing the document further, we see that there was to be no cessation of these atrocities but there was a callous intent to continue these feral operations:

> "I am in full agreement with the Commander of the SD
> in White Ruthenia that we are to liquidate every Jewish
> transport which hasnot been ordered or announced by
> our superior offices, so as to avoid further unrest in
> White Ruthenia," (Supra)

The Prosecution is of the opinion that the above stands as a stark contradiction of Jost's denials of knowledge and that his claims of ignorance and protests are hypocritical and empty.

VI. VOLUNTARY MEMBERSHIP IN THE SS AND SD AFTER 1 SEPTEMBER 1939

A. The Law

The International Military Tribunal, in its opinion and judgment, declared as follows in reference to the SD:

> "In dealing with the SD the Tribunal includes Amter III,
> VI, and VII of the RSHA and all other members of the SD,

49

including all local representatives and agents,
honorary or otherwise, whether they were technically
members of the SS or not, but not including honorary
informers who were not members of the SS, and members of the Abwehr who were transferred to the SD.
"The Tribunal declares to be criminal within the
meaning of the Charter the group composed of those
members of the Gestapo and SD holding the positions
enumerated in the preceding paragraph who became or
remained members of the organization with knowledge
that it was being used for the commission of acts
declared criminal by Article 6 of the Charter, or
who were personally implicated as members of the
organization in the commission of such crimes. The
basis for this finding is the participation of the
organization in war crimes and crimes against
humanity connected with the war; this group declared
criminal· cannnot include, therefore, persons who had
ceased to hold the positions enumerated in the preceding paragraph prior to 1 September 1939".

(Judgment of the International Military Tribunal,

  Vol. I, pages 267, 268).

"In dealing with the SS the Tribunal includes all persons
who had been officially accepted as members of the SS
including the members of the Allgemeine SS, members of
the Waffen SS, members of the SS Totenkopf Verbande, and
the members of any of the different police forces who
were members of the SS." (Judgment of the International
Military Tribunal, Vol. I, page 273).

"The Tribunal declares to be criminal within the
meaning of the Charter the group composed of those
persons who had been officially accepted as members
of the SS as enumerated in the preceding paragraph
who became or remained members of the organization

with knowledge that it was being used for the
commission of acts declared criminal by Article 6
of the Charter, or who were personally implicated
as members of the organization in the commission of
such crimes, excluding, however, those who were
drafted into membership by the State in such a way
as to give them no choice in the matter, and who had
committed no such crimes. The basis of this finding
is the participation of the organization in war
crimes and crimes against humanity connected with the
war; this group declared criminal cannot include,
therefore, persons who had ceased to belong to the
organizations enumerated in the preceding paragraph
prior to 1 September 1939". (Judgment of the International Military Tribunal. Vol. I, page 273).

B. THE FACTS

On 28 July 1934 the defendant Jost was officially accepted as
a member of the SS and of the SD (IIIA, page 4, NO-2896, Pros. Ex. 98).
Prior to this date he had joined the SA as "a simple soldier" and by 1934
he had attained the rank of Obersturmbannfuhrer (Lieutenant Colonel).
(R-1133). This rank was honored by officials of the SS and he was
accepted into the SS and SD as such. Through the course of the years
he worked on counter-intelligence matters (Surpa) and in 1939 – to be
more specific, on 20 April 1939 – he had attained the rank of Brigadefuehrer and Major General of the Police. (R-1133). (IIIA, page 4,
NO-2896, Pros. Ex. 98). In October 1939, after the reorganization of
the SD, he was appointed as the Chief of Amt VI of the RSHA. He continued therewith until September of 1941, at which time he transferred to the East Ministry under the now-deceased Rosenberg. He was and
remained a member of the SS and SD even at this time and received his
salary and orders from the FSHA. (R-1141, 1143). In his rank and
capacity as Brigadefuehrer, he undertook an information tour of the

Occupied Soviet Union in February of 1942, and in March of 1942 he was appointed Chief of Einsatzgruppe A and Commander-in-Chief of the Security Police and SD for the Eastland. (R-1147). Jost at no time resigned from the SS and SD, and remained a member of these organizations until the capitultion. As far as knowledge of the criminal nature of these organizations is concerned, his service therewith, considering his high position – first as Chief of Amt VI and later serving in the East with the Einsatzgruppen – is sufficient to impute the necessary knowledge. Further, he was aware of the Fuehrer Order to kill the Jews, which employed the SS and SD as the weapons for its executions. (R-1240).

In addition, the International Military Tribunal has stated:

> "The Tribunal finds that knowledge of these criminal
> activities was sufficiently general to justify
> declaring that the SS was a criminal organization to
> the extent hereinafter described. It does appear that
> an attempt was made to keep secret some phases of its
> activities but its criminal programs were so widespread,
> and involved slaughter on such a gigantic scale, that
> its criminal activities must have been widely known. It
> must be recognized, moreover, that the criminal activities
> of the SS followed quite logically from the principles on
> which it was organized." (Judgment of the International
> Military Tribunal, Vol. I, page 273).

C. CONCLUSION

In view of the above, it would be foolish for Jost to deny his voluntary membership in the SS and SD or to maintain that he was unaware of their criminal character.

VII. POSSIBLE DEFENSES

The defendant Jost has not seen fit to choose the well-known plea of superior orders, but has rather obviated this possibility by a categorical denial of the charges as set forth in Counts I and II of the

Indictment. He states that he repeatedly and persistently objected to his assignment in the East and further denies all knowledge of atrocities which took place in the East. He states that he strenuously objected to Heydrich, but we are well aware of Heydrich's attitude towards subordinates who refused to carry out his orders. He has said that Heydrich agreed to allow him to divorce himself of the "executive" tasks in the East and limited his command authority. It is at the very least safe to say that this is an illogical assertion. No one, especially a person of Heydrich's character and position would place an officer of Jost's rank in a commanding position and, at the same time, disrobe him of the mantle of command. He claims that his was only a temporary appointment. This is surely no defense, for all were appointed temporarily in furtherance of a plan to expose all high-ranking SS leaders of the RSHA to collective responsibility for the atrocities in the East.

He asserts that he told Jeckeln, the HSSPF, that he would not be involved in any actions against the Jews, (R-1163) but in speaking of Jeckeln he has stated:

> "I remember that during the summer months of 1942 he
> was in charge of a combat unit near Leningrad, temporarily.
> Two volunteer officers of this combat unit — did I say
> Estonian officers? — had taken an unofficial leave, and
> left for a short period of time, about twenty-four hours,
> and had travelled to Estonia. Jeckeln was informed about
> this or he somehow discovered this. They were put before
> a court-martial immediately. They were condemned to death.
> The sentence was confirmed by Jeckeln. The harshness shown
> in the measure proves how Jeckeln dealt in such cases."

Q. "Can you give us another example to characterize Jeckeln?"

A. "This harshness and strictness of Jeckeln I have already
explained this morning; that he was prepared to have shot
SS men whose nerves could not stand the strain. That
proves his harshness towards his subordinates. This court-
martial against officers also proves this. But how in his

personal sphere, down to the bitter end he could be so,

is shown by the fact that even one of his own children,

which was not quite sane, he had killed -- that is, he

used Euthanasia. That proves how hard this man was."

(R-1211, 1212, 1213)

After studying the above, it is difficult to believe that Jost

could have spoken to Jeckeln in the manner which he claims.

He claims that he objected to Himmler, but Himmler was a strict

disciplinarian. Jost says that in a discussion with Himmler he asked

to be released and, in Jost's own words:

"Himmler had given an order that when a superior was

greeted or saluted, the glove had to be taken from

the hand. In the Army it was the other way around;

the glove had to remain on the hand. Himmler said 'I

have given this glove order. There are many who believe

they do not have to bother about such an order because

they don't like it. Anyone whom I meet who does not

follow this order and obeys it in the strictest manner,

I shall punish him very severely and harshly, and even

if the contents of the order are ever so ridiculous, the

contents of the order don't matter; all that matters is

that it is an order and those who don't obey the glove-

order prove that they donot want to carry out orders

of great importance. Orders cannot be discussed or debated.

Orders have to be obeyed, and that principle you don't seem

to have realized yet'." (R-1176)

A man of this type would surely order the death of a disobedient

officer rather than inquire as to his health, as Jost claims he did.

Jost claims that he objected to Rosenberg, but this would seem a

rather foolish measure, as the International Military Tribunal found

Rosenberg sufficiently involved as a murderer himself to warrant his

death sentence.

54

In summation we might say that it is a startling coincidence, and quite convenient, that all of the people with whom he sought to plead and to whom he objected are no longer able to confront and contradict him. Heydrich met death at the hands of a Czech patriot striking a blow for freedom; Jeckeln died in the land which he had reddened with the blood of thousands; Himmler chose a coward's death by taking cyanide, rather than face his accusers; Rosenberg was conveniently sentenced and executed by the collective judgments of the Allied Nations as represented by the International Military Tribunal.

In consideration of the preceding it is respectfully submitted that the guilt of the defendant Jost, as charged in Counts I, II and III, has been adequately established.

RESPECTFULLY SUBMITTED FOR THE CHIEF OF COUNSEL

BY:

JOHN E. GLANCY

55

MILITARY TRIBUNAL II

CASE NO. 9

TRIAL BRIEF FOR THE

UNITED STATES OF AMERICA

-against-

ERICH NAUMANN

Benjamin B. Ferencz
Chief Prosecutor
Peter W. Walton
Arnost Horlik-Hochwald
John E. Glancy
Of Counsel

For:

TELFORD TAYLOR
Brigadier General, USA
Chief of Counsel for War Crimes

and

James M. McHaney
Deputy Chief of Counsel
for War Crimes
Director, SS Division

Mr. Alfred Schwarz
Mrs. Nancy H. Fenstermacher
Research Analysts

RESPONSIBILITY OF THE DEFENDANT NAUMANN

I.   THE CHARGES.

In Counts One and Two of the Indictment it is
charged that the defendant ERICH NAUMANN was a principal
in, accessory to, ordered, abetted, took a consenting
part in, was connected with plans and enterprises involving
and was a member of organizations or groups connected with
certain atrocities and offenses, constituting crimes
against humanity and war crimes. These offenses included
persecutions on political, racial and religious grounds,
murder, extermination, imprisonment and other inhumane
acts committed against civilian populations, in violation
of the Law of Nations, general principles of Criminal
Law and the Laws and Customs of War as defined in Control
Council Law No. 10.

The defendant NAUMANN is further charged with
membership in the SS and SD, organizations declared to
be criminal by the International Military Tribunal.

II.   CRIMES AGAINST HUMANITY AND WAR CRIMES WERE
      COMMITTED BY UNITS UNDER THE COMMAND OF THE
                  DEFENDANT NAUMANN.

    A.   THE DEFENDANT'S TIME OF COMMAND.

The defendant NAUMANN was the commanding officer
of Einsatzgruppe B from 1 November 1941 until February or
March 1943 (R. 147, Pros. Exh. 113, Doc. Book III-B, p.
11, NO-2970, Doc. Book III-B, p. 1, NO-4150, Pros. Exh.
112).

    B.   UNITS UNDER HIS COMMAND.

The defendant admitted that Sonderkommandos
7a and 7b and Einsatzkommandos 8 and 9 as well as the
Vorkommando Moscow and Trupp Smolensk were subordinate
to him as chief of Einsatzgruppe B (R. 810).

His contention that he was only in command from the end of November 1941 and not from the 1st of November, 1941, is refuted by his own SS Personnel Record showing him to have been in command from 1 November (Pros. Exh. 113, Doc. Book III-B, p. 11, NO-2970), the Einsatz Reports themselves listing Naumann as being in Smolensk on 12 November 1941 (Pros. Exh. 72, Doc. Book II-C, p. 20, NO-2830), the testimony of the defendant Steimle saying he met Naumann in Russia about the middle of November (R. 2027) and his own unsuccessful attempt to influence the testimony of the defendant Klingelhoefer by dropping a note into his cell saying: "The beginning of my duty, end of November 1941 (R. 881, Pros. Exh. 176, NO-5450). Naumann's statement that this was done solely "From a comradely attitude" (R. 884) is absurd. The attempted change in dates can be better understood as the "alibi" to evade the facts shown in the Einsatz Reports.

59

C. THE CRIMES COMMITTED.

The Einsatz report of 19 December 1941, describes 15 separate actions in 16 different localities by the Einsatzgruppe B which resulted in the murder of a total of 17,256 Jews, both male and female, as well as the deliberate killing of 16 children in a children's home (Pros. Exh. 62, Doc. Book II-B, p. 36-39, NO-2824).

The defendant has stated that all these executions took place before his time for although the report is dated 19 December it described events which took place four to five weeks earlier (R. 825-826) hence around the middle of November.

The report of 22 December describes the murder of hundreds of Jews in the Prisoner-of-War camps in

witebsk and Wjasma and the murder of additional hundreds
in other localities of Einsatzgruppe B (Pros. Exh. 114,
Doc. Book III-B, p. 19, NO-2833). Here again the defendant
Naumann relies on his statement: "That was before my time"
(R. 827). Even accepting his contention that reports
described events which took place four to five weeks earlier,
these killings would have occurred around the middle of
November.

His argument that he only took command on November 30 is thus a clear attempt to evade responsibility by
concealing the truth as shown by the evidence establishing
him as having been in command from the first of November.

Even if we accepted the defendant's statement
that he was not actually in command on the dates covered
by the reports of 19 and 22 December, he could not evade
responsibility.

One of the Reports covers specifically the executions by Einsatzgruppe B between 6 and 30 March 1942
(Pros. Exh. 66, Doc. Book II-B, p. 62, NO-3276). The
defendant Naumann has had to admit that he commanded
Einsatzgruppe B during that entire period (R. 871). The
report clearly shows that each of the units of Einsatzgruppe B carried out executions during that period including the murder of thousands of persons. In many instances, a reason is given for the killing, such as
"because of theft", or "attempted murder", or "sabotage",
or "spying", but these are very few and the vast majority
are listed as killed with a simple explanation "Jews" or
"Gypsies" or "Membership in the Communist Party". The
defendant's explanation for this report is that:

60

"The executions of Jews, Gypsies and Communist functionaries fell under the Fuehrer Order, membership in partisan bands and other crimes which are mentioned where various army orders applied."
(R. 828)

The defendant further explains that he had nothing to do with these murders (R. 828).

The defendant admitted that his unit had 2 or 3 gas vans and that "they were to be used to exterminate human beings" (R. 865). Asked how they were in fact used, he stated: "I know nothing about that" (R. 865) but explained that he had seen one carrying wood (R. 866).

Naumann commanded the Einsatz units in the Smolensk area. An official Soviet Commission investigating atrocities in that area found that during the German occupation 135,000 persons were put to death (USSR 48, 56, Pros. Rebuttal Doc. Book 5B). . . The Reports show that in the first 4 or 5 months of operation, Einsatzgruppe B killed over 45,000 people (Pros. Exh. 59, Doc. Book II-B, p. 15, NO-2825). The defendant admits commanding Einsatzgruppe B for 15 months (R. 146, 147, Pros. Exh. 112, Doc. Book III-B, p. 1, NO-4150) but refused to estimate the minimum number killed by his group (R. 860).

There can be no doubt that the units under the command of the defendant Naumann committed crimes against humanity and war crimes. It would indeed be naive to believe that the SS Brigadier General commanding these units knew nothing about and had nothihg to do with these grave offenses.

61

- 4 -

III. THE DEFENDANT IS RESPONSIBLE FOR THE CRIMES
      COMMITTED BY UNITS UNDER HIS COMMAND.

    A. NAUMANN HAD THE POWER TO COMMAND.

        The defendant has admitted upon cross-examina-
tion that he was the highest ranking officer in the Einsatzgruppe B and its Kommandos and that he had the power to
command (R. 866).

    B. HE KNEW HIS SUBORDINATE UNITS WERE KILLING
        AND WOULD CONTINUE TO KILL DEFENSELESS PEOPLE.

        The defendant has further admitted that at the
time he took command he knew that his subordinate units
were killing defenseless people (R. 854). Indeed two weeks
after he took command a report was submitted by Einsatzgruppe B showing that they had liquidated over 45,000
persons (Pros. Exh. 59, Doc. Book II-B, p. 15, NO-2825).
He also knew that they would continue killing defenseless
people, in accordance with their orders, after he took
command (R. 854).

        The defendant received orders from his military
superior to execute certain categories of persons. As he
admitted:

> "....I was ordered to Heydrich and
> I received clear orders from him for
> Russia. Now first of all I received
> the Fuehrer Order concerning the killing
> of Jews, Gypsies and Soviet officials..."
>   (R. 852)

He received and read reports from his subordinate Kommandos
(R. 854) and personally discussed with them the execution
orders (R. 855). He was therefore well aware that executions were being carried out during his time of command and
that he had personally been ordered to carry out such executions.

C. NAUMANN PERSONALLY ORDERED EXECUTIONS.

It is submitted by the Prosecution that the defendant Naumann personally ordered the executions which were committed by units under his command. As concerns the valuables of the victims, the defendant Ott swore in a pre-trial affidavit:

> "The valuables which were collected from these people were sent to Einsatz-gruppe B.
> This was ordered by command of Naumann, the head of Einsatzgruppe B, and the same was true for other executions."
> (Pros. Exh. 67, Doc. Book II-B, p. 64, NO-2993).

This was specifically denied by Naumann (R. 819-20). On cross-examination the defendant repeatedly denied that he had ever ordered anyone to be executed (R. 871, 872, 873). This was flatly contradicted by the evidence (Pros. Exh. 175, NO-5444, NO-5445, NO-5446, introduced loosely on 20 November 1947, R. 2724, R. 871-3). The Prosecution introduced 3 memoranda, each of which stated specifically that the person referred to in the memorandum was executed "by order of SS Brigadefuehrer Naumann of Einsatzgruppe B" (R. 874, Pros. Exh. 175). The defendant admitted that the scene of the executions was in his area and that he was there quite often (R. 872), that he knew one of the SS men mentioned in the memoranda (R. 891) and that he was indeed the person referred to as having ordered the executions (R. 876). As for the contents of the 3 separate memoranda, the defendant protested weakly "there must have been a mistake...." (R. 891).

Even if the incredible were accepted and it were believed that he did not personally order the executions, the defendant Naumann would still be responsible for the crimes committed by his units.

- 6 -

63

D.   EVEN IF HE DID NOT PERSONALLY ORDER EXECUTIONS
NAUMANN IS RESPONSIBLE FOR THE CRIMES OF HIS UNITS.

Naumann clearly knew that executions were carried on by the units of Einsatzgruppe B before his taking of command and that the executions continued.   When asked whether he controlled the executions to see that they were done in a humane and military manner, he replied:

> "During my visits the Commando leaders told me how executions had been carried out in the past. During my time, and I am now speaking about the chronological development, only a few or rather, fewer executions were carried out than before......"
> (R. 870)

and further he says:

> "The Commando leaders reported to me as to how they had carried out these executions so far and I had no objections to that."
> (R. 871)

64

Asked by defense counsel, Dr. Hoffman, whether he thought the Fuehrer Order was carried out to the full extent by the Einsatzkommando leaders, Naumann replied:

> "In my region, I think so."
> (R. 895)

Although the defendant has told us that he discussed these executions with his Kommando leaders (R. 855, 870) he does not cite a single instance where he, as commanding officer, did anything to try to stop, prevent, or hinder the slaughter of people he knew to be innocent (See R. 855).   On the contrary, he admitted that he would immediately have reported anyone who refused to carry out the order (R. 858).   This indicates that at least his attitude coerced his subordinates to carry out the extermination order to its full extent.

"The law of war imposes on a military officer in a position of command an affirmative duty to take such steps as are within his power and appropriate to the circumstances to control those under his command for the prevention of acts which are violations of the law of war."

(Judgment, Military Tribunal I, Case No. I, The United States of America against Karl Brandt et al, page 70)

"It is evident that the conduct of military operations by troops whose excesses are unrestrained by the orders or efforts of their commander would almost certainly result in violations which it is the purpose of the law of war to prevent. Its purpose to protect civilian populations and prisoners of war from brutality would largely be defeated if the commander of an invading army could with impunity neglect to take reasonable measures for their protection. Hence the law of war presupposes that its violation is to be avoided through the control of the operations of war by commanders who are to some extent responsible for their subordinates."

(Decision by the Supreme Court of the United States in Application of Yamashita, 66 Supreme Court 340-347, 1946)

Not only did the defendant Naumann fail to indicate that he did anything to prevent or mitigate the murder of defenseless people, but, under questioning by the Presiding Judge, openly admitted that he approved of the extermination order (R. 897, 899, 900). The question was asked:

"Yes, then you agreed that in order to win the war it was necessary to kill hundreds of thousands of defenseless people, men, women and children unarmed, did you agree with that?"

to which the defendant Naumann replied:

"Yes, Your Honor." (R. 897)

In view of the defendant's final admission that he approved of the extermination order, his contention that he failed to carry it out, pass it on to his subordinates, or to enforce it, becomes absolutely incredible.

65

IV.   NAUMANN WAS A MEMBER OF ORGANIZATIONS DECLARED
       CRIMINAL BY THE INTERNATIONAL MILITARY TRIBUNAL.

          Control Council Law No. 10, Art. II, provides
that:

          "(1) 'Each of the following acts is recognized
     as a crime': ......

          d) Membership in categories of a criminal
              group or organization declared criminal
              by the International Military Tribunal."

          The International Military Tribunal Charter

which is incorporated by reference into the Control Council

Law provides further that:

              "In any such case the criminal nature
          of the group or organization is considered
          proved and should not be questioned."
              (IMT Charter, Art. 10)

          The International Military Tribunal declared

certain groups of the Leadership Corps, the SS, the Gestapo

and the SD to be criminal organizations. The test to be

applied in determining the guilt of individual members

were clearly stated by the International Tribunal and

applied by Military Tribunal No. III in the case of

United States vs. Alstotter, et al, as follows:

              "Those members of an organization which
          has been declared criminal 'who became or
          remained members of the organizations with
          knowledge that it was being used for the
          commission of acts declared criminal by
          Article 6 of the Charter, or who were per-
          sonally implicated as members of the organi-
          zation in the commission of such crimes'
          are declared punishable."
              (R. 10711, Judgment, Court No. III,
              Case No. III) (Emphasis supplied)

A. MEMBERSHIP IN THE SS.

Certain categories of the SS were declared to
constitute criminal organizations:

> "In dealing with the SS the Tribunal
> includes all persons who had been offi-
> cially accepted as members of the SS
> Including the members of the Allgemeine
> SS, members of the Waffen SS, members of
> the SS Totenkopf Verbande, and the mem-
> bers of any of the different police forces
> who were members of the SS."
> (Emphasis supplied)
> (Trial of Major War Criminals, Volume I,
>   p. 273)

The defendant became a member of the Nazi Party
as early as 1929 (Pros. Exh. 112, Doc. Book III-B, p. 1,
NO-4150). He became a full time leader of the SA or Storm
Troops in 1933 (R. 804). In 1935 he joined the SS and be-
came a full time SS leader (Pros. Exh. 112, Doc. Book
III-B, p. 1, NO-4150).

His personnel record confirms his membership
in the SS and shows that the defendant was awarded the
Iron Cross First Class as well as numerous other decora-
tions (Pros. Exh. 113, Doc. Book III-B, p. 8, 6, NO-2970).
The defendant has nowhere even contended that his membership in the SS was not completely voluntary. The defendant
remained a member of the SS and in 1942 he was promoted to
Brigadefuehrer or Brigadier General (Pros. Exh. 113, Doc.
Book III-B, p. 4, NO-2970).

It cannot be denied that Naumann was "officially
accepted" into the SS and "became or remained" a member
of the SS with knowledge of its criminal activities. In
addition, the defendant was "personally implicated" as a
member of that organization in the commission of war crimes
and crimes against humanity as shown above.

B.   MEMBERSHIP IN THE SD.

The International Military Tribunal declared certain categories of the SD to be criminal:

> "In dealing with the SD the Tribunal includes Amter III, VI and VII of the RSHA, and all other members of the SD including all local representatives and agents, honorary or otherwise, whether they were technically members of the SS or not....."
> (Trial of Major War Criminals, Vol. I, p. 267-8) (Emphasis supplied)

The defendant admitted that in 1933 he became a full time leader in the SD (R. 804). This is confirmed also by his SS Personnel Record (Pros. Exh. 113, Doc. Book III-B, p. 7, NO-2970). It is clear from the defendant's own statements explaining why he joined the SD that his membership therein was completely voluntary (R. 804). He remained a member of the SD until the end of the war (Pros. Exh. 113, Doc. Book III-B, p. 4, NO-2970).

Again the defendant meets the test of having "become or remained" a member of the SD, with knowledge that it was being used for the commission of acts declared criminal by the IMT Charter. In addition the defendant was personally implicated as a member of the SD in the commission of crimes as shown above.

V.   THERE ARE NO MITIGATING CIRCUMSTANCES CONCERNING THE CRIMES OF THE DEFENDANT NAUMANN.

A.   SUPERIOR ORDERS.

For many reasons the plea of superior orders can have no applicability to the defendant Naumann. Although he concedes that through Heydrich he received the Fuehrer Order to kill the Jews, Gypsies and Soviet officials (R. 852) he denies that he personally passed on the order or did anything to carry it out (R. 856, 869, 870).

68

Since he denies that he carried out his orders it would be illogical to allow him any benefit from having carried them out under pressure of his military superiors.

The plea of superior orders is only applicable as a mitigating circumstance where a subordinate is forced to commit an act against his will under threat of death or punishment. Mitigation finds its justification in the fact that the deed was done against the will of the perpetrator. Where, however, the offender agrees with the order or carries it out enthusiastically it would be folly to say that he was forced or coerced to do an act against his will. The defendant Naumann has admitted that he, in fact, agreed with the Hitler Order to kill defenseless men, women and children (R. 897, 899, 900). The fact that the order happened to originate with a superior can, therefore, in no way mitigate anything done by Naumann in pursuance of the order of which he personally approved. It is clear that he was in no way coerced. Furthermore, the defendant has admitted that he would immediately have reported to higher authorities anyone who refused to carry out the order (R. 858). This clearly shows that he certainly made no attempt to evade the order, had no desire to evade the order, and in fact would have personally taken measures to see that it was carried out had any subordinate sought to evade it. Under such circumstances there can be no mitigation.

69

- 12 -

B. CHARACTER.

On the witness stand the defendant has
repeatedly made statements which were refuted by the
evidence. This was so, concerning his statements that he
took command only on 30 November (cf. pages 1-2 supra),
that he never ordered the valuables of persons executed
to be sent to him (cf. page 5 supra), that he never
ordered anyone to be executed (cf. pages 5-6 supra), that
he never passed on the Fuehrer Order (cf. pages 6-7 supra).

While in the Nurnberg jail he managed to drop
a letter into the cell of the defendant Klingelhoefer. In
that letter he carefully outlined his defense, listed
facts, names and places he thought Klingelhoefer might
contradict him on, assured him that the Prosecution's
proof was inadequate, and warned Klingelhoefer not to be
bluffed by the interrogator (R. 881-3).

This was a very obvious attempt to influence
what Klingelhoefer would have to say and to conceal and
distort the truth. Naumann's explanation that he wrote
this note simply "from a comradely attitude" (R. 884) is
as credible as his other testimony.

The true character of the defendant was shown
in his statement on the stand that he felt no guilt or
remorse about anything he did while commander of Einsatzgruppe B (R. 886-887).

In his opening statement, counsel for the
defendant stated that Naumann was not the type of person
described by the prosecution. To support that he stated
that:

> "The defendant Naumann endeavored in
> Holland to lighten the burden of occupa-
> tion wherever he had a chance to do so."
> (Opening Statement, Naumann, p. 6)

70

He cited general measures which were taken to help the
Dutch and

> "All this Naumann did though he was
> not competent to do so, and though he
> exceeded his competence by these actions
> and acted contrary to existing orders."
> (Opening Statement, Naumann, p. 6)

The absurdity of this is apparent from Naumann's own statement that he was an obedient soldier and carried out his
orders (R. 895) and the Official Police Report from the
Dutch government showing Naumann's complicity in the
murder of innocent Dutch citizens (Pros. Rebuttal Doc.
Book V-B, NO-5771).

VI.   CONCLUSION.

The defendant Naumann was a member of the SS
and SD after 1 September 1939, and remained a member with
knowledge of their criminal activities.

He was the commanding officer of Einsatzgruppe
B from 1 November 1941 to February or March 1943. During
that time the units of Einsatzgruppe B murdered thousands
of persons simply because they were Jews, Gypsies or Soviet
officials. The defendant when taking command of Einsatzgruppe B, received orders to exterminate these people. He
admitted that he was a good soldier and carried out his
orders but denied that it was necessary for him to do anything about the extermination order inasmuch as it was
already issued to the Einsatz units. The defendant's contention that he never ordered an execution is clearly refuted
by the evidence presented. Even if the defendant did not
personally order the murders however, he cannot evade

71

- 14 -

responsibility for their commission. He knew that such
crimes were being committed regularly by troops under
his command, and that they would continue to commit such
crimes. Yet the defendant Naumann did absolutely nothing
to hinder, evade, mitigate, or stop this slaughter of
defenseless people by his subordinates. He admitted
that he approved of the extermination order and would
have taken disciplinary action against any subordinate
who tried to evade it. He stated that he felt no guilt
or remorse.

In view of the foregoing, it is submitted
that the responsibility and guilt of the defendant for
the crimes charged in Counts 1, 2 and 3 of the Indictment
have been clearly established.

72

FOR THE CHIEF OF COUNSEL FOR
WAR CRIMES:

Benjamin B. Ferencz
Chief Prosecutor

- 15 -

M I L I T A R Y   T R I B U N A L   N O.   II

Case No. IX

CLOSING BRIEF FOR

THE UNITED STATES OF AMERICA

AGAINST

OTTO OHLENDORF

BENJAMIN B. FERENCZ
Chief Prosecutor
PETER W. WALTON
ARNOST HORLIK-HOCHWALD
JOHN E. GLANCY

For:

TELFORD TAYLOR
Brigadier General, U.S.A.,
Chief of Counsel for War Crimes

and

JAMES M. McHANEY
Deputy Chief of Counsel
for War Crimes

Alfred Schwarz
Nancy H. Fenstermacher
Research Assistants

Nurnberg, Germany
January 1948

Doc. 5

73

INTRODUCTION

Count One of the Indictment charges that between May 1941 and July 1943 Otto OHLENDORF was the Commanding Officer of Einsatzgruppe D, one of four Police Units, organized for the express purpose of eliminating all present and future threats to the security of the German Armed Forces in the conquered Russian territories. Count One further charges that he committed crimes against humanity in that he was a principal in, accessory to, ordered, abetted, took a consenting part in and was connected with plans and enterprises connected with the commission of such crimes. The crimes charged were a part of the National Socialist systematic program of genocide, deliberately aimed at the destruction of foreign races and ethnic groups by means of murderous extermination.

It is moreover charged in Count One that Otto OHLENDORF in becoming connected with the plans for the commission of these crimes and in acting as an Einsatzgruppen leader, organizer, instigator, and accomplice in the said crimes, became individually responsible for the acts of others performed in the execution of said plans and enterprises. (Paragraph 9 of Count One). It is charged that Einsatzgruppe D under the command of Otto OHLENDORF in the area of Southern Russia was responsible for the murder of 90,000 persons.

Count Two charges that the crimes of the Defendant Otto OHLENDORF were committed between 22 June 1941 and July 1943 against the persons and property of inhabitants of occupied territories and prisoners of war and such criminal acts were not justified by military necessity.

Count Three charges that Otto OHLENDORF was, subsequent to 1 September 1939, a member of the SS and the SD, organizations declared to be criminal by the International Military Tribunal.

The acts recognized as Crimes against Humanity and War Crimes are set forth in Paragraph 1 (b) and (c) of Article II of Control Council Law No. 10. Membership in organizations declared criminal by the International Military Tribunal is defined as a crime in Paragraph 1 (d) of the same Article.

- 1 -

Criteria of criminality are established by Paragraph 2 of Article
II of Control Council Law No. 10.

POSITIONS OF RESPONSIBILITY

The defendant Otto OHLENDORF was born on 4 February 1907 in Hohe-
neggelsen, Kreis Marienburg, in the province of Hannover. He was educated in the public schools and attended the universities of Leipzig and
Goettingen. His studies of law, political science and economics fitted
him for the field of state economy, and his political beliefs led him
to join the NSDAP in 1925 with the party number 6531. In 1926 he was
designated for service in the SD but left his native town and thus was
not given an identity number in the SD or the SS. In 1936 he formally
rejoined the SD and SD and was reissued his original SS number of 880.
The defendant retained his membership in those organizations until the
collapse of the Third Reich in May 1945. After 1936 his rise in the SD
was steady and he became an economic consultant. Due to difficulties
with high-ranking Party officials his connection with the SD for over a
year was largely honorary but in 1939 he was instrumental in reorgani-
zing the SD and so became the head of the SD organization within the
framework of the Reichssicherheitshauptamt (RSHA). (Doc. Bk. III D,
Page 32-33, Doc. NO-2857, Pros. Ex. 157).

In June 1941 he was detailed to organize and take command of the
Security Police Unit Einsatzgruppe D. At the end of his Einsatzgruppe
he invaded Russia in the rear of the Wehrmacht and was in command of
this unit until the month of June 1942. He saw service in this capacity
in the Southern part of Russia and the Crimean Peninsula, reaching as
far as the Caucausus. Upon the death of HEYDRICH, Chief of the Security
Police and SD, he was recalled to Berlin where under HIMMLER he was
appointed a Major General of Police. He held the post of Under-Secretary
in the Reich Ministry of Economy and in addition, continued as head of
Amt III (Chief of the Security Service) in the RSHA until 1945.

ACTIVITY IN EINSATZGRUPPE D

In June 1941 this defendant was designated by Himmler to command Einsatzgruppe D, and he knew of the impending attack on Russia some four weeks in advance. (Document Book I, page 35, Document 2620-PS, Pros. Ex. 9). Einsatzgruppe D was sub-divided into five units or kommandos designated as Sonderkommandos 10a, 10b, 11a, 11b and Einsatzkommando 12, with a total personnel strength of approximately five hundred men. These men were obtained from the State Police, Criminal Police, the Security Police (SD), the Waffen SS and the Order Police. (Document Book I, page 21, Document NO-2890, Pros. Ex. 5). The Einsatzgruppe was considered a mobile unit (R-514) and attacked to the 11th German Army (R-679). However, while the Army designated the areas in which the Einsatzgruppe functioned (Document Book I, page 35, Document 2620-PS, Pros. Ex. 9) and supplied the Einsatzgruppe with quarters, food, repairs, gasoline, etc., (Document NO-2890, cited supra) all operational directives and orders for the carrying out of executions were given through the Chief of the Security Police and Security Service (RSHA) in Berlin. (Document Book I, page 35, Document 2620-PS, Pros. Ex. 9).

The territory of operations of Einsatzgruppe D was that part of the Ukraine south of the Russian cities Czernowitz, Mogilew-Podolsk, Jampol, Ananjew, Nikolajew, Melitopol, Mariopol, Taganrog and Rostow, which included the Crimean Peninsula. Later on Einsatzgruppe D had charge of the Caucausus area. (Document NO-2890, cited supra).

The purpose and scope of the operations of Einsatzgruppe D under the commnd of the defendant Otto OHLENDORF is set forth in clear and unambiguous language in paragraph 6 of his own affidavit signed and sworn to on 24 April 1947, which states:

"The Einsatzgruppen had the following assignments: they were responsible for all political
security tasks within the operational area of the
army units and of the rear areas insofar as the
latter did not fall under the civil administration.

- 3 -

In addition they had the task of clearing the area of Jews, Communist officials and agents. The last named task was to be accomplished by killing all racially and politically undesirable elements seized, who were considered dangerous to the security. I know that the Einsatzbruppen were assigned partly to the reconnaissance of guerilla bands, and to military tasks and after completion of their basic assignments, were partly converted into combat units. All orders which pertained to the tactical and strategic situation or sphere of interest to the Army Group or Army, came from the Commander, the Chief of Staff or Counter Intelligence officer of the Army or Army Gruppe to which the Einsatzgruppe was assigned. Orders relating to clearing out undesirable elements went directly to the Einsatzkommandos and came from the Reichsfuehrer SS himself or by transmission through Heydrich. The Commander-in-Chief was ordered by Hitler to support the execution of those orders. Through the so-called Commissar Order, the Army units had to sort out political commissars and other similar undesirable elements themselves and hand them over to the Einsatzkommandos to be killed." (Document Book I, page 22, Document NO-2890, Pros. Ex. 5: see also R-515 and R-521).

As in all military and para-military units regular reports of their activities were dispatched to higher headquarters. Those of Einsatzgruppe D, when possible, were dispatched via radio weekly or bi-weekly and a comprehensive written report monthly, all reports going to the RSHA in Berlin. This Gruppe also made regular reports of their activities to the 11th German Army Headquarters. (Document Book I, page 21, para. 7, page 23; Doc. NO-2890; Pros. Ex. 5). These reports from all Einsatzgruppe in the conquered territories of the East were thereupon consolidated and issued as Operational Situation

77

Reports U.S.S.R. These Reports were published and distributed by
the Office of the Chief of the Security Police and the SD. (Document
Book I, page 25, Document NO-4327, Pros. Ex. 6).

MURDER OF RUSSIAN NATIONALS

In performance of its mission, Einsatzgruppe D murdered thousands
of Russian citizens. (Direct Testimony of OHLENDORF, R-534). The
Indictment in this case shows that Einsatzgruppe D between June 1941 and
July 1943 murdered more than 90,000 persons. (Count One, Paragraph 9 (A)
of Indictment, Case No. 9). This figure is neither fanciful or exaggerated
as claimed by the defense, when the evidence in this case is considered.
By a series of Operational Situation Reports issued from the RSHA in Berlin
the total number of executions performed by Einsatzgruppe D can be ascertained. In approximately four months of operation the Gruppe had executed
31,767 persons, the majority of whom were Jews (Document Book II D, page 18
Document NO-3159, Pros. Ex. 85). Five weeks later the number of executions of the unit had reached the total of 54,696 persons. (Document
Book II D, page 20, Document NO-2828, Pros. Ex. 86.) The regular ratio
of over 300 murders per day of operation was maintained in the next chro-
nological report of the 19th of January 1942, less than six months after
this Einsatzgruppe invaded Russian soil, when a sum total of 80,160 human
beings were reported as having been killed by Einsatzgruppe D (Document
Book II, page 31, Document NC-3338 (A). Pros. Ex. 88). The final Operational Situation Report showing a total number of executions introduced
by the Prosecution gives the figure of 91,678 executions. (Document
Book II, page 7, Document NO-3359, Prox. Ex. 84). This latter document
accounts for execution totals to the end of March 1942. According to the
defendant's own statement, he was away from early in March to the 26th
of April 1942. Then he was with his Einsatzgruppe until approximately
the 4th of June 1942 when he was recalled to Berlin following the death
of Heydrich and returned to the East only to relinquish command of this
Gruppe to his successor. (R-554-555). Therefore these totals of executions do represent the number of executions performed by Einsatzgruppe D

- 5 -

under the command of this defendant.

The Prosecution, however, does not rely wholly on this proof, but cites this defendant's testimony before the International Military Tribunal on the morning of 3 January 1946 when his memory for events in 1941-1942 was better and before he had completed a full year in confinement. This testimony is as follows:

"Q. Do you know how many persons were liquidated by Einsatz Group D, under your direction?

A. In the year June '41 to June '42, the Einsatzkommandos announced approximately 90,000 people as liquidated.

Q. Did that include men, women and children?

A. Yes.

Q. On what do you base those figures?

A. On reports submitted by the Einsatzkommandos to the Einsatz Groups.

Q. Were those reports submitted to you?

A. Yes.

Q. And you saw and read them?

A. I beg your pardon?

Q. And you saw and read those reports personally?

A. Yes.

Q. And it is on those reports that you base the figures you have given the Tribunal?

A. Yes."

(Page 2010 of the Official Transcript of the Record, IMT, see also Vol. IV "Trial of the Major War Criminals" – Official Copy – page 319).

Some two months earlier than his appearance in court as a witness, the Defendant OHLENDORF in a sworn statement, said on 5 November 1945:

"When the German Army invaded Russia, I was leader of Einsatzgruppe D in the southern sector, and in the course of a year, during which I was leader of Einsatzgruppe D, it liquidated approximately 90,000 men,

- 6 -

women and children. The majority of those liquidated were Jews, but there were among them some Communists functionaries too." (Document book I, page 35, Document 2620-FS, Pros. Ex. 9).

This portion of the then witness Otto OHLENDORF's affidavit was literally incorporated in the Judgment of the International Military Tribunal (Page 16, 897 of the Official Transcript of the Record IMT) as a finding of fact. (See also Vol. I "Trial of the Major War Criminals" - Official Copy - page 235).

The defendant again confirmed this testimony on cross-examination in this case (R-623).

The usual procedures employed in the collected and executing the victim was as follows:

When the kommandos of Einsatzgruppe D came into a town or in an area they generally solved the Jewish question first. Therefore they nominated a Jewish Council of Elders who were charged with registering the Jews in that locality (R-679) and assembling them. Those Jews were told that they would be resettled in another area. When the assembly took place usually in the market place of a town, the German authorities compared the registration lists with the names of the persons present. After this "roll call" the victims were taken via trucks to the place of execution some distance away from the place of assembly. The victims were then shot standing or kneeling and buried at the place of execution. The personal property and valuables were confiscated. The money and valuables went to the Reich Minister of Finance and the clothing of the victims was turned over to German Welfare organizations. (R-693-694).

An additional method of execution was inaugurated in the Einsatzgruppen, including Einsatzgruppe D, in the spring of 1942 when it was determined that women and children were to be executed by gassing in motorized gas vans. (R-694). Again, the victims were told that they were being moved away for purposes of resettlement and thus induced to enter the vans. These vans would accommodated 15 to 30 persons at a time. Approximately ten minutes treatment was enough to produce fatal results to the victims in these vans. (R-697). A few more details were given in his testimony before the International Military Tribunal which will serve here mrely to complete the account of this type of an execution. CHLENDORF there stated:

"The vans were loaded with the victims and driven to the place of burial, which usually was the same as that used for the mass executions. The time needed for the transportation was sufficient to insure the death of the victims." (Page 2010 of the Official Transcript of the Record IMT. See also Vol. IV, Trial of the Major War Criminals - Official Copy - page 322.

The apprehension and selection of Soviet Party members and Communist functionaries differed slightly in that those suspected of such classification were interrogated and the interrogating officer usually in collaboration with the kommando leader determined the "guilt" or innocence of the suspect. Automatically it followed that if he fell into a category considered to be a danger to the security of the German Armed Forces, then these two Einsatzgruppe offitcials passed judgment on the suspect (R-692) without trial of any kind (R-722).

81

These executions were usually reported to the RSHA in Berlin in the Operational Situation Reports U.S.S.R. periodically (See this Brief supra) and totals for Jews, Communists, Gypsies, Krimtchakes, partisans, saboteurs and asocial people as well as criminals, etc., were carefully accounted for. (See Document Book II D, page 28, Doc. NO-2834, Prosc. Ex. 87; Idem Document Book, page 7, Document No. 3359, Pros. Ex. 84; Idem Document Book, page 46, Document NO-3339, Pros. Ex. 93 and almost any other Operational Situation Report).

Another murderous activity in which the units under the command of this defendant engaged was the screening of the Prisoner of War and the transit camps for Communists, Party functionaries and NKVD (Soviet Intelligence) agents. These were to be turned over to the units of the Einsatzgruppe for immediate liquidation. The orders are so clear and unequivocal as to this mission of the Einsatzgruppen, that this subject was carefully avoided in the direct testimony of the defendant OHLENDORF. A brief consideration of the evidence offered by the Prosecution shows very clearly why any discussion on this subject was omitted.

On 17 July 1941, just after the Einsatzgruppen had been committed to its mission in the rear army areas, HEYDRICH, as Chief of the Security Police and SD, issued his Operational Order No. 8. On the distribution list attached to the order it is shown that copies were sent to Einsatz-gruppe D and to its kommandos. (Document Book I, pages 54 to 56, Document NO-3414, Pros. Ex. 14). The purpose of this order was to purge the prisoner of war camps which contained Soviet Russians. This would be effected by screening teams composed of one SS officer and four to six men. In the first supplement to this order, directions were given to the Einsatzgruppen chiefs to execute the purge of the transit camps with their own forces as far as possible. Detailed directions as to executions are also given, even to the locality where such affairs should be conducted. (Idem).

Supplementary directives and operational orders were issued for the "purging of prisoner of war and transit camps" and the attention of the Tribunal is respectfully directed to HEYDRICH's Operational Order No. 14 on 29 October 1941. (Document Book I, page 71, Document NO-3422, Pros. Ex. 19). This order based on Operational Order No. 8, (cited supra) was distributed for action to the Einsatzgruppen and to each kommando, in-cluding Einsatzgruppe D. In the third paragraph of this order it states:

".....the Einsatzgruppen will immediately detail
Sonderkommandos in appropriate strength under
the commnd of an SS officer. The kommandos have
to start their activity in the camps forthwith."

In a Top Secret enclosure to this order, it was directed (page 73 of Document Book I, that these screening kommandos could operate in-dependently of the Army and of the camp commandants. It also pointed out that the Russian soldier had forfeited the right to be treated as an "honorable soldier and in accordance with the Geneva Convention".

It was further directed (page 74 of Document Book I) that these screening teams would report weekly to the chief of their respective Einsatzgruppe on their activities for the report period. These significant statements in this directive appear on page 75 and are as follows:

"The chiefs of the Einsatzgruppen decide on the suggestions for execution on their own responsibility and give the Sonderkommandos the corresponding orders...

"Executions must be carried out unobtrusively at appropriate remote places and must, above all, not take place in or in the vicinity of the camps. Immediate and regular internment of the Corpses must be provided for.

"The special kommandos should, if possible, keep lists about the special treatment given; .....

"These lists (card file) are to be forwarded to the Chiefs of the Einsatzgruppen.

"The Chiefs of the Einsatzgruppen for their zone of operation, will submit to me monthly brief reports on the activity of the Sonderkommandos....."

As proof that these orders of HEYDRICH were put into effect, attention of the Tribunal is invited to the affidavit of Kurt LINDOW, formerly an official in the Gestapo Main Office (Amt IV RSHA). (Document Book I, page 65, Document 2542-PS, Pros. Ex. 16). SEIBERT, the Deputy to the defendant OHLENDORF, also knew of this activity of the SD on the Eastern Front, as he read all the reports from the kommandos. Furthermore he states in his affidavit of 1 April 1947, paragraph 5 (Document Book III D, page 34, Document NO-2859, Pros. Ex. 158) that he was aware that this screening of the prisoners of war and their execution took place. OHLENDORF on his cross-examination stated (R-725) that he commanded Einsatzgruppe D during the date the Operational Order No. 14 (Document Book I, page 71, Document NO-3422, Pros. Ex. 19) was issued. Every chance was

- 10 -

given this defendant to comment on this document which was specifically called to his attention by the Prosecution (R-725, cited supra) and he did not. Therefore it can be assumed that the defendant OHLENDORF received these directives and orders and that he himself issued the necessary orders to the kommandos to carry out the orders from Berlin.

This wholesale murder was performed for the purpose of the "momentary and permanent security" in the areas of operation of the Einsatzgruppen (R-521) more especially stated by this defendant:

> "In reference to the Eastern Jews, in the
> case of the Jews who were found in the Eastern
> campaign, it was the order that these Jews are
> to be killed for the reason that they were con-
> sidered as endangering the security of the German
> Reich." (R-627)

Yet the defendant in answer to a question stated:

> "Of course at a certain time there were
> persons when one could not have said that at
> that moment they were an immediate danger, but
> that does not change the fact that for us it
> meant a danger insofar as they were determined
> to be a danger, and none of us examined whether
> these persons at the moment, or in the future,
> would actually constitute danger, because this
> was outside our knowledge, and not a part of our
> task." (R-656).

He explained the killing of Jewish and Gypsy children in that they would offer a threat to permanent security when they grew up, since their parents had been killed by the German Armed Forces. (R-662). However, the defendant finally admitted that the killing of civilians in occupied areas, without trial, was murder (R-676).

The present and future security of the German armed might did not dictate the liquidation of human lives in every instance in which the

- 11 -

shooting of people occurred. Reports in at least two instances show that the insane were liquidated and these reports prove that Einsatzgruppe D contributed in some part to the Nazi euthanasia program. The Gruppe reports officially on 23 March 1942 that it had during the same month of March 1942 "rendered harmless" 800 Gypsies and insane people (Document Book II A, page 126, Document NO-3235, Pros. Ex. 54) while the defendant explains this by saying that in his opinion these reports must have been confused (R-705) when shown. The report made by his own sub-unit, Sonderkommando 11a, on the execution of one Vladimir ROMANENKO because he was considered insane (Document Book III D, page 12, Document NOKW-604, Pros. Ex. 150), OHLENDORF admitted that this victim did not offer any open threat to military security and that he was at a loss to explain the action of Sonderkommando 11 A (R-706).

As part of the res gestae Einsatzgruppe D actively participated in spoliation of property belonging to their victims and members of the civilian population in the occupied territories under the control of the Einsatzgruppe. In a report signed by OHLENDORF which he admitted (R-553) he gives in detail the disposition that was made of money and watches taken from Jews who were executed. (Document Book III D, page 14, Doc. NOKW-631). In this document it is clearly pointed out that these con- fiscations took place during "anti-Jewish actions". Had this been the only evidence of spoliation of the victims' property it probably would have been of little note in this case but when this practice is considered in the light of what the co-defendant Heinz SCHUBERT states in his affidavit it can be seen that spoliation of the victims' property was always a part of the action of murder performed by sub-units of Einsatzgruppe D. This affi- davit of SCHUBERT relating his participation in an execution of between 700-800 people goes into detail and outlines his duties in connection with such an incident. He says:

> "Para.3 (E).....to supervise that the collection of money, jewels and other valuables of the persons who were to be shot, be completed without the use of

85

force and the persons designated for this by the

special command 11b hand over the collected items

to the administration leaders and their deputies

in order to have them passed on to Einsatzgruppe D;"

"Para. 5.....when the condemned persons arrived at

the place of execution they were ordered to leave

their money, their valuables and papers at a place

designated for this. I watched that none of the

deposited items were kept by the SS or ORPO men

who were designated for the collection. The de-

positing of this property by the condemned persons

were finished without the use of force. I super-

vised this phase carefully in order that all the

valuables could be handed over to Einsatzgruppe D

for subsequent remittance to Berlin." (Document

Book I, p. 108, Doc. NO-3055, Pros. Ex. 28).

CONCLUSION

To the charges, the defendant has entered a plea of "Not guilty

in the sense of the Indictment" and has built his defense around the

concept of his obedience to the orders of his superiors as he was ob-

ligated to do by military law. The defendant further contends that

should he be found guilty of war crimes or Crimes against Humanity as

charged in the Indictment, because of this doctrine or superior orders,

his punishment must be mitigated to such a degree commensurate with his

chances of disobeying such orders and remaining alive.

The Tribunal in Case I (Medical) in its decision anent the Euthanasia

Program, which it found to be initiated and accomplished through decrees

(orders) from the Fuehrer, himself has evaluated such a defense. It

stated:

"Whether or not a state may validly enact legisla-

tion which imposes euthanasia upon certain classes of

its citizens is likewise a question which does not

enter into the issues. Assuming that it may do so, the Family_of Nations is_not_obliged_to give_recognition to_such legislation when_it manifestly_gives_legality to plain murder_and_torture_of defenseless and powerless human beings_of other nations." (Transcript of the Record, Case I, page 11, 395)(Emphasis supplied).

This condemnation of the theory of superior orders as defense in relation to active participation in the crime of murder and other crimes against humanity, was reiterated by the Tribunal in Case IV (WVHA). In its decision, the Tribunal stated:

"It is to be assumed that if this is the kind of national government (Police State) the people of Germany preferred, they were entitled to it. If they consented to surrender their human liberties to a police force, that was their privilege, and any outsider who intruded could well be told to mind his own affiars. But when the attempt is made to make provisions of such decrees extra-territorial in their effect, and to apply their totalitarian and autocratic police measures to non-Germans and in non-German territory, they thereby invaded the domain of international law, where reason still rules." (Transcript of the Record, Case IV, pp. 8096-8097).

After the beginning of the war, Himmler inaugurated a policy concernin promotions that effected every members of the SS from Obergruppenführer to SS-Mann. This policy was unknown even to the prosecution until it was brought out by the cross-examination of the defendant BLUME by counsel for the defendant BIBERSTEIN. Such revelation shows one personal reason each defendant in this case had for meticulous and prompt obedience to the

Fuehrer Order. A cursory examination of the position and service of the defendant BLUME in the SS organizations lends weight to his testimony when he swore:

"Q. Witness, in your activity as personal referent, about the directives Himmler gave concerning promotions, can you tell us anything about it?

A. Yes. After the beginning of the war, Himmler gave an order that suggestions for promotion within the Security Police were only to be submitted to him if they showed quite clearly that the person to be promoted had proved valuable in his assignment. If not, a statement was to be given why he had not been active on assignment as yet. The term Assignment Einsatz, meant any activity as a part of the German Wehrmacht or as part of the Security Police in any of the occupied territories. The result was that in the personal department of the Reichs Security Main Office, any suggestion for promotion was stopped for awhile if it did not fulfill these requirements. It was always the task of the person submitting the promotion to complete this".....

"Q. Was the Russian Campaign of special significance for this promotion which was proclaimed on 9th of November 1941; would the promotion also have been pronounced if the person concerned had been in another campaign?

A. Of course, the idea Assignment Einsatz included any activity in any occupied territory as part of the Security Police and the Army." (Transcript of the Record, Case IX, pp. 1925-1926).

All defendants in this case insist that they were drafted for service with the Einsatzgruppen and that they had no choice but to obey. It can be respectfully pointed out that all these defendants including OHLENDORF were highly trained police officers who wished to succeed in their

- 15 -

voluntarily chosen careers. Therefore their now stated reluctance to serve with the Einsatzgruppen cannot be accepted as true when each man was anxious to advance in his chosen career.

From a consideration of the evidence adduced both from documents and from witnesses it has been proven that these defendants are responsible for the suffering and death of whole sections of the popultions in their formerly occupied territories inhabited by Russian nationals. The contention that even small children were summarily shot because they would when grown, offer a threat to the security of Germany is as ridiculous as it is fantastic. The soldiers oath to obey a military order to murder in cold blood became a mockery of lip service to the honorable profession of arms. No defendant serving with the Einsatzgruppen, having of necessity knowledge of the criminal activities of the Security Police in these territories can successfully maintain his innocence of belonging to a criminal organization. The inescapable conclusion of reasons is that this defendant along with the others either actively particpipated in the crimes charged or ordered or acquiesced in them thereby becoming a joint principal in the crime of brutal and senseless murder of tens of thousands of human beings.

The Prosecution respectfully submits that Otto OHLENDORF ordered, aided, abetted and took a consenting part in the crimes of murder, spoliat: of property, persecution on political, racial and religious grounds, agains Russian Nationals. He became a party to War Crimes and Crimes against Humanity on a vast scale. He voluntarily joined the SS and SD. The Prosecution further submits that the defendant should be found guilty as char in the Indictment.

Nurnberg, Germany

    January 1948.

Respectfully submitted

on behalf of Chief of Counsel for War Crimes.

P.W. WALTON

89

MILITARY TRIBUNAL II

Case No. 9

TRIAL BRIEF FOR THE UNITED STATES OF

AMERICA

AGAINST

ERWIN SCHULZ

Benjamin B. Ferencz
   Chief Prosecutor
Peter W. Walton
Arnost Horlik-Hochwald
John E. Glancy
   Of Counsel

For:
TELFORD TAYLOR
Brigadier General, USA
Chief of Counsel for War Crimes

and

James M. McHaney,
   Deputy Chief of Counsel
   for War Crimes,
   Director, SS Division

Doc. 6

90

Mr. Alfred Schwarz
Mrs. Nancy H. Fenstermacher
   Research Analysts

INTRODUCTION

It is alleged in essence under Counts I and II (Crimes Against Humanity and War Crimes, respectively) that Erwin SCHULZ was a principal in, accessory to, ordered, abetted, took a consenting part in, was connected with plans and enterprises involving, and was a member of organizations or groups connected with: atrocities and offenses including, but not limited to, persecution on political, racial and religious grounds; murder, extermination, imprisonment and other inhumane acts committed against civilian populations including German nationals and nationals of other countries. It is further alleged that these acts, conduct, plans and enterprises were carried out as part of a systematic program of genocide aimed at the destruction of foreign nations and ethnic groups by murderous extermination. It is alleged under Count III of the Indictment that SCHULZ was a member, after 1 September 1939, of the SS, SD and Gestapo, organizations, declared to be criminal by the International Military Tribunal.

The acts recognized as War Crimes and Crimes against Humanity are set forth in paragraphs I (b) and (c) of Article II of Control Council Law Number 10. Membership in organizations declared criminal by the International Military Tribunal is defined as a crime in Paragraph I (d) of the same Article. The criteria of criminality are set forth in Paragraph 2 of Article II of Control Council Law No. 10, which reads in part as follows:

"2. Any person, without regard to nationality or the capacity in which he acted, is deemed to have committed a crime as defined in Paragraph 1 of this Article, if he was (a) a principal or (b) was an accessory to the commission of any such crime or ordered or abetted the same or (c) took a consenting part therein or (d) was connected with plans or enterprises involving its commission or (e) was a member of any organization or group connected with the commission of any such crime....".

I. POSITIONS OF RESPONSIBILITY

The defendant Erwin SCHULZ was born on 27 November 1900 in Berlin (SCHULZ R-903). He joined the Protective Police (Schutzpolizei) in Bremen in November 1923 (SCHULZ R-907). In 1924, he became a sergeant in the Police Force and passed his officer's examination in July 1925. After having received thorough training in all branches of the Police Department during the years from 1923 on, he was commissioned Lieutenant in 1926 (SCHULZ R-908).

In this capacity he was active in the Political Police of Bremen, the so-called Central Police Office (SCHULZ R-909). The defendant claims that, during his entire activities with the Political Police, previous to 1933, he never was politically active as he "was at all times of the opinion that a civil servant is a servant of the State and not a servant of the Party" (SCHULZ R-909). He stated that he joined the NSDAP as late as in May 1933, but that he sympathized with this Party already in 1932 (SCHULZ R-1060). Documentary evidence proves that he did not join openly the NSDAP before HITLER came to power in order to be in a position to render more valuable services to the Nazi-Party and SS in the Political Police, being a non-party member. Although this fact was explicitly

- 2 -

denied by the defendant (SCHULZ R-1060/1 cp. R-915), his own
hand-written note in the SS Service Record shows the contrary.
This note reads as follows:

"From the beginning of 1931, I occupied a particularly confidential position with regard to the SS and also to the Kreis-leadership of the NSDAP, because of my
position then as Referent in the Central Police Office
of Bremen (Political Police). My entrance into the Party only after 30 January 1933 resulted from the express
wish of the then SS-Unit Leader." (NO-4957, Pros. Exh.
176, R-1109).

It is, therefore, no wonder that SCHULZ rose rapidly in
the service of the Police in Nazi-Germany. He became a member of the Gestapo in 1933 (SCHULZ R-912) and a member of the
SS and SD in 1935. In the SD, he was "leader in the Main Office" (NO-4298, Pros. Exh. 144, Doc. Book III C, page 66,
SCHULZ R-916). When war broke out in 1939, SCHULZ already
was an SS-Obersturmbannfuehrer (Lt. Col.) (NO-4298, Pros. Exh.
144, Doc. Book III C, page 63). He was promoted SS-Standartenfuehrer (full Col.) in 1940 (ibid.), and SS-Oberfuehrer
(senior Col.), a position between full Colonel and Brig.
General, on 9 November 1941, not even 14 days after his return to Berlin from his assignment as Commanding Officer of
Einsatzkommando 5 in Russia. SCHULZ was promoted by HIMMLER
himself "because of outstanding service in the Einsatz" (NO-
4957, Pros. Exh. 176, SCHULZ R-1110). After having been confronted with HIMMLER's letter, the defendant had to admit
that he had been promoted for outstanding service with the
Einsatzgruppen in Russia (SCHULZ R-1110). In previous cross-

93

- 3 -

examination, he professed that he had no knowledge of the reason for his promotion, and that this promotion had been just a matter of routine (SCHULZ R-1109, cp. R-1062). In 1942, SCHULZ was promoted SS-Brigadefuehrer (Brig. General) and held this position until the collapse of Germany (NO-4298, Pros. Exh. 144, Doc. Book III C, page 66, SCHULZ R-1062).

When Austria was occupied by the Nazis in 1938, SCHULZ was assigned the task to take care of the security in Graz, and set up the Gestapo Office in this town (SCHULZ R-924). In the fall of 1938, when the so-called Sudetenland was occupied by Germany, after the Munich Agreement, he was in charge of an Einsatzkommando in Usti (Aussig) (SCHULZ R-924), and when the remainder of Czechoslovakia was occupied by the Germans in spring of 1939, he was again in charge of an Einsatzkommando and of the Gestapo Office in Olomouc (Olmuetz) and highest ranking Police Officer in this town (SCHULZ R-1064/5). In June of the same year, he was put in charge of the Gestapo Agency in Liberec (Reichenberg), also in the Sudetenland, and stayed there until spring of 1940 (SCHULZ R-1063, NO-3644, Pros. Exh. 26, Doc. Book I, page 97, Para 1). In Liberec, SCHULZ appointed an expert, one Police Inspector SPAET, who had to carry out and direct the confiscation of Jewish property. Reports of these activities were forwarded to the Ministry of Finance (SCHULZ R-1064). SCHULZ admits that, during his time of office in Liberec, people were arrested and sent to concentration camps. He only claims that decisions for such arrests were not made by him but by the RSHA. It is, however, obvious that the RSHA could only make decisions for arrests on the basis of reports and information received from the Gestapo, and SCHULZ admits that he reported to the RSHA on such subject (SCHULZ R-1064). SCHULZ further admits that, during his tenure of office in Olomouc (Olmuetz), German refugees and Czech citizens were arrested on the basis of lists which he had received from the RSHA (SCHULZ R-1066).

In 1940, SCHULZ was transferred to Hamburg as Inspector of the Security Police and the SD (SCHULZ R-926/7, NO-3644, Pros. Exh. 26, Doc. Book I, page 97, para 1) and in 1941, he was transferred to Berlin to the Headquarters of the Gestapo in the RSHA, as Chief of Group I B (Training and Education) (SCHULZ R-928, NO-3644, Pros. Exh. 26, Doc. Book I, page 97, para 1). In the same time, he became commander of the School for Leaders (Police Officers' School) (SCHULZ R-928, NO-3644, Pros. Exh. 26, Doc. Book I, page 98, para 3). From May to the end of September 1941, SCHULZ was commander of Einsatzkommando 5 (NO-3644, Pros. Exh. 26, Doc. Book I, page 98, para 3, page 101, para 8, SCHULZ R-930, R-966). When returning from Russia, he became again manager of the Police Officers' Training School and later became Chief of Group I A, the Personnel Office of the RSHA. When the Chief of the Department I of the RSHA, STRECKENBACH, joined the Waffen-SS, he was replaced by SCHULZ who became Chief of this Department (SCHULZ R-1020). In 1944, he was relieved from his duty as Chief of the Department I of the RSHA and became Commander of the Security Police in Salzburg. Shortly before the end of the war, he was appointed SS and Police Leader for the district of Salzburg (SCHULZ R-1021, NO-3644, Pros. Exh. 26, Doc. Book I, page 97, para 1).

- 5 -

In order to simplify the issue, the Prosecution has submitted that SCHULZ would not be charged with commission and knowledge of criminal acts, according to Count III of the Indictment, after his return from Russia in the beginning of November 1941 (R-1016).

II. PERSONAL PARTICIPATION IN CRIMINAL ACTIVITIES

In May 1941, the defendant SCHULZ who was then in charge of the Training School for Police Officers received from STRECKENBACH, Chief of Department I of the RSHA, the order to have his pupils trained for activities in the "Executive Staff". The reason for this particular type of training was the insufficient number of "leaders" in the Police Force, caused by the necessity to provide the Police Forces which operated in the numerous countries which had been occupied by the Germans during the war with Police Officers. The members of this Training School were transferred to Pretzsch and SCHULZ was informed that he was to become Chief of an Einsatzkommando (SCHULZ R-830). SCHULZ claimed that he was not present at Pretzsch when STRECKEN-BACH lectured on the task of the Einsatzgruppen, and he especially denied that he heard about the Fuehrer-Order to kill all Communists, Jews, and Gypsies which was handed down by STRECKENBACH at the meeting (SCHULZ R-933). He admits, however, having been in Pretzsch when HEYDRICH inspected the Einsatzgruppen (SCHULZ R-932) and at a meeting in the Prince-Albrecht-Palais in Berlin where HEYDRICH informed the Commanders of the Einsatzgruppen, Sonderkommandos and Einsatzkommandos about their tasks. In this lecture, HEYDRICH said:

"That every one should be sure to understand that,
in this fight, Jews would definitely take their part
and that, in this fight, everything was set at stake,
and the one side which gave in would be the one to be
overcome. For that reason, all measures had to be tak-
en against the Jews, in particular. The experience in
Poland had shown this." (SCHULZ R-934).

SCHULZ admits that he, in May 1941, became Commander of
Einsatzkommando 5 which was one of the four units of Einsatzgruppe C (SCHULZ R-938, NO-3644, Pros. Exh. 26, Doc. Bk. I,
p. 98). According to his own affidavit, he was relieved from
this position on or about 26 September of the same year (ibid.
p. 101, para 8). In contradiction to this pre-trial statement, SCHULZ testifies before the Tribunal that he was relieved from the command on 20 or 21 September (SCHULZ R-966).

As to the general tasks of the Einsatzgruppen and their
units in the East, reference is made to the Prosecution's
brief against the defendant OHLENDORF. That the main activities of Einsatzgruppe C were no different from the general
pattern of extermination of Communists and Jews is proved by
O.S.R. No. 128. This report reveals under the heading:

"B. Executive Actitities
As to purely executive matters, approximately 80,000
persons were liquidated until now by the Kommandos of
the Einsatzgruppe.

Among these are approximately 8,000 persons through investigations convicted of anti-German or Bolshevistic
activities.

- 7 -

The remainder was liquidated as a retaliatory measure.

Even though approximately 75,000 Jews have been liquidated in this manner, it is already at this time evident
that this cannot be a possible solution of the Jewish
problem. Although we succeeded, in particular, in
smaller towns and also in villages in accomplishing
a complete liquidation of the Jewish problem, again
and again it is, however, observed in larger cities
that, after such an execution, all Jews have indeed
disappeared. But, when, after a certain period of
time, a Kommando returns again, the number of Jews
still found in the city always considerably surpasses
the number of the executed Jews." (NO-3157, Pros.
Exh. 68, Doc. Br. II C, p. 3 - 4, emphasis supplied).

98 This report gives a survey of the activities of the
Einsatzgruppe up to 3 November 1941, the date of the report. SCHULZ was in command of one of the Kommandos of
Einsatzgruppe C, until 26 September. It needs no further
explanation that SCHULZ and his Einsatzkommando 5 participated in these "Executive Activities". In this connection, it should be noted that, according to the report, only approximately 8,000 persons, out of the total of 80,000,
i.e. ten percent, "were convicted through investigation of
anti-German or Bolshevistic activities", and that 75,000
of the victims were Jews. The wording of the report shows
clearly that none of these 80,000 victims were afforded as
much as a semblance of a trial, and that the killing of the
Jews was carried out as a "solution of the Jewish Problem".

The evidence shows that Einsatzkommando 5, under the
command of the defendant SCHULZ, participated in the pro-

gram of genocide, as set forth in the Fuehrer-Order. Einsatzgruppe C, with its units, among them Einsatzkommando 5, under the command of the defendant SCHULZ, left Pretzsch on 23 June and reached Lemberg on 2 July (SCHULZ R-937/8, NO-3644, supra). Immediately after the arrival of the Einsatzgruppe, large-scale arrests and executions were carried out by Einsatzgruppe C. Einsatzkommando 5 participated in these executions, and SCHULZ was present at least at one of them. He, himself, gives the following description of these events in his affidavit:

"4. On or about 23 June 1941, the Einsatzgruppe C, consisting of Sonderkommandos 4 A and 4 B, and the Einsatzkommandos 5 and 6, started to march in the direction of Gleiwitz. In the beginning of July, I cannot remember the exact date, we marched into Lemberg. It became known there that a number of persons from Lemberg had been killed before the retreat of the Russian troops. Shortly after our arrival in Lemberg Dr. RASCH, Chief of the Einsatzgruppe C, informed us that Jewish officials and inhabitants of Lemberg had participated in these killings. A Military Command post within the city had already created a local Militia. Dr. RASCH who was working in closest cooperation with the Militia, had instructed Kommando 4 B and, after their departure, Kommando 6, to support the Militia. Participants and suspected persons were arrested on the same or following day. In addition, the Kommando SCHOENGARTH (BdS Cracow) was put into action.

5. After completion of these arrests, approximately 2,500 to 3,000 people had been collected in the Sta-

dium which was situated right next to the quarters of the Einsatzgruppe C. Among these arrested, there were, so I was told, also non-Jews who had been suspected of having participated in the murders. On the following day, we were informed by Dr. RASCH that a Fuehrer-Order had come into force, according to which guilty persons or even strongly suspected persons were to be shot as reprisals for these murders. As far as I remember, the OKW-Order, that all political officials and Soviet-Russian commissars, if one could lay hands on them, were to be shot, was also published at that time. Approximately 4 days after our arrival, the executions of the persons arrested were started.

6. When I returned to my unit, Einsatzkommando 5, on midday of the same day, I was told by one of my leaders that Dr. RASCH had given orders that Kommando was to take over the carrying out of the executions for that afternoon. I immediately tried to get in touch with Dr. RASCH, but only succeeded in speaking to his Chief of Staff, Dr. HOFFMANN, who confirmed the order. I was going to try and rescind the order, as far as my Kommando was concerned; I did not, however, succeed. I repeated the order in front of my leaders and the troops and gave instructions that the executions were to be carried out in a serious and dignified manner. Useless tortures were to be avoided. I personally ascertained that the physician of the Einsatzgruppe C, Dr. KROEGER (a brother of the Leader of the Einsatz-kommando 6) was present during the executions. I was convinced that I had done all in my power to carry out

- 10 -

the executions in a military and humane way. My Kommando shot approximately 90 to 110 people.

I had subdivided my Kommando into three platoons; each platoon consisted of about 50 men. The persons to be executed were transported by lorriers to the place of execution. At each time, there were about 18 to 22 persons. I no longer remember the exact number of the lorriers. The first platoon was placed face to face with the persons about to be executed, and about three men, each, aimed at each person to be shot. I, myself, was present at the first volley of the execution, with my face turned away. When the first volley had been fired, I turned around and saw that all persons were lying on the ground. I then left the place of execution and approached the place where the second and third platoons were gathered. The first platoon which had carried out the shootings, was recalled, I inspected the men and then returned to my quarters. I noticed there that the detainees who were in the Stadium next to the quarters, some of whom were still to be executed, were driven across the Stadium by members of the Wehrmacht and tortured. I did not succeed in apprehending those responsible for the tortures. In order to terminate this spectacle, I had the rear door of the Stadium opened, and the detainees could march out through it. The members of the Wehrmacht who had participated in this affair, disappeared as well. As the remainder of the persons to be executed had also escaped, I informed my Kommando by means of a driver that the executions were terminated." (NO-3644, Pros. Exh. 26, Doc. Bk. I, p. 98 - 100).

101

- 11 -

O.S.R. No. 132 lists the execution total of Einsätzkommando 5 as 15,110, on 20 October 1941. The same report reveals that, between 23 September and 20 October, 2,476 persons, "political functionaries, people guilty of sabotage and looting and Jews" were liquidated by Einsatzkommando 5.

"The number of people executed by Einsatzkommando 5 amounted to 15,110, on 20 October 1941. From this number, 20 political functionaries, 21 people guilty of sabotage and looting and 1,847 Jews were shot, between 13 October 1941 and 19 October 1941. On 18 October 1941, 300 insane Jews of the Kiev lunatic asylum were liquidated, which represented a particularly heavy mental burden for the members of Einsatzkommando 5, who were in charge of this operation.

..... Between 28 September 1941 and 4 October 1941, Einsatzkommando 5 executed 8 political functionaries and 2 people guilty of sabotage in Kriwoj-Rog; between 28 September 1941 and 4 October 1941, 85 political functionaries, 14 people guilty of sabotage and looting, and 179 Jews were executed in Dnjepropetrovsk."
(NO-2830, Pros. Exh. 72, Doc. Bk. II C, p. 25).

As this report lists 2,476 executions between 23 September and 20 October and gives the execution total on a later date as 15,110, it is proved that, previous to 23 September 1941, not less than 12,634 persons were executed by Einsatzkommando 5. SCHULZ admittedly was Commander of this Einsatzkommando until at least 21 September (SCHULZ R-966). This evidence is corroborated by another O.S.R. which reveals that:

"In the period between 7 September and 5 October, 207 political officials, 112 saboteurs and looters, as well as 8,800 Jews, were liquidated by Einsatzkommando 5." (NO-3155, Pros. Exh. 79, Doc. Bk. II C, p. 57).

This entry proves conclusively that 14,096 had been executed by Einsatzkommando 5, until 20 October 1941.

Details of the activities of Einsatzkommando 5, when SCHULZ was in command, are apparent from the evidence in the Record. In the period between 31 August and 6 September 1941, 90 political officials, 72 saboteurs and looters and 161 Jews were liquidated by this Einsatzkommando. (NO-3146, Pros. Exh. 82, Doc. Bk. II C, p. 64).

O.S.R. No. 119 states:

"On 15 September 1941, Einsatzkommando 5 executed a further action in Bogusslav, since, according to reliable reports, partisans and parachutists were cared for by Jews. Through the execution of 322 Jews and 13 Communist officials, the town is now free of Jews.

In KOSCHEWETOJE also, partisans and parachutists were allegedly taken in by Jews. Therefore, all the Jews of this town were also liquidated by Einsatzkommando 5." (NO-3404-A, Pros. Exh. 75, Doc. Bk. II C, p. 41).

From this entry, it is apparent that Einsatzkommando 5 killed not only male Jews but also women and children, as it can hardly be assumed that, among the Jewish population of the two villages which were "freed from Jews" by the Einsatzkommando, there were only adult men. The same report proves that "a two-day action was determined for the combat of this source of danger (the Jews) in Uman". This action was planned for the time before 21 September, but according to the report, partly frustrated, as

"Contrary to the plan, it already came to excesses against the Jews by members of the Militia and with participation of numerous German Wehrmacht members, on 21 September 1941".

"During these events, the Jewish apartments were completely demolished and robbed of all utensils and valuables. In this, also almost only German Wehrmacht members participated. Spot examinations of the apartments of members of the Militia, which were undertaken immediately after the arrival of the train of Einsatzkommando 5 in Uman, remained without result.

Naturally, the systematic action of Einsatzkommando 5 suffered extremely by these planless excesses against the Jews in Uman. In particular, a large number of the Jews were not forewarned and escaped from the city. Besides the numerous Jews, many of the Ukrainian officials and activists still living in Uman, were warned by the excesses, and only two co-workers of the NKWD were found and liquidated. The results of these excesses were cleaned up immediately by Einsatzkommando 5, after its arrival.

For the rest, 1,412 Jews were executed by Einsatzkommando 5 in Uman, on 22 and 23 September 1941". (ebid. p. 38, emphasis supplied).

In an attempt to escape responsibility for the killing of these 1,412 on 22 and 23 September, SCHULZ tried to repudiate the statement in his affidavit, that he was relieved from the command of Einsatzkommando 5 "on or about 26 September" (644 supra); by stating that his successor arrived on 20 or 21 September, in order to take over the command (SCHULZ R-966). His pre-trial statement, made when he had no knowledge of the incriminating report, is certainly entitled to more weight than his self-saving statement which was made after SCHULZ had learned that evidence of crimes committed between 20 and 26 September by Einsatzkommando 5 had been submitted by the Prosecution. A document introduced by Defense Counsel for SCHULZ, a letter from the Office of the Chief of the Security Police and the SD to the defendant, releasing him from his assignment as Commander of Einsatzkommando 5, dated 26 September, proves in itself that SCHULZ certainly could not have left his position before this date. (SCHULZ Doc. Bk. I, Exh. 48, p. 106). But, assuming arguendo that SCHULZ, in fact, had handed over the command on 20 or 21 September, he would, by no means, be relieved of responsibility for the killing of the Jews in Uman, as it is clear from the report that the plan for these killings had been made already before the 21st of September. (NO3404-A, supra)

105

O.S.R. No. 88 shows the following entry:

"Between 24 August and 30 August 1941, Einsatzkommando 5 carried through 157 executions by shooting comprising Jews, officials and saboteurs." (NO-3149, Pros. Exh. 46, Doc. B'. II A, p. 89).

And O.S.R. No. 86 which is dated 17 September 1941 gives the following details of activities of Einsatzkommando 5, during the first part of September:

"The Einsatzkommando 5, for the time being, has been divided into troops, covering a larger territory, and is combing the villages of this area systematically. Among others, several Bolshevistic mayors and Kolchose-Vorstéher were taken care of. Besides that, several mentally handicapped persons, who had had the order to blow up bridges and railroad tracks and to carry out other acts of sabotage, were rendered harmless. It seems that the NKWD favored mentally retarded persons in the distribution of this kind of tasks, who, nevertheless, in spite of all inferiority, summoned enough energy for their criminal activities.

4 executions were carried out in Ulanow, 18 in Uledowka.

It was possible to take care of 229 Jews in the cleanup action carried out in Chmielnik. By that, this area which suffered especially from the Jewish terror, is extensively cleaned up. The reaction of the population here to the delivery from the Jews was so strong that it, finally, resulted in a Thanksgiving service.

Einsatzkommando 5 took care of 506 Bolshevists and Jews in the course of 14 days." (NO-3151, Pros. Exh. 73, Doc. Bk. II C, p. 29).

When questioned by the Presiding Judge in connection with the entry of the report that "it was possible to take care of 229 Jews" in Chmielnik, the defendant admitted that the phrase "take care of" meant that these people were executed (SCHULZ R-994). He questioned the correctness of the of the entry as to the number of victims, but admitted "that about 90 persons, including a number of Jews were shot" (SCHULZ R-996). He also claims that these individuals had been proved guilty of sabotage and acts of violence (SCHULZ R-998). He admitted further that two insane persons "who had orders to carry out sabotage" were arrested, but was silent about their fate (ibid.). The report proves that several mentally handicapped persons were rendered harmless (NO-3151 supra). Another O.S.R. reveals that 74 Jews were shot by the Einsatzkommando 5 (NO-2947, Pros. Exh. 82, Doc. Bk. II C, p. 71).

III. GENERAL DEFENSES

SCHULZ violently denies his participation in, or even knowledge of, criminal activities of Einsatzkommando 5. He alleges that, under his command, "only guilty people were executed" (SCHULZ R-1108). During the time when he was active as Commander of Einsatzkommando 5, he never obtained knowledge of the Hitler-Order and when he heard about the Order of HIMMLER which was communicated to him by the defendant RASCH in Shitomir at the end of the first week of August, he immediately requested and obtained his release from the assignment as Commander of the Einsatzkommando, and even was able to obtain the release for the members of the Police Officers' School from their various assignments with the Einsatzgruppen. He was very well known as being too soft and good-hearted and, therefore, his activities in the East were a failure, a fact which was commonly known to his superiors.

Not only the evidence in the Record, but also SCHULZ's own statements on the witness stand prove that this defense of his is entirely untrue and cannot be believed.

When testifying before the Tribunal, SCHULZ tried to justify the execution in Lemberg (see Part II, supra) as "reprisal measures". SCHULZ states that these reprisals were carried out, as

"we learned that, before the Russian troops had left, a very great number of Lemberg citizens, Ukrainians and Polish inhabitants of other towns and villages had been killed in this prison and in other prisons. Furthermore, there were many corpses of German men and officers, among them many Air Corps officers, and many of them were found mutilated. There was a great bitterness and excitement among the Lemberg population against the Jewish sector of the population." (R-938).

He states further:

"On the next day, Dr. RASCH informed us to the effect that the killed people in Lemberg amounted to about 5,000. It has been determined without any doubt that the arrests and killings had taken place under the leadership of Jewish functionaries and with the participation of the Jewish inhabitants of Lemberg. That was the reason why there was such an excitement against the Jewish population on the part of the Lemberg citizens." (R-939)

Questioned by the Presiding Judge, he amplified his statement explaining that the perpetrators had been allegedly Russian Communists, functionaries of Jewish Faith, office holders of the Soviet Nation who happened to be of the Jewish Race (SCHULZ R-939). He also stated that the alleged excesses had occurred before the occupation of Lem-

108

berg by the German Forces had taken place (SCHULZ R-941).
The Militia "had orders to arrest the Jewish population of
Lemberg and also those who were suspected of having participated in the killings" (SCHULZ R-941). On the basis of
an order of HITLER, all "guilty ones and the participants
in these murders which were against International Law, were
to be executed in reprisal", and according to his recollection, "in connection with this decree, the Army Command Order
was also made known, according to which the political commissars and functionaries were to be executed" (SCHULZ R-942).
This order also stated that the Einsatzkommandos "have to be
especially careful about the Jews, they have entered into
an embittered fight. The Jews also are carriers of destruct-
ive tendencies in the rear of combat troops" (SCHULZ R-943).

SCHULZ admits that Einsatzkommando 5, under his command, participated in the execution of the victims of these
"reprisal measures" (SCHULZ R-944/5) and that approximately
90 to 110 persons were shot by his Kommando alone (NO-3644,
Pros. Exh. 26, Doc. Bk. I, p. 110 comp. SCHULZ R-1095).

The self-saving statement of SCHULZ, that the killing
of the Jews in Lemberg was a reprisal measure does not carry any credibility. A well-trained and experienced Colonel
of the Police (see Part I, supra), SCHULZ must have known,
and undoubtedly knew, that the German occupation forces
had no right or reason for the carrying out of reprisals
for the killing of Poles and Ukrainians which had taken
place before this occupation. These Poles and Ukrainians,
who were the alleged victims of the Communists and Jews of
Lemberg, were not members of the German Armed Forces; they

- 19 -

were not citizens of a country allied to Germany; on the
contrary, they were Nationals of countries which had been
attacked by Germany in breach of International Treaties
and in disregard of International Law. There is no evidence
in the record, and it is not even contented by the
Defense that the alleged killing of 5,000 Poles and Ukrainians
was an act of illegitimate warfare, on the part of
the Red Army, aimed against the German Armed Forces. As
it is the commonly accepted theory that reprisals are acts
of retaliation, resorted to by one belligerent against the
enemy individuals or property for illegal acts of warfare,
committed by the other belligerent, it is perfectly clear
that the murder of these 5,000 Poles and Ukrainians could,
under no circumstances, have justified reprisals on the
part of the German Armed Forces. It should be further noted
that the victims of these alleged reprisals were themselves
Polish and Ukrainian nationals, so that the defense put forward
by SCHULZ amounts to the preposterous assertion that
Ukrainians and Poles were killed in reprisal for criminal
acts committed against Ukrainians and Poles. It is also
unexplainable, and SCHULZ, therefore, was unable to explain,
when examined by the Tribunal, why the German Armed Forces,
which had executed Polish civilians in countless numbers -
hundreds of thousands - would suddenly demand reprisals because
Poles had allegedly been executed by the Russians
(SCHULZ R-1127/8). It is clear from the evidence and from
the contradictory statements of SCHULZ that the expression
"reprisal" was used in the Operational Situation Reports
of the Einsatzgruppen in a form which must be considered
as an euphamistic expression for murder. For example, the

killing of the entire Jewish population of Kiev, approximately 34,000 people, is described as a reprisal measure in the reports, (NO-3157, Pros. Exh. 68, Doc. Bk. II C, p. 3) and it is reported that 1,160 Jews were shot as a reprisal for the fact that "the corpses of a total of 10 German members of the Wehrmacht had been found" (NO-2938, Pros. Exh. 44, Doc. Bk. II A, p. 81). SCHULZ claims, however, that the so-called reprisals in Lemberg were also carried out for the alleged killing of members of the German Armed Forces (SCHULZ R-949), but he could not, or would not state how many of them had allegedly been killed (SCHULZ R-1087). He stated only that HITLER ordered a reprisal measure "for the entire killings in Lemberg". In order to back up the reprisal story, SCHULZ and his Counsel refer to two documents. One of them, which was admitted in evidence as Pros. Exh. 116 (NO-4537 Doc. Bk. III B, p. 20) is silent, as to the killing of members of the German Armed Forces. The other, which was introduced in rebuttal by the Prosecution, proves that 7 German pilots (who had been taken prisoner were found murdered in the vicinity of Lemberg". As reprisal for the killing of these 7 pilots, 7,000 Jews were arrested and shot; only 73 of whom had been identified as officials and informers of the NKWD and 40 more who could be convicted as accessories (NO-2651, Pros. Exh.   Rebuttal).

It goes without saying that, with the exception of the defendant BLOBEL, every one will consider that murder of 1,000 persons for the killing of every flyer, is a criminal exaggeration of the right of reprisals.

It should be further noted that the affidavit by WEBER which was introduced by Defense Counsel for SCHULZ and re-

ports the happenings in Lemberg is silent as to the fact that
members of the German Wehrmacht werekilled there (SCHULZ Doc.
Bk. I, Exh. 44, p. 71). The affidavit of HENNICKE, introduced also by the Defense, contains only the sentence "corpses were being placed there by the inhabitants of Lwow and by
members of the German Wehrmacht". It is obvious that HEN-
NICKE has no knowledge whether German soldiers were killed
in Lemberg or not (SCHULZ Doc. Bk. I, Exh. 45, Doc. 21, p.
75).

SCHULZ offered no explanation why it was ordered "to
arrest the Jewish population of Lemberg and also those who
were suspected of having participated in these killings"
(SCHULZ R-941); but he admitted that all or "at any rate,
a great part of the Jewish population" had been arrested
(SCHULZ R-1086). He admitted that approximately 2 - 3,000
Jews and some non-Jews were affected by these measures.
He, thereby, made himself a difference between persons
who were suspected of having committed the crimes and of
those who were arrested, as they were racially undesirable.
The Operational Situation Report of 31 July submitted by
him, proves that not less than 7,000 Jews were arrested
and shot (NO-2651, Pros. Exh.   Rebuttal).

SCHULZ further stated that all these persons were in-
vestigated within 48 hours, at the utmost, and that, on
the basis of these investigations, the perpetrators were
ascertained (SCHULZ R-948). It was made absolutely clear
from his testimony that no trial against the alleged perpetrators took place (SCHULZ R-1090). When questioned by the
Tribunal, SCHULZ admitted that the executions were conducted

by him, without having received as much as a report concerning the guilt of the persons who were to be executed
or even a list with their names (SCHULZ R-1093/4).

Thus, it is proved that the executions in Lemberg
were nothing less than a measure carried out in execution
of the HITLER-Order, which provided for the killing of
Communists and Jews; and that SCHULZ participated in them
with full knowledge of the criminal nature of these measures.

The contention of SCHULZ that he was ignorant of the
HITLER-Order as he had not been present at the lecture of
STRECKENBACH in Pretzsch (SCHULZ R-937) becomes even more
grotesque in the face of the documents which prove that
this order was actually carried out by Einsatzkommando 5
during the entire period when he was in command of this
unit. (See Part II, supra). The testimony of SCHULZ is
full of contradictions on the point of his knowledge of
the HITLER-Order. In his direct examination, he answered the question of his Counsel:

> "Q: It is mentioned in the documents that, in Pretzsch,
> the Fuehrer-Decree was made known. You told me
> that this Decree was not known to you before your
> assignedment, is that correct?
>
> A: Yes, that is correct, I only heard about the so-
> called STRECKENBACH-Decree when Herr WARTENBERG,
> on Good Friday of this year, interrogated me <u>for</u>
> the first time." (SCHULZ R-933, emphasis supplied).

In another part of his direct examination, SCHULZ testified that he reported to STRECKENBACH about the Order he

113

had received in Shitomir, on 28 or 29 August, in detail.
He "told him what order SS-Obergruppenfuehrer JECKELN had
issued through Dr. RASCH, in particular, that women and
children were not to be saved". He then went on to say:

"When I read the text of the order to him, just as
RASCH had issued it, he told me that such an order
would just mean plain murder. In this connection, I
would like to emphasize that this statement on his
part referred to the form of the order, which was passed on by RASCH and which stated, as a reason for this
measure, that women and children should be shot so that
no vendetta would arise." (SCHULZ R-961)

and

114

"Several days passed, because HEYDRICH was not there.
If I am not mistaken, he was at Prague, at that time.
Several days later, STRECKENBACH asked me to come and
see him and he told me on that occasion that HEYDRICH
also had misgivings about the manner in which this order had been issued. However, he told me that, at the
prevailing facts, nothing could be changed because a
Fuehrer-Order demanded that these measures should be
maintained as long as the opponent was also using
these measures, and as long as they were necessary."
(SCHULZ R-962/3).

When confronted in cross-examination with the incred-
ibility of this story, he stated, "Well, I can remember,
Mr. Prosecutor, that STRECKENBACH was also very excited
about this way of issuing orders, for I expressed my conviction about it to him." (SCHULZ R-1077), and

- 24 -

"I cannot remember the wording of this order, and,
please, try to imagine yourself in my situation, for,
when I came to STRECKENBACH, I still did not know that
this order had been given, already announced at
Prétzsch. <u>That this Fuehrer-Order actually existed,
he did not keep from me.</u>" (SCHULZ R-1078, emphasis
supplied).

This proves in itself that his statement, that he heard
about the order for the first time when interrogated by Mr.
WARTENBERG on Good Friday of 1947 (SCHULZ R-933) is entirely
incorrect. Moreover, SCHULZ failed to give any explanation
for the fact that STRECKENBACH who knew the HITLER-Order and
handed it down to the Commanders of the Einsatzgruppen and
Einsatzkommandos, should have been very excited about it
and would have told SCHULZ that "such an order would just
mean murder" (SCHULZ R-961), instead of telling SCHULZ that
these measures, criminal as they were, were ordered by HITLER
and, therefore, had to be obeyed by everybody.

Comparison between the statements of SCHULZ, concerning
the meeting with STRECKENBACH on 28 or 29 August, in direct
examination (SCHULZ R-933), and in examination by the Tribunal (SCHULZ R-1079/81), and cross-examination (SCHULZ R-
1077/9, 1081/2), makes it clear that the testimony of the defendant is untrue and fabricated. That is clear also from
the fact that SCHULZ further testified that he was on excellent official and personal terms with STRECKENBACH and that
STRECKENBACH knew that SCHULZ was "too soft" for the position of Commander of an Einsatzkommando. STRECKENBACH allegedly knew that SCHULZ "was absolutely an opponent of any
brutality measures" (SCHULZ R-1082/3). SCHULZ could offer

115

no explanation why STRECKENBACH who was Chief of the Personnel Department of the RSHA and, therefore, had decisive influence on such an assignment, would have chosen him who was known to be "too soft" for the job of killing innocent and defenseless people. SCHULZ admitted further that he had knowledge of excesses on the part of the Nazis against Jews, Communists and other enemies of National Socialism (SCHULZ R-1071). He knew of the anti-Jewish pogrom which was carried out as a result of the assassination of a member of the German Ambassy in Paris, von RATH, by the Jew GRYNSPAN (SCHULZ R-921). He knew of the "intolerance" of the Nazis toward the Jews (SCHULZ R-958), but when he heard HEYDRICH state, during the meeting in the Prince-Albrecht-Palais in Berlin, that "also against Jewry, one would have to take more severe measures", he allegedly was of the opinion that only those Jews who were considered dangerous were to be arrested (SCHULZ R-1072/3). It is entirely incredible that a Colonel of the SS, a man who was in high positions in the Gestapo from 1933 on, should have been ignorant of the policy against the Jews as it was advocated and carried out by his Chief, HEYDRICH.

SCHULZ admitted that the defendant RASCH informed him that SS-Obergruppenfuehrer JECKELN had handed down an order of HIMMLER, according to which all "suspected Jews" were, thefefore, to be shot. Consideration was to be given only where they were indispensable as workers. Women and children were to be shot also, in order not to have any revengers remain" (SCHULZ R-954). SCHULZ professed having been horrified and having raised objections against this order (SCHULZ R-955), but maintains that even then he had not been informed

about the fact that HITLER had ordered similar measures
(SCHULZ R-955/1096). It goes without saying that the
only possible reaction to such objections on the part
of RASCH would have been to inform SCHULZ that these
measures were to be carried out in execution of an order
of HITLER himself.

SCHULZ also claims in his defense that the Higher SS
and Police Leader JECKELN was in charge of the program of the
execution of the Jews and not Einsatzkommando 5. He stated
that JECKELN "had major units of the Regular Police with him
who were exclusively destined to carry out executions of
Jews" (SCHULZ R-957/8). He alleged that the Staff Leader
of Einsatzgruppe C, Sturmbannfuehrer HOFFMANN, reported
the number of persons killed by these Police Forces as having been exterminated by the Kommandos of Einsatzgruppe C
(SCHULZ R-976). From the evidence in the record, it is,
however, apparent that the killing of Jews which was carried out by the units of the Higher SS and Police Leader
is reported separately in the Operational Situation Reports.
Operational Situation Report No. 94 states, for example,

"The units of the Higher SS and Police Leader, during
the month of August, shot a total of 44,125 persons,
mostly Jews." (NO-3146, Pros. Exh. 81, Doc. Bk. II C,
p. 65).

The same report contains the following entry, concerning the activities of Einsatzkommando 5,

"Einsatzkommando 5, for the period between 31 August
and 6 September 1941, reports the liquidation of 90

political officials, 72 saboteurs and looters, and
161 Jews." (ibid. p.64).

Operational Situation Report No. 88 shows the following entry,

"On 1 and 2 September 1941, leaflets and inflammatory
pamphlets had been distributed by Jews in Berditschev.
As the perpetrators could not be found out, 1,303 Jews,
among them 875 Jewesses over 12 years, were executed
by a unit of the Higher SS and Police Leader."

and also in this report, the activities of Einsatzkommando
5 are listed separately,

"Between 24 August and 30 August 1941, Einsatzkommando
5 carried through 157 executions by shooting comprising Jews, officials and saboteurs," (NO-3149, Pros.
Exh. 46, Doc. Bk. II A, p. 89, emphasis supplied).

118

These entries prove conclusively that the contention
of SCHULZ that the executions listed in the reports as having
been committed by Einsatzkommando 5, actually were committed
by JECKELN and his Police Forces, has no foundation. Moreover, it is obvious that the reports from Einsatzgruppe C to
the RSHA, which allegedly were made by HOFFMANN, were compiled on the basis of reports of the different Kommandos of the
Einsatzgruppe. SCHULZ admitted that, as far as Einsatzkommando
5 was concerned, reports were made by commanders of the subunits of the Einsatzkommando and sent via Einsatzkommando 5
to Einsatzgruppe C. He received these reports and read them
before they were forwarded to Einsatzgruppe C (SCHULZ R-1103).

This admission alone removes any possibility that SCHULZ should have been ignorant of what was actually reported to the RSHA about the activities of Einsatzkommando 5.

SCHULZ not only claims complete ignorance of the HIT-LER-Order, but also states that, after he had heard from RASCH that all "suspected Jews", men, women and children, were to be killed, he undertook immediate steps to be relieved from the command of Einsatzkommando 5, as he had a personal revulsion against such an order. As he was an excellent official and on personal terms with STRECKEN-BACH, he succeeded and was relieved from this command. As a result of his good-heartedness, which was considered by his superiors as softness, his activities in Russia had been a failure and his discharge was carried out because he "was not hard and severe enough" (SCHULZ R-1108). Documentary evidence and the testimony of SCHULZ prove that his statement is not in accordance with the facts.

SCHULZ stated in his testimony that not only he personally, but also the numerous pupils of the Training School for Police Officers were recalled to Berlin on his request (SCHULZ R-965). It may be possible that an individual is recalled from duty in an Einsatzkommando because he is not "hard and severe enough"; it may be possible that he can persuade a friend who is in charge of the superior Personnel Department to relieve him from an unpleasant and distasteful assignment, but that this friend would go so far to recall, in times of war, a great number of Police Officers who were obviously sent to the East for training in ruthlessness, is entirely incredible and practically

- 29 -

119

impossible. It is clear from the testimont of SCHULZ that the members of the Police Officers' Training School, who were to be trained for activities in the "Executive Staff" in the occupied territories (SCHULZ R-930) were sent to the East in order to get the practical training in the ruthless and inhumane methods which were required for these "Executive activities". It is obvious that the time of three months was sufficient for such training and, therefore, SCHULZ and the members of his school returned after this time to Berlin. SCHULZ's alleged softness and unwillingness to carryout executions had nothing to do with his transfer to Berlin. It should be noted that his alleged revulsions against the order to kill women and children did not prevent him, at a later date, when he became Chief of the Personnel Office of the RSHA (Part I, supra) from assigning some of the defendants and other SS officers to similar duties in the Einsatzgruppen. Moreover, it is proved by documentary evidence that SCHULZ was promoted SS-Oberfuehrer a few days after his return from the East for outstanding performance of his duties as Commander of Einsatzkommando 5. HIMMLER gave expression to his appreciation of SCHULZ's activities with Einsatzkommando 5. The letter of promotion to SCHULZ reads,

"I, hereby, promote you, effective 9 November 1941, to SS-Oberfuehrer, because of outstanding service in the Einsatz". (NO-4957, Pros. Exh. 176, SCHULZ R-1110).

Before he had been confronted with this letter of HIMMLER's, SCHULZ had confessed complete ignorance of the reasons for his promotion (SCHULZ R-1109). It goes without saying that this document destroys completely the story of the de-

120

fendant that he was not "hard and severe enough" as commander of an Einsatzkommando and, therefore, was recalled. Viewed in the light of this evidence, his entire testimony cannot be considered credible.

As to the plea of superior orders which might eventually be put forward by SCHULZ as mitigating his guilt, reference is made to the Prosecution's Brief on this subject. It should be pointed out here that, with the exception of the executions in Lemberg, SCHULZ does not even claim having acted under such orders. On the contrary, he disclaims every knowledge of an order of HITLER which provided for the executions which were carried out by Einsatzkommando 5, under SCHULZ's command. (Part II, supra).

CONCLUSION

The defendant SCHULZ was a member of the SS, the Gestapo and the SD. In the SD, he was leader in the Main Office and rose in the SS and Gestapo to Brig. General.

In his capacity as Gestapo Officer, he was active as the Chief of Einsatzkommandos and Highest Gestapo Offices in different towns of Austria and Czechoslovakia, after the occupation of these countries by Nazi Germany. Under his command, citizens of these countries were imprisoned without trial and sent to concentration camps.

SCHULZ was Commander of Einsatzkommando 5 which was a unit of Einsatzgruppe C, from May until 26 September 1941. In this capacity, he was a direct subordinate to the defendant RASCH. Under the command and supervision of the

- 31 -

defendant SCHULZ, Einsatzkommando 5 executed approximately 10,000 to 12,000 defenseless persons, men, women and children. SCHULZ conducted at least one of those executions personally. A great majority of the unfortunate victims of the activities of SCHULZ had committed no crime and done no wrong but they "had been born in the wrong part of the world, of forebears whom their murderers detested" (Judgement Tribunal No. 2, Case No. 4, USA vs. POHL et al. 24) or they had been members of the Communist Party. None of the victims was afforded as much as a semblance of a trial. These murders were carried out in pursuance of a program of genocide which aimed at the extermination of so-called sub-humans, Communists, Jews and Gypsies.

The Prosecution submits that the evidence proves that SCHULZ was a principle in accessory to, ordered, abetted, took a consenting part in, and was connected with plans and enterprises involving atrocities and offenses, including, but not limited to, murder, extermination, imprisonment, and other inhumane acts, carried out as part of the systematical program of genocide; and that his guilt has been established under Counts I, II and III of the Indictment.

FOR:

U.S. CHIEF OF COUNSEL

A. HORLIK-HOCHWALD
Attorney

Nuremberg, Germany
15 January 1948

- 32 -
(END)

MILITARY TRIBUNAL II

CASE NO. 9

TRIAL BRIEF FOR

THE UNITED STATES OF AMERICA

-against-

FRANZ SIX

Benjamin B. Ferencz
    Chief Prosecutor
Peter W. Walton
Arnost Horlik-Hochwald
John E. Glancy
    Of Counsel

For:

TELFORD TAYLOR
Brigadier General, USA
Chief of Counsel for War Crimes

and

James M. McHaney
    Deputy Chief of Counsel
    for War Crimes
    Director, SS Division

Mr. Alfred Schwarz
Mrs. Nancy H. Fenstermacher
    Research Analysts

Doc. 7

123

RESPONSIBILITY OF THE DEFENDANT SIX

124

I. THE CHARGES.

In Counts One and Two of the Indictment it is charged that the defendant FRANZ SIX was a principal in, accessory to, ordered, abetted, took a consenting part in, was connected with plans and enterprises involving and was a member of organizations or groups connected with certain atrocities and offenses, constituting crimes against humanity and war crimes. These offenses included persecutions on political, racial and religious grounds, murder, extermination, imprisonment and other inhumane acts committed against civilian populations, in violation of the Law of Nations, general principles of Criminal Law and the Laws and Customs of war as defined in Control Council Law No. 10.

The defendant Six is further charged with membership in the SS and SD, organizations declared to be criminal by the International Military Tribunal.

II. THE DEFENDANT SIX WAS THE COMMANDING OFFICER OF THE VORKOMMANDO MOSCOW OF EINSATZGRUPPE B FROM 22 JUNE 1941 UNTIL AT LEAST 28 AUGUST 1941.

The defendant Six admitted that he was called to Berlin on 20 June 1941 and that he was given command of the Vorkommando Moscow though he contends that he commanded only from 16 July to 20 August (Doc. Book III-B, p. 77, NO-4546, par. 5, Pros. Exh. 127).

The defendant Six stated that he regarded his personnel record as accurate (R. 1432). Part of his personnel record states that the defendant was in the Security Police Einsatz or East Einsatz from 22 June 1941 to 28 August 1941. This is further supported by the testimony of the defense witness, Veronika Vetter, who

- 1 -

125

testified that she saw Six in Smolensk on 23 August 1941
and is certain of the date because of an entry in her
diary (R. 5164). She testified further that she saw
Six there when she received a letter dated 31 August.
1941 from "Vorkommando Moscow of Einsatzgruppe B" (R. 5165).
(Doc. Book V-B, p. 137, NO-5855, Pros. Exh. 241). The
defendant Six has attempted to limit his period of command
in order to establish an "alibi" that he had left before
many of the executions reported in the documents took
place (See R. 1444).

III.   DURING SIX'S TIME OF COMMAND THE VORKOMMANDO
       MOSCOW COMMITTED WAR CRIMES AND CRIMES AGAINST
                        HUMANITY.

       A.   PRINCIPAL TO EXECUTIONS.

           There can be little doubt that one of the prin-
mary purposes of all Einsatzgruppen was the extermination
of Jews, Gypsies and Communist officials in pursuance of
the Fuehrer's Order. The Vorkommando Moscow is mentioned
many times in the Einsatzgruppen reports and in every
single instance it is shown as a Kommando of Einsatzgruppe B.

            (Report of 16 July 1941, not introduced but
            made available to defense, Report of 23
            July in Doc. Book III-B, p. 82a (loose),
            NO-2956, Pros. Exh. 128; Doc. Book II-B,
            p. 6a, NO-2837, Pros. Exh. 58; Doc. Book
            II-B, p. 26, NO-2844, Pros. Exh. 61; and
            all later references to Vorkommando Moscow.)

The defendant has admitted that he was stationed in the
building in which Einsatzgruppe B had its headquarters
(R. 1340) and that he turned the Vorkommando Moscow
over to Einsatzgruppe B when he returned to Berlin
(R. 1439-1440). He has sought to deny, however, for
obvious reasons, that Vorkommando Moscow was a part of

Einsatzgruppe B (R. 1439). During his admitted time of
command the reports clearly indicate that Vorkommando
Moscow was part of Einsatzgruppe B, but Six stated that
these reports were wrong (R. 1439). He attempted to
explain these away by saying that Nebe, the commander of
Einsatzgruppe B had deliberately made these misleading
reports (R. 1438-9). He further stated that Nebe was
able to report about Vorkommando Moscow in one instance
because one of the commanders of Vorkommando Moscow had
an inflammed jaw (R. 1345) and at another occasion, one
of the leaders of Vorkommando Moscow had an appendicitis
attack and both men passed through Minsk where Nebe was
located at the time and reported verbally to him (R. 1347).
The defendant would have us believe, therefore, that
Nebe deliberately sent inaccurate reports to Berlin about
Vorkommando Moscow, a unit with which he was supposedly   127
not connected, showing that the Vorkommando Moscow was
part of Einsatzgruppe B. To this interesting concoction
the defendant somehow adds a jaw inflammation and appendicitis hoping it will thereby be made credible. We submit
that this attempted explanation of the documents does
not detract from their face value. That Vorkommando
Moscow was in fact part of Einsatzgruppe B is further
clearly established by Prosecution Rebuttal Document NO.
5846, a letter issued by Vorkommando Moscow in Smolensk
while Six was still there stating specifically
"Vorkommando Moscow of the Einsatzgruppe B of the
Security Police and the SD" (Doc. Book V-B, p. 137, Pros.
Exh. 242, see R. 5165).

        The defendant admitted that he was in command
until 20 August. Prosecution Exhibit 61 shows the total

of executions by all the units of Einsatzgruppe B up to
the 20th of August. It states that the Headquarters
staff (of Einsatzgruppe B) and Vorkommando Moscow
liquidated 144 persons (Doc. Book II-B, p. 27, NO-2844).
The defendant testified that this report was wrong
(R. 1354) and an arbitrary action on the part of Nebe
(R. 1354). However, the same Einsatz report states:

> "The Vorkommando 'Moscow' was
> forced to execute another 46 persons
> amongst them 38 intellectual Jews who
> had tried to create unrest and dis-
> content in the newly established Ghetto
> of Smolensk" (Doc. Book II-B, p. 26).

When questioned about this by his defense counsel, Six
stated:

> "I have no explanation whatever
> for this report" (R. 1355).

Yet, shortly thereafter he attempted to explain it by
stating:

> "...This explanation then that
> the execution of the 46 people, in-
> cluding those 38 Jews in Smolensk,
> judging by the receipt of the reports
> from the Einsatzkommandos to the
> Einsatzgruppe must have happened at a
> time when I was no longer in Smolensk."
> (R. 1358)

The defendant Six testified that the defendant
Klingelhoefer became a member of Vorkommando Moscow
when it was organized (R. 1332). Klingelhoefer confirmed
this in his testimony that he was a member of Vorkommando
Moscow from 10 or 11 July until the middle of September
(R. 3904). Klingelhoefer was therefore asked to explain
the activities of Vorkommando Moscow:

128

- 4 -

"Q. Do you know that any Jews were shot by
     Vorkommando Moscow while you were
     there? (R. 3903)

 A. While I was in Advance Kommando Moscow
     of course I know that executions were
     carried out by the Department for Jewish
     Affairs. Of course I know that. I said
     that I know that the groups staff and
     also the Advanced Kommando Moscow
     constantly carried out executions, and
     operations. I never denied that. But
     I do not know the details." (R. 3903)
                  (Emphasis supplied)

Later Klingelhoefer testified:

            "...I knew in general that the
     group staff itself, as well as the
     advance commando Moscow continually
     carried out executions. Of course
     I knew this, (R. 3912)
                  (Emphasis supplied)

     B. ACCESSORY TO EXECUTIONS.

          The main point of defense presented by the

defendant Six has been that he merely collected documents

and archives while he was at the Eastern Front (R. 1339)

and that this was the mission of Vorkommando Moscow (R.

1330-1335).

          A careful examination will establish that

this was simply a part of the organized and systematic

extermination program.

          The defendant Blume, Chief of Sonderkommando

7A of Einsatzgruppe B, who admitted that a total of 200

people were killed under his command (R. 1898) testified

as follows:

129

- 5 -

Q. "You stated in your direct examination
that in several localities you were
kept busy collecting archives and documents for the purpose of study. That's
correct, isn't it?"

A. "Yes, that's correct."

Q. "Was that part of the task of all Einsatzkommandos?"

A. "Yes, certainly. We had to take care
that interesting and relevant communist
material would be seized and used."
(R. 1869)

The defendant Six testified that his unit, the
Vorkommando Moscow occupied part of the NKWD building in
Smolensk, and that the staff of Einsatzgruppe B occupied
another part of the same building (R. 1338, 1340); (see
also Doc. Book III-B, p. 33, NO-2954). He also stated
that he seized important materials there (R. 1347-8).
It was not mere chance that the Vorkommando Moscow was in
the NKWD building seizing important materials. The Fuehrer
had ordered that all communist functionaries were to be
killed (R. 3902) and in order to accomplish this systematically a list of all officials was necessary. This information was essential if a thorough job was to be done.

Thus one of the reports specifically based in part
on "the report of Standartenfuehrer Dr. Six" (Doc. Book
III-B, p. 33, NO-2954, Par. 1, Pros. Exh. 117) states
that "neither important material nor communist officials
can be seized" (Op. cit. par. 3, p. 34). The meaning
of this activity is further clarified by the Einsatzgruppe B Report stating (In welish) :

"Moreover files on the membership to the
Komsomol and to the Communist Party could
be secured in the NKWD building".
(Doc. Book II-B, p. 9, NO-2837,
Pros. Exh. 53)

Welish was in the area of Einsatzgruppe B. And another

- 6 -

report:

> "Apart from the 215 Jewish and Bolshevist
> officials 15 more NKWD agents were shot in
> Bialystock. The NKWD office was completely
> burned down. Only in the cellar vaults was
> it possible to secure various lists.
>   (Doc. Book II-B, p. 2, Pros. Exh. 57,
>   NO-2937)

Another report reads:

> "The whole Jewry had to be liquidated in
> Vileyka. During the search of the buildings
> and archives, lists of the NKWD leaders and
> the District Wilna were found, also lists of
> the political officials, the election agitators
> and confidential agents, and the young communists
> ....Interesting political material was found
> and secured in the NKWD building of Wilna.
> The same kind of material was seized in
> Gobilew. The membership files of the communist
> party, which were found, are of special impor-
> tance. A personnel file with photographs and
> a Bolshevist library with works in German were
> found in the NKWD building in Grodno."
>   (Emphasis supplied)
>   (See NO-2652, Doc. Book II-C, p. 11)
>   (See NO-2937, Doc. Book II-B, p. 2)

131

Why these files in the NKWD building were important

and how they were used is explained a few paragraphs later

with the report that party officials and NKWD agents were

liquidated in Wilna and Grodno and Bialystock (NO-2652,

Doc. Book II-C, p. 11). Bialystock, Grodno and Wilna

were in Einsatzgruppe B's area (NO-2937, Doc. Book II-B,

p. 2, 3).

The entire pattern was made crystal clear by the

defendant Klingelhoefer. He explained that his part of

Sonderkommando 7B was in the NKWD building investigating

documents (R. 3900). He further stated:

Q. "So, therefore, you found some lists giving you the names of all party functionaries in that area and you just gave that list to Rausch (Kommando Chief), is that correct?" (R. 3900)

A. "Yes, that was my duty." (R. 3901)

...Q. "I asked you witness, didn't you know that when you were giving him these lists of communist party functionaries that he was going to exterminate all those he could? You either knew it or you didn't know it." (R. 3901)

A. "Of course I did." (R. 3901)

The defendant Steimle too used the lists of communist party officials when he dealt with partisans (R. 2002).

It is therefore apparent that putting a unit of the Einsatzgruppe or the Einsatzgruppe Headquarters into the NKWD building to study their files was merely the initial stage of the systematic exterminations. Once the names of communist officials were obtained, they were liquidated. When the defendant Six, therefore, admits that he was quartered in the NKWD building and going through their files it becomes apparent that he was acting as an accessory before the fact to the contemplated murders.

IV. THE TESTIMONY OF THE DEFENDANT SIX IS INCONSISTENT, CONTRADICTORY AND REFUTED BY THE EVIDENCE.

1. TESTIMONY —   Q. "Isn't it true that you were promoted on the 9th of November because of your exceptional service with the Einsatzgruppe?"

A. "The date of my promotion and the list does not say anything about special merits. I am quite certain of that." (R. 1451)

Q. "You say that you did not get promoted because of exceptional service in the Einsatz; was it because of exceptional service someplace else that you got promoted a few weeks after you left the Einsatzgruppe?"

A. "That is not known to me. I only know that there were no special merits concerned with my promotion, nor was it in the least in the Einsatzgruppe." (R. 1452)

EVIDENCE - Letter "To the SS-Standartenfuehrer Dr. Six, Franz Alfred (SS No. 107480 SD Main Office).

I hereby promote you, effective 9 November 1941 to SS Oberfuehrer for outstanding service in Einsatz.

Signed: H. Himmler"
(Doc. Book V-B, p. 33, NO-4768, Pros. Exh. 237)

2. TESTIMONY - ..."It is quite unimaginable that in 1945 again special merits in the past should be mentioned in my promotion." (R. 1457)

EVIDENCE - Document - "Memorandum: The Reich Main Security Office requests the promotion of SS Oberfuehrer Dr. Six to Brigadefuehrer, effective 31 January 1945.......SIPO Einsatz: 22 June 1941 - 28 August 1941, East Einsatz....
On 9 November 1941, Six was promoted by the RFSS to SS Oberfuehrer for outstanding service in Security Police Einsatz in the East." (Doc. Book V-B, p. 36-37, NO-4768, Pros. Exh. 237)

3. TESTIMONY - Six made no reports to Einsatzgruppe B (R. 1343)

EVIDENCE - Under the heading of Report of Einsatzgruppe B dated 26 July, it states:

"Part of the Voraus Kommando (6 men) is in Smolensk, NKWD Building.
Smolensk, according to the report by Standartenfuehrer Dr. Six is as thoroughly destroyed as Minsk.....It was therefore not possible to have the entire Vorkommando follow to Smolensk."
(Doc. Book III-B, p. 33, NO-2954) (Emphasis supplied)

133

- 9 -

4.   TESTIMONY -   "The Advance Commando Moscow
                           was a special Commando of the
                           Reich Security Main Office. It
                           was not an Einsatz Kommando"
                           (R. 1334).
                                "I inspected the archives of
                           the town. The archives of the
                           Administrative district; all
                           cultural organizations, institu-
                           tions, universities, and other
                           places like churches......."
                           (R. 1339)

     EVIDENCE   -   Letter dated 3 April 1942
                           from SS Operational Main Office:
                           "Subject: Release of SS Unter-
                           sturmfuehrer of the Reserve Prof.
                           Dr. Franz Alfred Six, commanded
                           to the Chief of the Security
                           Police and the SD.
                                To the SS - Personnel Main
                           Office
                                ...The Reichsfuehrer SS has
                           ordered that SS Untersturmfuehrer
                           of the Reserve Prof. Dr. Franz
                           Alfred Six be released immediately
                           from the Waffen SS, since S. has
                           already been assigned as commander
                           of the Security Police and the SD
                           in the East."....
                                (Doc. Book V-B, p. 34, Doc.
                                NO-4768, Pros. Exh. 237)

134
                                "Herr Dr. Augsburg always
                           said that Professor Six was a very
                           good man and that he was very sorry
                           for him that he had come just into
                           this organization."
                                (R. 5195 - Testimony of defense
                                witness Vetter)

5.   TESTIMONY -   Vorkommando Moscow was not
                           a part of Einsatzgruppe B (R.
                           1439, 1334, 1348)

     EVIDENCE   -   Report dated 23 July lists
                           Vorkommando Moscow among the
                           Kommandos of Einsatzgruppe B
                           (Doc. Book III-B, p. 82a (loose)
                           NO-2956).

                                Report dated 26 July under
                           heading of Einsatzgruppe B re-
                           ports on location of Vorkommando
                           Moscow and mentions the defend-
                           ant Six (Doc. Book III-B, p. 33,
                           NO-2954).

Report dated 29 August lists
Vorkommando Moscow under units
of Einsatzgruppe B (Doc. Book
II-B, p. 6a, NO-2837) and reports activities of Vorkommando
Moscow which the defendant confirms (R. 1349).

Report listing executions by
Einsatzgruppe B as of 20 August
1941 begins with the "Staff and
Vorkommando Moscow". Defendant
admits that Nebe, Chief of
Einsatzgruppe B assigned persons
from Einsatzgruppe B to Vorkommando Moscow (R. 1331-2).

Letter, issued while Six was
still in command carries heading
"Vorkommando Moscow of Einsatz-
gruppe B" of SIPO and SD.
(Rebuttal Doc. Book V-B, p. 137,
NO-5855, Pros. Exh. 241)

Vorkommando Moscow occupied
the same building as the Headquarters Staff of Einsatzgruppe
B (R. 1340).

Defendant admits turning
Vorkommando Moscow, which he
contends was a completely independent unit, over to Einsatzgruppe B (R. 1440).

Later reports continue to
list Vorkommando Moscow as part
of Einsatzgruppe B (Doc. Book
II-B, p. 53, NO-3143; Doc. Book
II-B, p. 62, NO-3276; Doc. Book
II-B, p. 54, NO-3160).

6.   TESTIMONY -

"...I myself - and I have to
make a point in stating this -
had no knowledge about the
general elimination of Jewry,
especially about the extermination of women and children. As
I said, I had no knowledge and
never received any knowledge"
(R. 1334)

135

- 11 -

CROSS-EXAMINATION -   Q. "when did you first learn
                                   of the order to annihilate
                                   the Jews?" (R. 1461)
                              A. "I learned of this between
                                   7th and 10th of July 1941"
                                   (R. 1462)
                              Q. "where"
                              A. "In Minsk"
                              Q. "From whom?"
                              A. "From Untersturmfuehrer
                                   Lutter, who arrived first
                                   from Einsatzkommando 9 in
                                   Minsk" (R. 1462)
                              Q. "what did you do when you
                                   learned of this order to
                                   annihilate the Jews?"
                              A. "I said to him that my com-
                                   mando would not have to
                                   carry out executions of
                                   Jews" (R. 1463)

7. TESTIMONY -   Q. "But one of your positions
                                   at least was to be an SS
                                   Colonel?"
                              A. "yes, it was an honorary
                                   position" (R. 1428) (See
                                   R. 1427, also R. 1313)

    CROSS-EXAMINATION -   Q. "was it any more honorary
                                   than any other SS rank or any
                                   other SS position?"
                              A. "No more and no less" (R.
                                   1428)
                              Q. "In other words you were an
                                   SS Colonel, the same as
                                   other SS Colonels?"
                              A. "yes". (R. 1428)

       Compare also: Q. "...will you please tell me
                                   if it was any different from
                                   any other SS Colonel?"
                              A. "yes, owing to the fact that
                                   I had been commanded to this
                                   assignment...." (R. 1428).

8. TESTIMONY -   people assigned to Six and
                                   Vorkommando Moscow by Einsatz-
                                   gruppe B were either inter-
                                   preters, or had local know-
                                   ledge of Moscow or had scien-
                                   tific knowledge of archives.
                                   Noack was one of them. (R.
                                   1331-2)

    EVIDENCE -   Noack was the "commisar
                                   for Jewish Affairs in Vor-
                                   kommando Moscow" (R. 5165)
                                   Noack was in charge of
                                   executions while Klingelhoefer
                                   was in Vorkommando Moscow.
                                   (Doc. Book III-B, p. 58,
                                   NO-4235, pros. Exh. 124)

136

9. TESTIMONY –   "I said in Smolensk there
                      were no synagogues...(R. 1404)

    EVIDENCE –   Ghettos were established in
                      Smolensk. (Doc. Book III-B,
                      p. 37, NO-2949)

                      There were Jews in Smolensk
                      and they worked in the yard of
                      the building occupied by Six
                      (R. 5200).

10. TESTIMONY –   Speaking of Amt VII of the RSHA
                      "...The reason why Heydrich
                      founded such an institute
                      during the war can only be seen
                      from his own snobbishness. He
                      just wanted to have his own
                      office of science, which would
                      so-to-speak be a decorative
                      office in his RSHA (R. 1321-
                      1322).

    EVIDENCE –   In declaring certain cate-
                      gories of the SD as criminal
                      the IMT specifically included
                      Amt VII of the RSHA (Trial of
                      Major War Criminals, Vol. I,
                      p. 267-8).

                      Organization Charts of the
                      RSHA show sections on Jewry,
                      Freemasonry, political churches,
                      and other opposing groups
                      (Doc. Book V-B, p. 73, 104,
                      No. L-185 and L-219, Pros. Exh.
                      239, 240).

11. TESTIMONY –   In Section VII of the RSHA,
                      headed by Six, there was no
                      special section concerned with
                      the Jewish question (R. 1394-
                      1395)

    EVIDENCE –   Organizational Chart showing
                      the division of work in the
                      RSHA as of 1 January 1941 shows
                      Sec. VII-B 1 concerned with
                      "Freemasonry and Jewry" (Doc.
                      Book V-B, p. 105-6, Doc. L-185,
                      Pros. Exh. 73).

137

Organizational Chart
showing the Division of work
in the RSHA as of 10 Oct. 1943
shows Sec. VII-B 2 concerned
with "Judaism" and headed by
SS Hauptsturmfuehrer Ballensiefen (Doc. Book V-B, p. 135,
Doc. L-219, Pros. Exh. 240).
The defendant admitted he knew
Hauptsturmfuehrer Ballensiefen
and that the latter was in
charge of several departments
(R. 1395)

12. _TESTIMONY_ -

Q. "Isn't it a fact that you did
agree at some time to the
general elimination of the
Jews?" (R. 1466)
A. "No". (R. 1466)
Q. "I ask you a simple question,
and it is surprising that you
have a loss of words. Isn't
it a fact that as a good
National Socialist you favored
the program to exterminate the
Jews? That you spoke in favor
of it, if you want me to be
more specific. Yes or No?"
A. "No". (R. 1467)

EVIDENCE -

Document "Confidential work-
Session of the Consultants on
Jewish Questions of the German
Missions in Europe.
Krumhubel, 3 and 4 April 1944

"Greetings by Ambassador Prof.
Dr. Six, who gives the chairmanship to Ambassador SCHLEIER.
In his opening speech he deals
with the tasks and aims of the
anti-Jewish action abroad.
Ambassador Schleier points to
the faith of the Fuehrer in the
racial principal of the people...
Ambassador SIX speaks then
about the political structures
of world Jewry.... The physical
elimination of Eastern Jewry
would deprive Jewry of its
biological reserves...The Jewish
question must be solved not
only in Germany but also inter-
nationally."

138

Embassy counsellor v. THADDEN
speaks about the Jewish-political
situation in Europe and about
the state of the Anti-Jewish
executive measures...(As the
details of the state of the
executive measures in the various
countries, reputed by the consultant, are to be kept secret,
it has been decided not to
enter them in the protocol)"
(Doc. Book V-B, p. 45-47,
3319-PS, Pros. Exh. 238)

Six admits that he was present at the meeting and that
he made a speech (R. 1467) but
denies that he made the statements quoted (R. 1469).

The defendant's attempt to deceive is further
clarified when it is recalled that this "learned professor"
was in hiding as a farm hand after the war until he was
caught in 1946 (R. 1391). On the stand he stated that he
protected the churches (R. 1340) and exerted his influence
to have the churches reopened so that the civilian population could worship (R. 1372-1405). But when asked by
the tribunal:

Q. "What did you do between June 22nd and
August 20, 1941, while you were in that
occupied territory, to restore political
liberty and freedom to the civilian
population?"

the defendant replied:

A. My function in the East during the march
was not of such a nature that I would
have had the possibility to carry out
such principles. I could not do anything at all." (R. 1375-6)

The defendant contended that he was able to be
promptly released from duty on the Eastern front by simply
writing a letter and sending a cable to Berlin (R. 1342,
1448). Other defendants testified that it was impossible
to ask to be released from an assignment which had been
ordered (R. 1772).

The defendant testified that as section chief of the RSHA he was officially concerned with the Jewish church, but only from the point of view of cultural research (R. 1396). His section on Jewry had as its main and sole task the writing of historical thesis and "No, never for a moment" would he be interested in using that material or making it available for others to use against the Jews. (R. 1397, see 1400). Yet the defendant admitted he knew that one of the basic policies of Hitler's program was war on the Jews (R. 1399) and he had taken the oath of inviolable allegiance to Hitler (R. 1399).

The defendant stated he never received the letter from Himmler which was addressed to him (R. 1454) and it was not until 1947 that he learned why he had been promoted in the SS (R. 1488). At one point he stated that Heydrich had "reproached me very severely", "accused me with desertion", and "was not pleased with my attitude during the last few years and he reproached me and said I had been unfaithful and disobedient". (R. 1450) Yet when questioned about his promotion he said it must have been signed by Heydrich or Himmler (R. 1452) and that it was suggested and proposed by Streckenbach or Heydrich (R. 1455, see 1456). Questioned about his co-defendants, six refused to answer (R. 1417). His record stated, and he did not deny, that he was "an active and proven National Socialist" (R. 1461) (Doc. Book V-B, p. 37, NO-4768, pros. Exh. 237). He had been a Nazi since the age of 21 (R. 1391). He testified that he regarded Jewish males as justifiable victims of Hitler's extermination order (R. 1413) and that he as an officer would have carried out the order had he received it (R. 1385).

Six admitted that he was willing to deviate from the oath he gave to Hitler (R. 1485). Can there be any doubt that he deviated from the oath he took in court?

V. THE DEFENDANT SIX WAS A MEMBER OF ORGANIZATIONS DECLARED CRIMINAL BY THE INTERNATIONAL MILITARY TRIBUNAL.

Control Council Law No. 10, Art. II, provides that:

"1) Each of the following acts is recognized as a crime:....
(d) Membership in categories of a criminal group or organization declared criminal by the International Military Tribunal."

The IMT Charter which is incorporated by reference into the Control Council Law provides further that:

"In any such case the criminal nature of the group or organization is considered proved and should not be questioned."
(IMT Charter, Art. 10)

The International Military Tribunal declared certain groups of the Leadership Corps, the SS, the Gestapo, and the SD to be criminal organizations. The test to be applied in determining the guilt of individual members was clearly stated by the International Tribunal and applied by Military Tribunal No. III in the case of United States vs. Alstotter, et al., as follows:

"Those members of an organization which has been declared criminal 'who became or remained members of the organizations with knowledge that it was being used for the commission of acts declared criminal by Article 6 of the Charter, or who were personally implicated as members of the organization in the commission of such crimes' are declared punishable." (R. 10711, Judgment, Court No. III, Case No. III) (Emphasis supplied)

(A) MEMBERSHIP IN THE SS.

Certain categories of the SS were declared to constitute criminal organizations:

> "In dealing with the SS the Tribunal includes all persons who had been officially accepted as members of the SS including the members of the Allgemeine SS, members of the Waffen SS, members of the SS Totenkopf Verbande, and the members of any of the different police forces who were members of the SS."
> (Emphasis supplied)
> (Trial of Major War Criminals, Vol. I, p. 273)

The defendant Six fits within the SS categories named as criminal and meets the test of criminal responsibility. He became a member of the SS in 1935 as a Lieutenant and admitted that this was not an honorary title (R.1392). By 1938, he had been promoted to SS Colonel and by 1945 he was an SS Brigadier General (R. 1392-1393).

Six was also an officer in the Reserve of the Waffen SS until April 1942 (Doc. Book V-B, p. 32, NO-4768, Pros. Exh. 237) having volunteered in the spring of 1940 (R. 1322).

There can be no doubt therefore that the defendant was "officially accepted" as a member of the SS.

The defendant admitted that he learned about the order to annihilate the Jews in July of 1941 (R. 1461-2). It is therefore clear, without any further reference to the mass of other evidence proving such knowledge that he "remained a member of the organization with knowledge that it was being used for the commission of acts declared criminal". That is adequate to establish guilt under the law. In addition, the defendant was personally implicated in the commission of war crimes and crimes against humanity as shown above.

142

(B) MEMBERSHIP IN THE SD.

The International Military Tribunal declared
certain categories of the SD to be criminal.

"In dealing with the SD the Tribunal
includes Amter III, VI and VII of the
RSHA, and all other members of the SD
including all local representatives and
agents, honorary or otherwise, whether
they were technically members of the SS
or not...(Trial of Major War Criminals,
Vol. I, p. 267-8) (Emphasis supplied)

The defendant Six voluntarily joined the SD in
1935 (R. 1319). In November 1939 he became Chief of Amt
VII of the RSHA which was specifically included by the IMT
in its declaration of criminality. He remained Chief of
Amt VII until March 1943 (R. 1393)

Six also meets the test here of having remained
a member of the SD with knowledge that it was being used
for the commission of criminal acts. He cannot deny that
what he observed being done on the Eastern front by units
of the SD he did not recognize as crimes. The defendant,
in addition, was personally implicated in the commission
of such crimes and was in fact promoted for his outstanding
service in the Security Police and SD (Doc. Book V-B, p.
33, NO-4768, Pros. Exh. 237). The IMT found Amt VII a
criminal organization because of its criminal acts. No
further proof of these acts was offered in this trial for
by the very terms of the IMT Charter which is embodied
in Law No. 10 "the criminal nature of the group or organization is considered proved and shall not be questioned."
(IMT Charter, Articles 9 and 10).

The IMT judgment would be rendered meaningless
and senseless if the chief of a group declared criminal
were not to be held responsible. All members of that

- 19 -

group, Amt VII of the RSHA, are subject to automatic arrest and ten years confinement, in accordance with the rulings of the IMT and subsequent orders of the Office of Military Government for Germany (U. S.) (Letter, OMGUS, "Arrest by German Police of Members of Organizations Found Criminal by the IMT" dated 9 July 1947; OMGUS Regulations, Title 2, Change 1, Sec. 2-220.2, dated 21 October 1946). The Chief of that office must bear a greater responsibility than any of its members.

VI. CONCLUSION.

The defendant FRANZ SIX was the commanding officer of Vorkommando Moscow of Einsatzgruppe B. During his time of command, Vorkommando Moscow, together with the Headquarters staff of Einsatzgruppe B murdered 144 people. Vorkommando Moscow alone executed 38 intellectual Jews during that time. The defendant was promoted to SS Colonel by Himmler because of his outstanding service in the Einsatz. His later promotion to General in the SS was also based in part on his outstanding service with the Security Police Einsatz in the East. The contention of the defendant that he was not part of the Einsatzgruppe B is clearly refuted by the many documents showing Vorkommando Moscow as part of Einsatzgruppe B, and his own letters of promotion.

Other defendants have explained that all Einsatz units had to seek lists of political functionaries in the Soviet Intelligence Buildings. These lists were then used to find those officials who were to be executed in accordance with the Fuehrer's Order. Therefore, even if we accepted the defendant's claim that he was merely collecting documents while in the Intelligence Building at Smolensk, it would be apparent that he was acting as an accessory to the contemplated killings.

The testimony given by the defendant Six was inconsistent, contradictory and refuted by the evidence. Although admittedly a Nazi since the age of 21, he stated that he did not favor the anti-Jewish program. Yet the captured minutes of a speech given by him show his clear advocacy of the physical elimination of Eastern Jewry.

The defendant was regularly promoted in the SS and reached the rank of Brigadefuehrer or Brigadier General. He was Chief of Amt VII of the RSHA, specifically named by the International Military Tribunal when they declared the SD a criminal organization. From his rank, position and activities, there can be no doubt that he knew of the criminal activities of the SS and SD while he remained a member.

In view of the foregoing, it is submitted that the responsibility and guilt of the defendant FRANZ SIX for the crimes charged in Counts 1, 2, and 3 of the Indictment have been clearly established.

Respectfully submitted,

For the Chief of Counsel for War Crimes:

Benjamin B. Ferencz
Chief Prosecutor

PERSECUTION OF ALIEN PEOPLES--RESPONSIBILITY OF
BERGER FOR THE PERSECUTION OF THE JEWS.

The defendant's responsibility for the spreading of anti-Jewish propaganda has already been discussed. Because this offense was in itself considered a substantive crime by the International Military Tribunal, the evidence on this point was treated separately. As we have already pointed out, whether the charge of incitement to anti-semitism stands or falls depends on whether or not the defendant did commit these acts with knowledge of the then contemporary extermination of the Jews. The specification already discussed is therefore dependent upon the instant one for proof of guilty knowledge. The evidence in this connection demonstrates amply that the defendant not only had guilty knowledge of the planned persecution program, but actually took an active hand in bringing it about.

Although he now professes to denounce him in no uncertain terms, the fact is that the defendant was the close confidante of Heinrich Himmler. He was described by the Prosecution witness Bach as "Himmler's mouthpiece" and "the power behind the throne" (Tr. pp. 4293, 4294). He was the only SS Fuehrer whom Himmler called by his first name (Tr. p. 4292). Another equally unflattering but accurate epithet to which BERGER himself admitted was "the almighty Gottlob" (Tr. p. 7115). The defense witness Albrecht described him as coming "from the closest entourage of the Reichsfuehrer SS" (Tr. p. 6264). The twelve main office chiefs, of which he was one, were referred to as "Himmler's twelve apostles". (Tr. p. 7115) But there is no need to rely on cliches. That BERGER frequently functioned as Himmler's deputy in matters over and above his duties in the SS Main Office is proven by documents to which we shall later refer.

In July, 1942, BERGER was appointed liaison officer between Heinrich Himmler and Reichsleiter Alfred Rosenberg, the Minister for the Occupied Eastern Territories. (Doc. NO-3631, Pros. Exh. 1100, Doc. Bk. 44, p. 17)

The civilian administration of the Occupied Eastern Territories --perhaps the best contemporary counterpart for purposes of comparison would be military government--was centered in the Ministry for the

Occupied Eastern Territories. Reichsleiter Rosenberg headed this administrative hierarchy. Subordinate to him were the several Reichskommissars (Reich Commissioners) and Generalkommissars (Commissioner Generals), each competent for a particular segment of the occupied East. Subordinate in turn to these men were numerous other territorial officials (Gebietskommissars, etc.) administering smaller component parts of the Occupied East.

The mailed fist behind the civilian administration was not the Army, in the immediate vicinity of the front. In all other areas, the SS and Police were charged with the maintenance of order. SS military administrative districts similar to those in the Reich were set up by Himmler, each headed by a Higher SS and Police Leader. Sometimes the areas administered by the Higher SS and Police Leaders corresponded to the areas administered by the civilian administration, but more often it over-lapped them. In theory at least, there was no concurrent jurisdiction, for Himmler's men were theoretically subordinate to Rosenberg's civilian administration for the area, receiving their orders from Himmler via the civilian administration. But this was in theory only. In point of fact, there was much friction between the two sets of administrations, engendered by the fact that the SS and Police, working in secrecy, received their orders through SS and Police channels directly from Berlin. (Testimony of witness Bach, Tr.pp. 4287, 4288) The civilian administration was often not even apprised of what was going on in its own territory. More frequently than not, it sought to resist the more immoderate and radical policies of the SS.

It was the job of the defendant, as Himmler's representative with Rosenberg's Ministry, to see to it that the brutal and criminal policies of Himmler and the agencies which had formulated these policies were carried through to fulfillment in the East, notwithstanding occasional resistance of a few administrators. BERGER was, in effect,

147

"the political whip of the SS".* BERGER's personal advisor was in fact also his man for SD matters, the liaison officer between the RSHA and the East Ministry, SS Hauptstuermfuehrer Brandenburg. (Testimony of Eppenauer, Tr. p. 8144)

In this capacity, if in no other, the defendant had a complete insight into what went on in the East. He received copies of all reports of so-called anti-partisan warfare from the office of the Reichsfuehrer. (Doc. NO-1473, Pros. Exh. 2371, Doc. Bk. 66-B, p. 34) In addition, file copies of all other matters pertaining to the East in which the SS had a hand were sent to him for scrutiny. (Doc. NO-3631, Pros. Exh. 1100, Doc. Bk. 44, p. 17; Doc. NO-2563, Pros. Exh. 2402, Doc. Bk. 67, p. 3; Doc. NO-3129, Pros. Exh. C-211)

The defendant could have wielded this power for good or for evil. He chose the latter course and elected to compel the civil administration to carry out the criminal policies of his Reichsfuehrer.

The best illustration of this is afforded by an instance that happened in the summer of 1943, at a time when the "final solution of the Jewish question" had reached the operational phase in the East on an unparalleled scale. The Commissioner General of White Ruthenia, Gauleiter Kube, had vigorously resisted the liquidating activities of the SD Einsatzkommandos in his territory, and word of this heresy had reached Himmler. On 14 August 1943, Himmler's adjutant sent BERGER copies of the complaints against Kube, stating:

> "The Reichsfuehrer-SS requests you to inform Reichs-
> minister Rosenberg about this confidentially..."
> (Doc. NO-5888, Pros. Exh. 2372, Doc. Bk. 66-B, p. 35)

The enclosures to this letter are appalling in the clarity of their disclosures, and lend themselves to no two interpretations. The first enclosure is a file memorandum by Strauch, the chief of an SD Einsatzkommando operating to effect a final solution of the

---

*Even the defense witness Albrecht admits that the purpose of BERGER's assignment to the Ministry was to enforce Himmler's insane policies in the East. (Tr. pp. 6267, 6292)

Jewish question in the vicinity of Minsk. As will be seen from the following quotations, it involves a shocking instance of systematized murder.

> "On Tuesday, 20 July 1943, at about 7 o'clock, I arrested the 70 Jews employed at the General Commissioner White Ruthenia, and made them subject to Special Treatment.
>
> On the same day at 10 o'clock I received a telephone call from the office of the General Commissioner that the Gauleiter would like to see me at once.
>
> I complied with the request.
>
> Although the outward appearance of the Gauleiter seemed to be calm, his manner of speaking betrayed that he was in a state of extreme excitement. He asked me how dare I arrest the Jews employed with him; I declared that I had received a strict order to carry out this action. He asked me for a written order. I replied that I was satisfied with an oral order, since I had to carry out such an order exactly as a written one. Gauleiter Kube emphasized then that this constituted a serious violation of his jurisdiction; the Jewish workers were subordinated to him and it was not permissible that the Reichsfuehrer SS or the Obergruppenfuehrer von dem Bach interfere with his jurisdiction as General Commissioner...
>
> Kube asked me then whether I had cared with the same diligence for the transports of livestock to the Obergruppenfuehrer BERGER as I had cared for his Jews. I replied that I did not know anything about such transports of livestock. Kube thought this strange, since, after all, it was the duty of the Police to prevent such illegal procedures.
>
> ...
>
> I emphasized that I could not understand how German men could quarrel because of a few Jews; I was again and again faced with the fact that my men and I were reproached for barbarism and sadism, whereas I did nothing but fulfill my duty. Even the fact that expert physicians had removed in a proper way the gold fillings from the teeth of Jews who were designated for Special Treatment had been made the topic of conversations. Kube replied that this method of our procedure was unworthy of a German man and of the Germany of Kant and Goethe. It was our fault that the reputation of Germany was being ruined in the whole world. It was also true, he said, that my men literally satisfied their sexual lust during these executions. I protested energetically against that statement and emphasized that it was regrettable that we, in addition to having to perform this nasty job, were also made the target of mud-slinging.
>
> That was the end of the conversation.
>   (signed) Strauch
>   SS Obersturmbannfuehrer"

(Underscorings added) (Doc. NO-4317, Pros. Exh. 2373, Doc. Bk. 66-B, p. 37)

Another enclosure sent to BERGER at the same time was a copy of a formal report from the same Einsatzkommando chief to von dem Bach, the chief of Antipartisan Units. The tone of this report is the same as the foregoing memorandum; it was a violent denunciation of Kube for the uncooperative attitude shown by him and by his civilian administration towards the "final solution of the Jewish question" by the SS and Police. Strauch substantiated his report with a number of examples where Kube and his staff had resisted the SS in its planned program of liquidation. The report reads in part as follows:

150

> "I have composed the report from evidence which is available with the Commander of the Security Police and the SD for White Ruthenia. The rumor-mongering about Gauleiter Kube is, as is well known, boundless. I have, therefore, in my report kept almost exclusively to facts which are based on documents or to which I myself am a witness. I have tried to point out that Kube is completely incapable in administrative and leadership spheres, that he is hostilely disposed toward the SS and Police and that he finally displays an almost impossible attitude towards the Jewish question.
>
> • • •
>
> It is noteworthy that the administration is never on hand for large-scale actions of the SS and Police in order to take up their work immediately after the pacification. In the face of this, practically all actions are illusory.
>
> • • •
>
> Attacks of this kind on my officers and men were daily routine. An action against the Russian Ghetto at Minsk was to take place on 1 March 1942. The Commissioner General had been informed previously. The action was intended to be camouflaged by telling the Council of Elders that 5,000 Jews of the Minsk Ghetto were to be resettled. They were to be selected and to be made available by the Council of Elders. Each Jew was permitted to carry 5 Kg. of luggage. It can be proved that the Commissariat General disclosed the actual intentions of the Security Police. Those Jews, who were employed with the Commissariat General, were not returned to the Ghetto for several days, but were kept at the Commissariat General. From this, the Ghetto Jews already realized that the statement of the Security Police was not correct. Still further indiscretions were committed, as appears from reports of secret agents. At that time it was not possible to clear these happenings unobjectionably. But it is an established fact that the Gauleiter used his knowledge for rescuing his Jews. Due to the treachery, no Jew reported at the given time. We had no choice but to herd the Jews together by force. Because there was some resistance, the agents assigned had to make use of fire arms. In the worst situation, when everything had to be done to break the resistance, the Gauleiter appeared...The Gauleiter immediately overwhelmed me with abuses concerning the unheard-of happenings which allegedly occurred when the Jews were herded together. He claimed that shots were fired repeatedly in the Ghetto, so that ricochets were found outside of the Ghetto also...In my capacity as a referent

for Jewish questions and as an SS
officer, I feel considerably hurt
by the behavior of the Gauleiter...
These abuses continued for days...
The Commissioner General went to
Wileika on 3 March 1942 because he
was informed that anti-Jewish actions
would take place at Wileika and
Molodetschno also. He went to the
local branch office of the Security
Police and requested a report. He
obviously hoped to be able to blame
the Security Police for its activity
at these places, too.

. . . .

During a conference about Jewish
labor, at which a greater part of
the responsible men were present, I
stated that the Jewish question in
White Ruthenia would be completely
solved by the beginning of Winter.
An official objected that it would
be necessary under these circumstances
to notify all army and civilian offices,
as well as all establishments in which
Jews were employed. I replied that
there was no necessity for this, since
the Gauleiter had in several speeches,
demanded the solution of the Jewish
question. The chief of the department
answered spontaneously that the dissen-
sion of the Gauleiter was well known
to me.

. . . .

In the course of a large-scale action
in the Ghetto, confidential agents
revealed that the security service of
the German Jews, consisting mainly of
war veterans, were prepared to put up
resistance by force of arms. To avoid
the shedding of blood on the German
side, this security service was concen-
trated at a different site. It was
explained to them that a fire had
broken out in the city and that they
had to keep themselves at disposal
for fire-fighting activities. The
Jews were loaded on trucks and given
Special Treatment. This affair also
came to the ears of the Gauleiter,
through unexplainable channels. He
got very excited first because it is
brutal to annihilate the former front
line soldiers, and that, secondly, the
manner of execution was unheard of.

In the communication of 28 April
1942, already mentioned by me, Kube
elaborates that he would like it
best of all if all Russian Jews were

151

brought as quickly as possible to
their just desserts. Here again he
exempts the German Jews.

.   Kube has often emphasized to me
personally, that the Jews evacuated
from Germany could be kept without
difficulty, because they did not
speak the language of the country
and therefore could not become
dangerous in respect to partisans.

From all these experiences I
have come to the conclusion that he,
from the bottom of his heart, is an
opposent of our Jewish actions. If
he does not show it outwardly, then
it is only for fear of the consequences.
He would agree to it as far as the
Russian Jews are concerned, because
he can quiet his conscience because
they are preponderantly helpers of
the partisans. . .
              (signed) Strauch
                       SS Obersturmfuehrer"
(Pros. Exh. 2374, NO-2262, Bk.66-B,p.40)

Did BERGER react to these shocking reports?

Did he react to Kube's valiant attempts to resist

152   the murderous policies of the SS? He certainly

did -- but not as a decent man should.

Heinrich Himmler's political whip went into

action. The man whose job it was to see that SS

policies were enforced in the East took his assign-

ment seriously. He paid a visit to Reichsleiter

Rosenberg and put on the pressure. Four days later

he reported back to Brandt:

> "During the next few days, Reichs-
> leiter Rosenberg will send Gauleiter
> Meyer to Minsk to give Kube a serious
> warning." (underscoring supplied)
> Exh. 2375, NO-4315, Bk.66-B, p. 56)

BERGER clashed with Kube again with respect to

the proposed resettlement of the Minsk Jews. After

having attended a meeting of leading figures in the

Rosenberg Ministry and the civilian administration

as the SS representative, the defendant reported to

Himmler:

"Upon order of the Reichsfuehrer SS,
the Jews in Minsk have to either be
resettled or brought into a concentration camp. Now, Kube has in his district a large Panje cart factory with
4,000 Jews and says that he would have
to close down this factory immediately
if the Jews were taken away. I urged
him to turn to the Reichsfuehrer SS
via the Higher SS and Police Leader
and possibly to turn this factory into
a concentration camp. This would
certainly signify that he wanted to
be rid of them, but since, as he
claims, his concern was only the
production of carts, this would entail
no sacrifice for him." (Pros. Exh.
2376, NO-3370, Bk. 66-B, p. 58)

BERGER requested orders from the Reichsfuehrer as

to what he should do. Some time later he received

orders from Himmler that:

"... the Jews are to be taken out of
Minsk and to Lublin or to another
place. The present production can be
transferred to a concentration camp."
(Pros. Exh. 2377, NO-3304, Bk.66-B, p.61)

These are no isolated instances of the implementa-

tion of a policy which only incidentally affected a

few hundred or a few thousand Jews. These episodes

are part and parcel of a program of genocide applicable

in the first instance to all the Jews of the occupied

Eastern territories. The SS was the spearhead of

liquidation in the East, and the defendant well knew

what was at stake from the very first. In July 1942,

a few days after BERGER became liaison officer to the

Eastern Ministry, Himmler informed him of the strategy:

"I urgently request that no ordinance.
regarding the definition of the word
'Jew' be issued. We are only tying our
own hands by establishing these foolish
definitions. The occupied territories
will be purged of Jews. The Fuehrer
has charged me with the execution of
this very hard order. No one can release
me from this responsibility in any case,
and I strongly resent all interference.
You will receive a memorandum
Lammers in a short time." (Pros. Exh.
2378, NO-626, Bk. 66-B, p. 62)

153

The defendant now claims that no one ever spoke
to him of "liquidation" and he did not know what was
going on. (Tr. p. 6085) Even if we give the defendant
the benefit of the doubt and look at this document in
a vacuum, the conclusion is inescapable that, having
freed the Reich proper of Jews and shipped them to the
East, the many millions of Jews in the East would have
to go somewhere, if the East was to be "purged", or
else their liquidation was portended. Since the defendant only claims to have heard of a plan for the
evacuation of Jews from Germany proper, (Tr. p. 6085)
death alone could be the intention of the Reichsfuehrer
when he spoke of "purging" the occupied territories
as well.

But all these logical calisthenics are pointless,
for this is no vacuum, there are other documents, and
the defendant knew what was transpiring and even
helped to bring it about.

In the first place, the "final solution of the
Jewish question" was the first point on the SS program,
and it was not by any means confined to the East.

Himmler spoke quite frankly about that subject
at the conference of his SS Gruppenfuehrers at Posen
on 4 October 1943. He said:

> "I also want to talk to you, quite
> frankly, on a very grave matter.
> Among ourselves it should be mentioned
> quite frankly, and yet we will never
> speak of it publicly. Just as we did
> not hesitate on June 30, 1934, to do
> the duty we were bidden, and stand
> comrades who had lapsed up against the
> wall and shoot them, so we have never
> spoken about it and will never speak
> of it. It was that tact which is a
> matter of course and which I am glad
> to say is inherent in us, that made
> us never discuss it among ourselves,
> never speak of it. It appalled every-
> one, and yet everyone was certain that
> he would do it the next time if such
> orders are issued, and if it is
> necessary.

"I mean the clearing out of the Jews,
the extermination of the Jewish race.
It's one of those things it is easy
to talk about--'The Jewish race is
being exterminated' says one Party
member, 'that's quite clear, it's
in our program--elimination of the
Jews, and we're doing it, extermina-
ting them.' And then they come, 80
million worthy Germans, and each one
has his decent Jew. Of course the
others are vermin, but this one is
an A-1 Jew. Not one of all those who
talk this way has witnessed it, not
one of them has been through it.
Most of you must know what it means
when 100 corpses are lying side by
side, or 500 or 1000. To have stuck
it out and at the same time---apart
from exceptions caused by human
weakness---to have remained decent
fellows, that is what has made us
hard. This is a page of glory in
our history which has never been
written, for we know how difficult
we should have made it for ourselves,
if,-with the bombing raids, the burdens
and the deprivations of war---we still
had Jews today in every town as secret
saboteurs, agitators and troublemongers.
We would now probably have reached the
1916/17 stage when the Jews were still
in the German national body.

"We have taken from them what wealth
they had. I have issued a strict
order, which SS-Obergruppenfuehrer
Pohl has carried out, that this
wealth should as a matter of course,
be handed over to the Reich without
reserve." (Doc. 1919-PS, IMT U.S.
Exh. 170, Pros. Exh. 2368, Bk. 66-B,
p. 1)

Although the defendant admitted being present at

the Posen conference at which these policies were

discussed by Himmler, (Tr. p. 6085) he flatly denied

the foregoing passages of the Himmler speech. Testify-

ing under oath, he said:

"I can say with certainty that he did
not speak about the extermination of
the Jews, because the reason for this
meeting was to equalize and adjust
these tremendous tensions between the
Waffen SS and Police." (Tr. p. 6086)

On cross examination, BERGER took the same position.

(Tr. p. 7115-7117) Learned counsel for the defense went

even further to prove their point. They brought in

155

SS Obergruppenfuehrer and General of the Police Udo
von Woyrsch. (Tr. p. 5921-5973) Through the medium
of this witness, the defense also attacked the
authenticity of the German document submitted by the
Prosecution as the Posen speech. The matter was
developed by a lengthy direct examination: (Tr. p.
5925-5938)

> "Q. Now there is one certain specific
> portion which I am particularly
> interested in. In that portion refer-
> ring to the plans concerning the Jews,
> and at least so the Prosecution says,
> Himmler supposedly spoke of extermina-
> tion. 'Ausrottung' and complete
> extermination of the Jews in that
> speech, and now I ask you, did Himmler
> in that speech speak of the extermina-
> tion of Jewry?
>
> A. Counsel, I must definitely say no
> in answer to that question. The word
> 'Judenausrottung', extermination of
> Jews, was not used, because I, if
> you permit me to say so, being a man
> of very critical mind, would have
> noticed that in some form or other.
> The word was not used." (Tr.p.5935)

156

. . . . . .

> "Q. . . . What statement do you wish
> to make regarding the contents of the
> document and the contents of the
> speech respectively?
>
> A. Counsel, first of all let me say
> the following, generally speaking.
> The speech which you gave me and which
> I now have before me was never the
> speech held by the Reichsfuehrer.
> Really, I have checked and rechecked
> into my recollection and conscience.
> Possibly there are certain portions,
> even sentences, perhaps, which may
> possibly have been said, but the
> speech as such which has been intro-
> duced here as an exhibit was never
> the speech held by the Reichsfuehrer. ."
> (Tr. p. 5935-5936)

On cross examination, reminded that he was under
oath and might suffer the consequences of perjury, the
witness von Woyrsch persisted in his denouncement of
the document. (Tr. p. 5949-5951) It seems the theory

-63-

on which the document was attacked, apart from its content, was the fact that Himmler spoke from notes, and that this could not therefore have been the text from which he spoke. In taking this position, the defense conveniently overlooked the fact that certain parenthetical observations of the reporter interspersed in the text of the document itself made it quite clear that this was not the speech from which Himmler spoke, but rather a transcript of what he said.

The credibility of the witness von Woyrsch and of BERGER himself was badly shaken by the subsequent introduction by the Prosecution of a recorded transcript of the Posen speech following right on the heels of BERGER's denial of the document. (Tr. p. 7115-7126)

---

*The Prosecution submits that the testimony of the witness von Woyrsch should in all respects be disregarded in view of the general proven unreliability of the witness. The witness proved himself to be untruthful in respect to several other matters in addition to the Posen speech. On direct examination the witness said:

> "Referring to those Auschwitz exterminations, I have to tell you, Counsel, that I heard of them for the first time when I was here, in 1946. The locality of Auschwitz, and I remember this very well, was only made known to me for the first time in 1944--first came to my knowledge then, when the Senior SS and Police Leader of Silesia, on the occasion of my birthday, paid me a visit on my estate and he told me 'I am now going to Auschwitz.' I asked him 'What is Auschwitz' and he said 'I have a concentration camp there'." (Tr. p. 5929)

The witness took the same view on cross examination, Tr. p. 5964). The Prosecution then submitted a document conclusively establishing that von Woyrsch had taken part in the pacification of Auschwitz in 1939. (Doc. NOKW 1006, Pros. Exh. 3480, Bk. 96, p. 1)

Questioned as to his own part in the liquidation of Polish Jews during two weeks of campaigning (after which the Wehrmacht disgustedly recalled him) the witness angrily denied such acts. (Tr. p. 5956-5961) The file notes of Lt. Col Lahousen submitted by the Prosecution in rebuttal in this connection, read as follows:

(footnote continued on next page)

Except for the fact that the document contains certain grammatical corrections by the reporter, it corresponds in its entirety, word for word, with the German recording of the speech. (NO-5909, 5909A, Pros. Exh. 3507, 3508, Bk. 96, p. 68)

Discussed, therefore, at this conference at which BERGER was present, was the extermination of the Jews, which had been promulgated at the State Secretaries conference on January 20, 1942, the genocidal plans of the SS for the Eastern peoples, the warring plans of the SS for the creation of a pan-Germanic Reich, and many other points that touch on crimes charged against the defendant in the instant case.

But the Prosecution does not rest its case either with the Eastern Jews or with general intentions.

In addition to his activities in the East, the defendant was intimately associated with Himmler in the execution of the ultimate liquidation of the Jews of Hungary, Czechoslovakia and Denmark, which had been planned and prepared by the defendants von Weizsaecker, von Steengracht, Woermann, Ritter, Erdmannsdorf, and Veesenmayer, among others.

------

footnote continued:

> "G-2 further reports about unrest in that army area arising from the partly illegal measures taken by Einsatzgruppe von Woyrsch (mass shootings, especially of Jews). It was especially annoying to the troops that young men, instead of fighting at the front, are testing their courage on defenseless people."
> (Exh. C-202, 3047-PS)

Finally, although he denied ever having fostered the criminal policies of the SS, on cross examination, the witness admitted that in the earlier days of Nazi strongarm tactics, three of his men had kidnapped a political opponent in his car, and murdered him. (Tr. p. 5961)

In the case of Hungary, the defendant's initial
interest was one of exploitation. He sought to obtain
pengo credits for purposes of paying family allowances
to families of Waffen SS men recruited from Hungary.
In this connection, he wrote on 23 July 1942 to the
Chief of the Gestapo, SS Gruppenfuehrer Mueller (with
whom, incidentally, he employed the intimate "per du"
form of address). We quote from the latter:

> "Now a certain Baron Collas proposed
> to get hold somehow of the property
> situated in Hungary belonging to the
> German Jews. He estimates it at many
> million pengoes. I would be very
> grateful to you, if you would examine
> this question and if you would inform
> me as soon as possible whether this
> means is at all practicable." (Pros.
> Exh. 2381, NO-2250, Bk. 66-B, p. 67)

A report was subsequently made to Himmler on the
subject on 13 August 1942; and on 19 August 1942, an
order was issued evidently authorizing the proposal.
Unfortunately, the Prosecution did not have those
reports. It did, however, have a letter dated 24 November 1942 from a member of Gestapo Mueller's staff
to Himmler on the subject, and referring to the above
orders. (Pros Exh. 2382, NO-2408, Bk. 66-B, p. 68)
The writer stated in part:

> "In the execution of the above mentioned
> orders, I discussed with the SS Main
> Office, the questions in connection with
> the procuring of pengoe for the recruit-
> ment of Volunteers for the Waffen SS in
> Hungary / Granting family support to
> the relatives of the Volunteers. Due
> to certain circumstances, it is not
> possible, at least not in the near
> future to realize pengoe for the
> intended purpose from the in Hungary
> remaining property of German Jews. ."

Accordingly, the writer informed Himmler that it
was proposed to raise the 30 million pengoes BERGER
needed in a different fashion, namely by ransoming
Slovakian Jews "similar to the method carried out in
the occupied Dutch districts. The writer concluded:

159

"With regard to the financial details, the Chief of the SS Main Office will place an SS Fuehrer as specialist for foreign currency at your disposal . . . I request your agreement."

The defendant's only comment on these documents is that what he terms "Mueller's reply" came too late to do him any good in any event (Tr.p.6088/6090). This is in the usual blithe disregard of the fact that a short time after the original BERGER proposal was sent to Mueller --- three weeks later, in fact --- further conferences were had with the SS Main Office which resulted in an order on the subject. The second letter was not a reply to the first by any means, it was an item of correspondence much further along in the proceedings, reporting that the necessary sum requested by BERGER could not be obtained through the enforcement of that order, and suggesting that other Jewish monies be used.

160

The defendant having successfully transformed one such proposal into a Reichsfuehrer order, the Prosecution believes that it can rely on the fact that the second proposal was also put into force, unless rebutted by something else than the generally unreliable testimony of the accused. In any event, the episode clearly shows the propensity of the defendant to exploit the Jewish problem to his own advantage, from which the Tribunal may judge the truth or untruth of some of the other overstrong disavowals that are in the record.

The defendant knew of the German plans to liquidate the Jews of Hungary as early as April 1943. In that month, he wrote Himmler a letter, reporting on the various rumors circulating in Hungary regarding the possible formation of an Axis-led League of States.

He boasted to the Reichsfuehrer that through Amtsgruppe D (the

Germanic Directorate) he had:

> "...connections in Hungary with men directly sub-
> ordinate and personally very closely linked to the
> Prime Minister."

Reporting on the Jewish question, BERGER said:

> "In Hungarian Government circles there exists a
> well-founded fear that the accession to the
> consideration will be tied up with compulsion
> to liquidate the Jews. Hungarian Government
> circles hope that they will be able to evade
> this anticipated German desire by being allowed
> to postpone the liquidation of the Jews until
> the end of the war. The Government would then
> join, for it would thus have saved its face
> towards us, without being compelled to make a
> change in its most decisive question." (underscoring added)

> "The basic attitude of the Hungarian Government
> is to give the Jews as fair a treatment as possi-
> ble, so as to be able to prove this basic atti-
> tude to the Anglo-Americans as being firmly
> established." (Doc. NO-628, Pros. Exh. 2383, Doc. Bk.
> 68B, p. 71)

When he took the stand, the defendant, in commenting on this

document, claimed that from the first to the last, he was merely

reporting what was discussed in Hungarian circles, without giving

any comment or opinion of his own. (Tr. p. 6090) The description

of the Hungarian Government's fear of the liquidation of the Jews

as "well-founded" is about as clear an expression of opinion as can

be found, and certainly presages knowledge on the part of the defen-

dant of the Reich plans for the Hungarian Jews.

The defendant's later actions confirmed that knowledge, for

when the final deportations in Hungary subsequently began in 1944,

BERGER was there to do his part. The Hungarian Minister of the

Interior, Gabor Vajna, tells us what took place:

> "Upon invitation of the Reichsfuehrer-SS Himmler and
> on orders of the National leader Szalasi, I travelled
> to Himmler's headquarters on the Western Front in the
> vicinity of Neukoeln. Himmler received me at that time
> in his special train in the presence of Obergruppen-
> fuehrer BERGER, who, in the best of my knowledge, was
> his deputy. We discussed the evacuation of Hungary,
> establishment of 5 commands each of Gendarmerie and
> Police and a Central Registration Office in Germany,
> which should register all Hungarian persons living in
> Germany, including the Jews; Himmler ordered in the
> presence of BERGER that the details would have to be
> discussed the next day with BERGER and Kaltenbrunner
> in Berlin. Himmler stated that the Jews were well
> treated in Germany, because they work and that the
> output of the Jaegerprogramme had risen 40% since Jews
> were working there. Himmler declared that Obergrup-
> penfuehrer Winkelmann and mainly Obersturmfuehrer

Eichmann were his deputies in Hungary."

. . .

"At the meeting with BERGER in Berlin, between 8 and 16
December 1944, BERGER personally confirmed Himmler's
requests and ordered Kaltenbrunner to negotiate the
details," (underscoring supplied) (Doc. NO-1874,
Pros. Exh. 2384, Doc. Bk. 66-B, p. 73)

Vajna then narrates how he "negotiated the details" with Kaltenbrunner
and the notorious Eichmann, referent for Jewish questions. The
resulting stream of deportees--men, women and children headed in
railroad boxcars for the gas chambers of Germany's concentration
camps--is already a matter of record, and well known to the Tribunal.

The defendant found the charge of deportation of the Slovakian
Jews even more embarrassing. It is a charge arising out of the defendant's activities as the German Military Commander in Slovakia,
a position he held from 1 September to 19 September 1944 (Tr. pp.
6094, 6098).

The Prosecution witness Kastner (Tr. pp. 3616-3659) was a
Jewish lawyer and President of the Zionist Organization of Hungary
(Tr. pp. 3622, 3633). In this capacity he negotiated with the
German authorities, with the Gestapo, with Eichmann's Einsatzkom-
mandos and with the staff of SS Standartenfuehrer Kurt Becher,
Himmler's special representative, to save the lives of countless
Hungarian Jews, if necessary by ransoming them. (Tr. pp. 3652-3656)
There were 85,000 Jews in Slovakia, and in 1942, some 60,000 of them
were deported by the Germans to extermination camps. (Tr. p. 3630)
As a consequence of this major wave of anti-Jewish measures insti-
tuted by the Germans in Slovakia, many Slovakian Jews fled to
Hungary, and the witness formed a committee for the rescue and help
of these refugees. (Tr. p. 3622) Through Papal intervention with
Tiso, the deportations were then stopped and the 20,000-25,000 Jews
remaining in Slovakia were put to work. (Tr. pp. 3630,3631)

In 1944, rumors of new anti-Jewish measures against the Slovakian Jews reached the witness. Accordingly, he again entered into
negotiations with SS Obersturmbannfuehrer Kurt Becher, Chief of the
Economic Staff of the SS at Budapest, who acted as Himmler's representative in these matters. (Tr. p. 3631) (Kastner had negotiated

162

-69-

successfully with Becher before. (Tr.p,3652, 3654,3656))

> "A. Well, these negotiations had a clear purpose,
> to try and save the lives of the remnants of
> the Jews in Hungary, in Slovakia, and of those
> who were still living in the concentration
> camps. Well, it was our hope that we will
> succeed to keep alive these 20,000 Slovakian
> Jews. It proved once again a vain hope because
> starting from September, 1944, new anti-Jewish
> measures were being taken by the German authori-
> ties in Slovakia and we were informed by our
> friends that deportation is once again
> threatening them. I went to Bratislava. I was
> there about three or four times to be informed
> and to try to help them. As I saw that it can
> not be done on a local level, I asked Mr.Becher
> to intervene with Himmler in order to stop
> the carrying out of the execution of these
> measures." (Tr.pp.3631-3632)

It was the defendant BERGER in his Slovakian capacity

whose recommendations to Himmler brought an end to

these negotiations and culminated in the extermination

of these Jews.

> "Q. You say you asked Becher to intervene with
> Himmler to stop these deportation proceedings?
> A. Yes.
> Q. What did Becher tell you about the results
> of his interview with Himmler?
> A. Becher told me, after having been in the
> headquarters of Himmler, that Himmler refused
> to cancel the dispositions taken concerning
> the Slovakian Jews. He told me that Himmler
> stated that Obergruppenfuehrer BERGER, their
> military commander of Slovakia, sent him
> reports that the Slovakian Jews joined the
> Slovakian revolt and generally had the
> behavior that they had to be wiped out
> militarily.
> Q. Did you say that BERGER's recommendation
> as reported to you by Becher was that the
> Jews be wiped out militarily?
> A. Yes.
> Q. Now what subsequently did happen to these
> Slovakian Jews?
> A. Subsequently they were deported to Auschwitz."
> (Tr.p.3632)

On cross examination, defense counsel only succeeded

in confirming Kastner's story:

> "Q. . . . . What did Becher tell you at the time
> about the result of his conversation with
> Himmler, as far as the motives which moved

163

him to turn down his requests were concerned?
A. I duscussed that in detail this morning.
Q. I only wanted to know whether Becher told
why Himmler turned it down.
A. As far as I remember in the course of the
conversation, Himmler is supposed to have told
Becher that he had been informed by Berger that
the Jews in Slovakia were supporting the cause
of the insurgents, and that they must be liquidated militarily. I don't quite realize why
babies and sick persons and old people must
be liquidated as insurgents, but that is what
happened.
Q. And this statement, in your opinion, was
made in October, 1944?
A. That is when Herr Becher told me, you mean?
   Yes, it must have been about October.
Q. But then the revolt had already been
suppressed.
A. I wasn't talking about the revolt. I was
talking about the liquidation of the Slovakian
Jews, and that had not been finished. That was
still going on.
Q. May I point out that BERGER, on or about
the 17th or 19th of September, returned to
Berlin from Slovakia?
A. I don't know that. All I know is that his
orders were carried out; even in his absence.
There was no hurry about deporting the Jews
in Slovakia. It was not so urgent as the
revolt. There was time for that." (Tr.pp.3658/59)

164

Kastner's testimony was that SS Standartenfuehrer

Becher, Himmler's contact man in these negotiations,

reported his conversation with Himmler only about the

beginning of October. (Tr.p.3658) Since the defense

claims BERGER left Slovakia about September 19th, they

have stressed this difference of dates, we take it,

either to impeach Kastner or to demonstrate that the

deportations did not take place until after BERGER

had gone. (Tr.pp. 3657-3659)

No matter how hard the defense works at it, there

is no discrepancy between Kastner's testimony and the

facts. We do not think it is usual that it should

take two weeks (a) for Himmler in Berlin to receive a

report from BERGER in Slovakia, (b) for Himmler to

act on that report, (c) for Himmler to receive Becher

and tell him of his decision and (d) for Becher to tell Kastner of the interview. Two weeks is a reasonable length of time in which this could take place; in fact Kastner's testimony is not even a bar to the inference that the deportations recommended by BERGER started while he was still in office.

The witness Kastner has testified to what subsequently happened to these "partisan suspects"; — — they wound up in the gas chambers of the extermination camps.

From the premise (which we feel is false) that the deportations took place only after BERGER left Slovakia, defense counsel draws the conclusion that BERGER was not responsible for such deportations. Such a conclusion is also a non-sequitor of the first order. While the prosecution contends that these measures against the Jews took place while BERGER was in office, and the evidence bears this out, the theory of the Prosecution's case is not even affected by the contrary conclusion. The witness Kastner testified that Himmler had acted on the strength of BERGER's recommendations made while he was Military Commander in Slovakia. We feel that the time when those murderous recommendations were carried into effect in no way detracts from the fact that they were initially made. They were made in line of duty to the competent agency, with the intention that they should be followed, and they were in fact followed, resulting in death in the gas chambers of thousands of Slovakian Jews. Whether or not the deportation of the Jews started in BERGER's administration, this defendant bears the major responsibility for the action.

165

In this connection, see Tr.p. 5178, in which the defendant Schellenberg said:

> "Only the Chief of the RSHA himself was an Obergruppenfuehrer, and the rest of the chiefs of the other 11 SS main offices which constituted the SS hierarchy. These chiefs of the SS Main Offices were the next collaborators and closest collaborators of Himmler. They influenced his decisions basically, and if I may remind you of Kaltenbrunner, they influenced him in a disadvantageous manner against my plans."

Finally, there is the deportation of the Danish Jews. An order signed by the General Keitel, and dated 23 September 1943, provided that "SS Obergruppenfuehrer BERGER is in charge of the deportation of the Danish Jews." (Doc.NOKW-356, Pros.Exh.1670, Doc. Bk.60-B, p.16 at p.22) The deportation of the Danish Jews is already a matter of record with this Tribunal. It was to be supposed that the participation of this defendant was unequivocally established by this document. BERGER's defense is novel only to the extent that it taxes the credulity of the Tribunal. The solemn and formal order of the Chief of the wartime German High Command, Field Marshal Keitel, is met with the explanation that this was all a big mistake. Said BERGER:

> "... .it was a mistake of Keitel. He mixed up a few things." (Tr.p.6102)

We need hardly point out to the Tribunal that this is not the first document which the defendant has answered in this fashion. Of course, the defendant has found a willing echo to his chorus in the person of SS Obergruppenfuehrer Werner Best. Best, sentenced to death in Copenhagen for his own part in the deportation of the Danish Jews, gave the defense several affidavits.

(BERGER Defense Doc.21, Berger Defense Exh.17, Berger
Doc.Bk. III, p.48; BERGER Defense Doc.30, Berger :
Defense Exh. 31, Berger Doc.Bk.IV, p.3) The first told
us that "it must have been a typographical error",
and the second affidavit reiterated that contention.
Best then applied the whitewash freely in his own
interest and informed all who cared to read that
like BERGER, he too did not participate in the
deportation. The Prosecution is informed to the
contrary and submits Document NG-4807, Pros.Exh.1668,
Doc.Bk. 60-B, p.11 by way of rebuttal. We have waived
the right of cross examination on this witness. The
self-serving declarations of a man who is himself implicated in the crime which is charged are hardly
credible. There is a presumption that when an order
is given, especially such a high echelon order as
this, it will be carried out. The Prosecution does
not feel that the statements unsupported in evidence
of the accused and his accomplice serve to shift the
burden of proof imposed by that presumption.

They say that every German war criminal has his
conveniently rescued "Haus Jude" or"House Jew", whom
he employs as a defense of any charge that is brought
against him. In this respect, BERGER is no exception.
He testified:

> "I had nothing to do with Jewish affairs at any
> time. During any time in my life I never had
> anything to do with executive of police func-
> tions. I am not suited as a policeman anyhow.
> During the war I had something to do with
> Jews because people came to see me --- as
> Heydrich put it in 1942, he said they came
> to the Wailing Wall on the Fehrbelliner Platz
> in Berlin, where they intervened for acquain-
> tances, and in one case for relatives, and

167

-74-

asked me to do something to help them. I did
that, and I assume that some witnesses will
appear to testify about that. . . ."(Tr.p.6084)

In this case, the "House Jew" must have had a
change of address, for that is the last we heard of
him. But the defendant needs more than a "House Jew"
to extricate him from his present predicament in
any event.

We have discussed the bulk of material pertaining
exclusively to BERGER's persecution of the Jews in
the instant section. But there is much material
which the Prosecution has offered in evidence in
connection with other charges and specifications
which touches collaterally upon the subject of
Jewish persecution, and this will be discussed in
subsequent sections of this brief.

168

Into this category, for instance, fall the crimes
committed by the Special Commando Dirlewanger.

III. COUNT V

1. Persecution of Jews

It is charged under Count V of the Indictment that the defendant von KROSIGK participated in persecutions on political, racial and religious grounds. His guilt under this count has been overwhelmingly proven. As will later be shown, this defendant signed the infamous decree of July 1943 under which the Jews were deprived of all judicial process and left at the mercy of Himmler's police. The "Final Solution" had arrived.

The IMT branded this persecution as "a record of consistent and systematic inhumanity on the greatest scale" (p. 247), and, after summarizing the anti-Jewish policy formulated in the Party Program, continued (p. 248-249):

> "With the seizure of power, the persecution of the Jews was intensified. A series of discriminatory laws was passed, which limited the offices and professions permitted to Jews; and restrictions were placed on their family life and their rights of citizenship. By the autumn of 1938, the Nazi policy towards the Jews had reached the stage where it was directed towards the complete exclusion of Jews from German life. Pogroms were organized, which included the burning and demolishing of synagogues, the looting of Jewish businesses, and the arrest of prominent Jewish business men. A collective fine of 1 billion marks was imposed on the Jews, the seizure of Jewish assets was authorized, and the movement of Jews was restricted by regulations to certain specified districts and hours. The creation of ghettos was carried out on an extensive scale, and by an order of the Security Police Jews were compelled to wear a yellow star to be worn on the breast and back. "

Doc. 9

169

-75-

These measures against the Jews were enacted during a meeting presided over by Goering on 12 November 1938 with several high officials as participants, among them von KROSIGK. The minutes of this meeting are contained in Doc. 1816-PS, (Exh. 1441, Bk. 59, p. 9). At this meeting Heydrich reported that 101 synagogues were destroyed by fire, 76 synagogues demolished and 7500 stores destroyed during the pogrom on 10 November 1938 (p. 15) and estimated the total damage at 25 million RM (p. 19). As consequence of all this, Goering, in agreement with all participants of the meeting of 12 November 1938, decided that the insurance companies "have to make payment for the damage the Jews have suffered, but not to the Jews but to the Minister of Finance" (p. 18), and imposed a "Fine of Atonement" in the amount of 1 billion marks on the Jews (p. 39-40). Furthermore, the "Aryanization" of Jewish stores and commercial enterprises, the exclusion of Jewish children from schools, the restriction of Jews to certain districts of cities, the forcible emigration, the wearing of a yellow star, etc., were introduced.

The defendant von KROSIGK testified under direct examination (Tr. p. 23286) with regard to the pogrom:

> "At the time when this occurred, and ever since, I have always considered this to be a disgrace on the character of the German people."

Moreover, he testified that he had remained in Hitler's Cabinet "to raise the voice of reason and justice" (Tr. p. 22923).

These statements must be compared with his attitude during the meeting in question. The corresponding part of his cross examination reveals:

"Q. . . . . Now, may I ask you, after experiencing the injustice and inhuman actions inflicted on the Jews, as told at that meeting, did you then voice your reason and right at the meeting which was held by Goering?

A. No, not at that meeting.

Q. And you didn't object to any decision made during that meeting?

A. No, not at that meeting." (Tr.p.23903)

He did not only refrain from making any objection, he even stressed the urgency of the measures agreed upon. When Minister Fischboeck suggested that those measures should be carried out "during the next week", von KROSIGK stated:

"They have to be taken during the next week at the latest." (1816-PS, Exh.1441, Bk. 59, p. 49; and Tr.p. 23903-23904)

In pursuance of Goering's decree concerning the "Fine of Atonement" von KROSIGK issued an ordinance dated 21 November 1938, levying an assessment of 20% of the property of Jews, to be paid in four installments, in order to collect the fine. (1411-PS, Exh. 2103, Bk. 57-B, p. 100). This ordinance is signed by the defendant von KROSIGK only. On 19 October 1939 he issued a further decree increasing the assessment to 25% (NID-13853, Exh. 2104, Bk. 57-B, p. 103), and on 10 December 1938 he signed detailed instructions as to how to exact the payment, especially with regard to securities, mortgage bonds, real estate and the like to be taken from the Jews if they were not in a position to hand over sufficient amounts in cash. (NG-4902, Exh. 2424, Bk. 75)

171

-77-

In other words, the defendant von KROSIGK was in complete charge of enacting all legal and administrative measures for carrying out the collection of the "fine." In reality it was nothing more than forceful confiscation.

A former official of the Ministry of Finance, Amtsrat Parpatt, has described in his affidavit (NG-4625, Exh. 2428, Bk. 75) the way in which the Ministry of Finance, the only competent authority in these matters, realized the securities received by the Reich by various methods. Parpatt who handled such matters pointed out that the utilization of securities handed over by or confiscated from Jews was the task of the Ministry of Finance. For this purpose it made use of the Prussian State Bank (Seehandlung) and the Reich Main Pay Office (Reichshauptkasse). It is of no avail to set forth here how the realization of the securities took place in particular. In any case, it always remained under the supervision of the Ministry of Finance. Von KROSIGK has not denied that he was in charge of realizing all securities fallen to the Reich whether they were confiscated or captured:

> "Q. Now, witness, is it correct that all securities which came into the hands of the Reich for various reasons were administered and utilized by the Finance Ministry from the end of 1933 on?
>
> A. All securities you say, yes.
>
> Q. And didn't all the higher agencies which concerned themselves with confiscated and captured securities report to the Finance Ministry whenever these securities were delivered to them?
>
> A. Securities?

Q. Securities, yes.

A. Yes, that was the order in effect."
(Tr. p. 23907-23908)

Referring to the Reich Main Pay Office, the defendant von KROSIGK stressed under direct examination, "that it was not a pay office of the Reich Ministry of Finance but much rather it was the Joint Main Pay Office of all the departments". (Tr. p. 23135-23136). This shall not be disputed, however, it must be emphasized that the Main Pay Office is mentioned in the Trial Brief on von KROSIGK only insofar as that office acted on his directives. Von KROSIGK admitted:

> "The Reich Main Pay Office was sub-
> ordinated to the Reich Ministry of
> Finance in respect to personnel and
> in respect to disciplinary measures.
> The Reich Finance Minister was also
> responsible for orderly books in
> questions of fundamental importance,
> or in questions of doubts it was up
> to the Reich Minister of Finance to
> rule." (Tr. p. 23135)

He, furthermore, admitted that also with regard to the other ministries in some way "the entire assets were under the control of the Reich Finance Ministry". (Tr. p. 23138)

We will revert to this matter of confiscation and utilization in connection with the 11th Decree to the Reich Citizenship Law. First of all, the background of von KROSIGK's anti-Jewish activities must be discussed.

In 1937, relative to the firing of Jewish employees in governmental agencies, von KROSIGK issued an order, dated 19 June 1937, to all supreme Reich authorities and Reich governors stating:

"After agreement with the Reich and
Prussian Minister of the Interior I
ask you that the question of the scope
of dismissal from public service of
employees in public administrative
offices and enterprises - in accordance
with Article IAOGO - who are Jews or
of Jewish descent and whose termination of contract is contractually
prohibited either permamently or for
a period of more than one year or
made dependent upon important reasons,
be decided along the same lines as
the decision of the dismissal or
retaining of public officials on
active service." (NG-1277, Exh. 3914,
Bk. 212)

His participation in the anti-Jewish policy of

Hitler and the Ministry of Interior was conclusive.

The decree concerning the Fine of Atonement of

12 November 1938 was followed by a series of additional

anti-Jewish decrees promulgated, for the most part,

by the Ministry of Interior. They are dealt with in

the Trial Brief on the defendant Stuckart. Von

KROSIGK had knowledge of them and knew the ruthless

trend of legislation enacted against the Jews.

The importance of the concentration camps as

means for oppressing and torturing Jews is commonly

known. The IMT states with regard to the concentra-

tion camps (p. 234):

"They were first established in Germany at the moment of the seizure of
power by the Nazi Government. Their
original purpose was to imprison without trial all those persons who were
opposed to the Government, or who
were in any way obnoxious to German
authority. With the aid of a secret
police force, this practice was
widely extended, and in course of
time concentration camps became places
of organized and systematic murder,
where millions of people were destroyed."

-80-

Von KROSIGK was concerned in many respects with
the concentration camps. He has not denied that he
knew the number of those camps up to the outbreak
of war. (Tr. p. 23350). According to the "Budget of
the Armed Units of the SS and of the Concentration
Camps for the fiscal year 1939" (NG-4456, Exh. C-62,
Bk. 212) there were six concentration camps (p. 9 of doc.)
with an average of thirty thousand inmates at that
time (p. 101) in each camp.

As to the money needed for the maintenance of
                                                    it
the Concentration Camps and Death Head Units, belonged
to a budget provision of the Minister of Interior
(Tr. p. 24114), but was allocated by the Minister of
Finance. When the break-down budget was established
KROSIGK received knowledge of it. Of it, KROSIGK
said under cross examination:

> "Q. And you were aware of the SS
> expenditures for the maintenance of
> concentration camps?
>
> A. Yes." (Tr. p. 23897)

His knowledge went even further, however. He
also took the opportunity of visiting a concentration
camp together with Ministerial Director von Mantenffel
and stayed there about two hours. According to his
testimony he had "not the slightest impression of
atrocities," (Tr. p. 23302) and allegedly nothing in
particular struck him. Yet, his companion von
Mantenffel felt "that the head of the camp looked
like a beast in the shape of a man." (witness Mayer,
Tr.p. 16790). This "beast in the shape of a man"
had the inmates of the camp lined up to sing for
von KROSIGK (Tr. p. 16790), but KROSIGK did not feel

-81-

shocked at this repugnant travesty. He testified that
he "can only say that the installations, as far as
the outward order and sanitary arrangements and so
forth are concerned, made a model impression". (Tr. p.
23301-23302). Under cross examination KROSIGK admitted
that he knew of incidents in the concentration camps
as early as 1938. (Tr. p. 23811)

Whenever Himmler desired to enlarge a concentration camp, he contacted the Minister of Finance for
financial approval. This is evidenced by the letter
of the Reichsfuehrer SS to von KROSIGK, dated 1 October
1941, requesting the budgetary approval for the pur-
chase of a mill urgently needed for the enlargement
of the Auschwitz concentration camp and "in conformity
with the political tasks of the camp." (NG-5545, Exh.
3915, Bk. 212). Further evidence in this respect is
the letter of 7 November 1942 by SS Obergruppenfuehrer
Pohl to the Minister of Finance requesting authorization
for a further enlargement of the same concentration
camp. The letter stated in part:

> "The tasks allotted by the Reich Fuehrer
> SS require an enlargement of the area of
> the Concentration Camp Auschwitz to the
> limits which have already been marked on
> the map. (total area about 4640 ha)....
> the formation of such an estate district
> presupposes, that the total area is the
> property of the Reich.. . This area con-
> sists of the following estates: 1) agri-
> cultural and forestry estates belonging
> to Poles and Jews..... 2) urban property
> and several business enterprises owned
> by Poles and Jews.... 3) landed property
> which formerly belonged to the Polish state
> ..... 4) Municipal Property..... 5) Eccle-
> siastical property..... 6) property of
> persons of German blood." (1643 PS, Exh. 2442, Bk 75)

In a conference on this topic, held on 17 and 18
December 1942, "the representative of the 'Referat
Maedel' of the Reich Ministry of Finance, Regierungs-
rat Keller, pointed out that there is no objection to

176

the cession of church property within the area of
the Auschwitz concentration camp to the Reichsfuehrer SS. " (1643-PS, Exh. 2422, Bk. 75, p.10-11).
The document further shows that the concentration
camp was enlarged thereby.

On the other hand, when the finances of the
Party later on became strained the Party Treasurer
again got in touch with the Minister of Finance suggesting that the Reich should buy the concentration
camp of Dachau, and adding:

> "I should also welcome the sale of
> the Dachau camp inasmuch as the
> Party would benefit from it in
> financial respects - and because of
> the fact that this real property is
> now being used almost exclusively
> for the State, i.e. for the purposes
> of the Waffen SS and as a concentra-
> tion camp." (NG-5550, Exh. C-98,
> Bk. 212)

In the same way the sale of the SS Cadet School
at Bad Toelz was offered to the Ministry of Finance,
and von KROSIGK promptly came to the assistance of
the Party and bought the Cadet School and the concentration camp of Dachau at 17 million marks as shown
in his letter of 15 May 1940. Incidentally, by
this letter he simultaneously allotted 289.6 million
marks "for the needs of the NSDAP". (NG-5550, Exh.
C-98, Bk. 212).

KROSIGK's sphere of influence and knowledge
was not limited to the concentration camps.
In 1941 the mass deportations of Jews to the
East commenced on a large scale. KROSIGK's Ministry
of Finance had a considerable share in these activities. By printed circular letter of 4 November 1941
the Minister of Finance informed all Oberfinanzpraesidents of the impending deportation by the

Gestapo stating "The property of the Jews to be
deported will be confiscated in favor of the Reich".
The letter then continues:

> "The deportation has already begun
> in the districts of the Finance -
> Presidents Berlin, Hamburg, Weser-
> Ems in Bremen; Kassel, Cologne,
> Duesseldorf. Shortly additional
> 8000 Jews will be deported from
> the Finance-District of Berlin.
> .... The administration and
> utilization of the confiscated
> property of the Jews is my task."
> (NG-4905, Exh. 2452, Bk. 75)

To accomplish this task detailed instructions
were given concerning all kinds of property. Significant for the dominant position of the Minister of
Finance with regard to utilization of the Jewish
property is the following directive contained in
the same letter:

> " I request to examine, before
> furniture is utilized otherwise,
> which objects can be used for the
> Reich Finance Administration. Into
> consideration are to be taken: For
> the outfit of offices (offices of
> the chiefs and referents, office
> rooms):
>   writing desks, bookcases, arm-
>   chairs, carpets, pictures,
>   typewriters and so on.
> For the outfit of recreation homes
> and schools of the Reich Finance
> Administration:
>   Bedrooms, beds, music instru-
>   ments and especially bed linen,
>   table linen, towels, etc. "
> (NG-4905, Exh. 2452, Bk. 75)

This letter is signed "by order" by Ministerial
Dirigent Schlueter. The defendant von KROSIGK, when
questioned under direct examination as to whether
this letter of Schlueter had come to his knowledge,
stated:

> "A. No, I don't think that I pre-
> viously knew this circular letter,
> but I do know that as far as the
> technical handling of the property
> was concerned which deported Jews
> left behind them, this matter was
> reported by Schlueter." (Tr. p. 23339)

178

It can be added that in this instance it was apparently unnecessary to inform KROSIGK in advance, for he had no objections to such a procedure.

Some months later, on 21 March 1942, the same Ministerial Dirigent Schlueter issued, by order of KROSIGK, instructions to all Oberfinanzpraesidents (except Prague) concerning the seizure of Jewish literature and other cultural and artistic works of Jewish origin. These works of literature and art were to be handed over to the operational staff of Rosenberg, and the Oberfinanzpraesidents were ordered to inform Rosenberg, if such material was available from confiscated or forfeited property. (NG-5340, Exh. 3919, Bk. 212)

KROSIGK was fully aware of the meaning of the mass deportations. He attended the session of the Reichstag on 30 January 1939. At that time Hitler delivered a speech stating that if

> "International Jewry in and outside
> Europe should succeed in plunging
> the people of the world once again
> into world war, then the result
> would be . . . the annihilation of
> the Jewish race in Europe." (2360 A-PS
> Exh. 3906, Bk. 211a).

Still more precise and definite was Hitler during the war. In his speech of 30 January 1942, published in the official Nazi publication, the "Voelkischer Beobachter", of 1 February 1942, Hitler said:

> "I have already declared on 1 September
> 1939, in the German Reichstag, and I
> am careful today not to make premature
> predictions - when I say today that
> this war will not turn out the way the
> Jews think it will, that the European-
> Aryan peoples will not be wiped out,
> but that the result of this war will
> be the annihilation of Jewry." (PS-2360B,
> Exh. 3906, Bk. 211-C)

Time and again Hitler repeated this threat with unmistakable determination. On 30 September 1942 he once more delivered a speech reiterating his prophecy that Jewry will be wiped out (PS-2360 C, Exh. 3906, Bk. 211 C), and in his Proclamation of 24 February 1943 he said that

> "this war will find its end with
> the annihilation of Jewry in Europe."
> (PS-2360 D, Exh. 3906, Bk. 211 C)

The same brutal and "most radical counter-measures" were announced by Goebbels when he harangued a crowd in the Berlin Sportpalast on 20 February 1943. The speech was, of course, published in the papers and broadcasted over all German radio stations. (PS-2360 E, Exh. 3906, Bk. 211 C)

The Protestant Bishop Wurm was one of the few Germans who was courageous enough to warningly express his dismay about a situation which had become clear to everyone; namely, that the privileged Mischlings were

> "in mortal danger, now that the non-
> Aryans have already been eliminated
> to a large extent in the areas which
> are under the power of Germany."

This letter of the Bishop was addressed to Hitler and the members of the Reich Cabinet under the date of 16 July 1943. (NG-5874 A, Exh. C-241, Bk. 211 C).

Before 1941 German Jews were forced to emigrate or succeeded in escaping from Germany. They were not allowed to take along their property. A legal transfer was prohibited. Their bank accounts were frozen. A "legal" device of confiscating their property had not yet been enacted, hence confiscation took place at random. Arbitrary actions of

-86-

the Gestapo were prevalent after the Jews were deprived of their citizenship. Yet, in July 1941 Himmler ordered that safeguarded property of Jews against whom a proceeding of de-naturalization was pending should be sold by auction prior to the conclusion of the proceedings. Since considerable quantities of such confiscated property was stored in custom houses, Himmler asked the Ministry of Finance to instruct the custom houses to hand over the property under custom seal to the State Police. The reaction of the Ministry of Finance to this request, dated 8 July 1941, read: "There are no objections to this." (NG-4906, Exh. 2430, Bk. 75) This letter is signed by Ministerial Director Wucher, head of Section II of the ministry. There can be no doubt that he would not have given this unusual and illegal instruction without consent of his chief, the defendant KROSIGK.

To render the theft of property of emigrated Jews simpler, the 11th Decree to the Reich Citizenship Law, dated 23 November 1941, was issued. It provided that all Jews living abroad would lose their citizenship and hence their property. The decree is co-signed by State Secretary Reinhardt "as deputy of the Reich Minister of Finance." (NG-2499, Exh. 1536, Bk. 75, pp. 113-116) On 7 July 1941 the Ministry of Interior had invited several top officials, among them the defendant von KROSIGK, to attend a meeting on the subject. The corresponding letter stated that

"According to information received from the Reich Chancellery, the Fuehrer does

not deem it necessary that a regulation
as comprehensive as previously provided
for should be made at this time. The
Fuehrer rather considers it as sufficient
to issue a regulation, which deprives
the Jews who live abroad of their citizenship and which declares their property as forfeited to the Reich." (NG-2499,
Exh. 1536, Bk. 75)

A draft of the decree to be discussed was attached
to that letter.

After the enactment of the decree an ordinance
to it seemed necessary to fill certain gaps of the
regulations, and to secure the cooperation of the
Ministry of Finance and its subordinate agencies for
carrying out the confiscation. Again the Ministry
of Finance received the corresponding draft, this
time by a letter of the Reich Security Main Office,
dated 27 November 1941. (NG-5373, Exh. 3917, Bk. 212).
On 8 December 1941 a conference was held in the Ministry of Finance where Krosigk was represented by
Dr. Maedel and Dr. Schwarzat. The Gestapo representatives asked for a discussion of the draft, transmitted on 27 November 1941. The document reveals:

"A general statement was made to
the effect that the Reich Ministry
of Finance had no objections to the
draft."

The document further states that individual cases
were discussed with the following result:

"1) The Commissioner for enemy
property is to transfer to the Oberfinanzpraesident of Berlin all assets,
which, on the basis of available documents belong to Jews who meet the
conditions of art. 1 and 10 of the
ordinance

. . . . . .

4) Jews who are residing in Palestine
have hitherto been treated as foreign
Jews. In future, it will no longer be
assumed that these Jews have acquired
Palestinian citizenship. Their assets
will thus be transferred from the

Commissioner for Enemy Property to
the Oberfinanzpraesident of Berlin,
for his administration and utilization." (NG-5373, Exh. 3917, Bk. 212)

It must be stressed here that the Oberfinanzpraesident Berlin as well as all other Oberfinanzpraesidents were subordinates of the Ministry of Finance.
This has been confirmed by von KROSIGK. Transcript
page 23905 reads:

> "Q. Well, was the Oberfinanzpraesi-
> dent of Berlin a subordinate of yours?
>
> A. Yes, he was."

However comprehensive the regulations for the
confiscation of property of emigrated Jews had become by that time, one particular phase was not
taken into consideration. The 11th Decree and the
ordinance to it applied to all Jews who resided
abroad on or after the day when the 11th Decree came
into effect, i.e. on 25 November 1941. It, therefore,
didn't apply to those Jews who had committed suicide
or had died before that date. Their property consequently belonged to their heirs. "Such cases are
very numerous" reported the Oberfinanzpraesident of
Badenia to the Minister of Finance in a letter of
2 February 1942:

> "The 11th Decree to the Reich Citizen-
> ship Law of 25 November 1941 does not
> apply to Jews who were to be expelled
> from Baden on 22 October 1940 but who
> preferred suicide to deportation."

Nevertheless, the Oberfinanzpraesident of Badenia
suggested the confiscation of the property of those
dead Jews:

> "....without consideration to the fact
> whether they elected to commit suicide
> thus avoiding deportation or whether
> they were no longer alive when the 11th
> Decree to the Reich Citizenship Law
> came into force. The simplest way
> would be to carry out such confiscation
> of the property of expelled Jews with

183

retroactive effect from the date of expulsion, ... Such confiscation retroactive to the date of expulsion would prevent the possibility of inheritance claims on confiscated assets which in many cases have already been utilized." (NG-5371, Exh. 3918, Bk. 212)

As a matter of fact, the Ministry of Finance followed this shameless suggestion, and informed the Reich Main Security Office accordingly by letter of 16 May 1942 which reads in part:

"In order to avoid any claims by the heirs to these properties, I should like to ask you to announce confiscation with retroactive effect as of 15 October 1940. Please send the confiscation orders directly to the Oberfinanzpraesident for Baden, in Karlsruhe."

When questioned regarding this letter von KROSIGK testified:

"A. Yes, the Oberfinanzpraesident of Baden was my subordinate." (Tr.p. 23906)

A similar letter of the same date was sent by the Ministry of Finance to the Reich Security Main Office concerning the Jews who were scheduled for expulsion from Pomerania for 12 February 1940 but had avoided deportation by suicide. (NG-5371, Exh. 3918, Bk. 212).

The defendant von KROSIGK stated under re-direct examination that he considers this letter "a very regrettable document in its contents", and denied that he knew about it. (Tr. p. 24106). Yet, it is most unlikely that his competent Referent neither informed him of the report by the Oberfinanzprzesident of Baden nor of the report of the Oberfinanzpraesident of Pomerania nor of the two letters to the Reich Security Main Office. It is all the more unlikely as

184

this was by no means a routine matter but an exceptional one, which could not be settled according to prevailing laws or instructions. Assume KROSIGK had no knowledge of this matter, he nevertheless cannot evade responsibility for it. That is to say, there are only two possibilities, either von KROSIGK had conferred general authority to give such instructions to his competent Referent, or he had neglected to see to it that matters of this importance were submitted to him. He cannot escape responsibility.

Referring once more to the 11th Decree to the Reich Citizenship Law it may be pointed out that an analogous decree, dated 2 November 1942, was enforced in the Protectorate of Bohemia and Moravia. It declared all Jewish Bohemians and Moravians who had established their domicile abroad devoid of citizenship and property. This decree was signed by the defendants von KROSIGK and Stuckart. (NG-180, Exh. 2453, Bk. 75). In Norway the 11th Decree was already implemented by the Reich Commissioner in Spring 1942. Before doing so the Reich Commissioner had informed the Minister of Finance of his plan, and the latter's answer read:

> "I approve your draft of an ordinance
> for the implementation of the 11th
> Ordinance concerning the Reich
> Citizenship Law dated 25 November 1941."
> (NG-4039, Exh. 2455, Bk. 75, pp.19a and
> 19b)

In 1939 KROSIGK, together with Ribbentrop and Frick, signed a decree of 3 October 1939 which revoked citizenship of persons who had committed actions in foreign countries hostile to the Third Reich. It authorized the Minister of Interior, the Foreign

Minister, and the Reich Protector of Bohemia and
Moravia to revoke citizenship of wives and children
of such persons, and to confiscate their property.
(NG-3744, Exh. 638, Bk. 15 B). On 4 October 1939,
KROSIGK signed, together with Frick, a decree which
authorized the confiscation of property of persons
within the Protectorate who had committed actions
hostile to the Third Reich. (NG-3745, Exh. 635,
Bk. 15 B). On 24 October 1942, KROSIGK's State
Secretary Reinhardt, together with the defendant
Stuckart, had issued the "Decree amending the decree
concerning the confiscation of property in the
Protectorate of Bohemia and Moravia" according to
which the Reich Protector and the Minister of Interior
were to determine "what activities are considered
detrimental to the Reich". (NG-3794, Exh. 636,
Bk. 15 B). These decrees were the forerunners of
the aforementioned decree of 2 November 1942, specifically aimed at Jews and implementing the 11th
Decree to the Reich Citizenship Law in the Protectorate. (NG-180, Exh. 2453, Bk. 75)

        With regard to Belgium and France, a conference
was held in the Ministry of Finance on 11 and 12
December 1942, and "the subject under discussion
was the question of seizure, administration and
utilization of present and future accrual of Jewish
property in the zones of command of the Military
Commanders" in those countries. The basis of the
discussion was the implementation of the 11th Decree
on Jews who had emigrated to Belgium and France.
All particulars were discussed. The minutes of the
meeting conclude:

                        -92-

"Concerning the suggestion made at
the conference of 1 June 1942
(O 5210 Fr. I VI) to the effect
that small assets up to 3000 RM
should be exempt from confiscation,
it was unanimously agreed that no
general minimum could be fixed."
(NG-5369, Exh. 3920, Bk. 212)

The application and execution of the 11th Decree
to the Reich Citizenship Law was of immediate concern to the Ministry of Finance. Officials of the
Ministry of Finance were engaged in activities pertaining to the confiscation, liquidation and utilza-
tion of Jewish property. They included, among others,
Ministerial Dirigent Mayer of Section I, Ministerial
Dirigent Wucher (head of Section II), Ministerial
Director Maass (head of Section IV), and Ministerial
Councillor Maedel of Section VI . A task which
involved at least four out of seven sections of the
ministry was certainly not a sideline job. The
following documents bear out this contention.

On 13 December 1941 the Ministry of Finance
furnished various banking institutions still keeping
Jewish accounts with instructions to be followed
in the registration and sale of Jewish property.
These instructions were issued, as the note on the
copy shows, "to cause no delay in the delivery of
securities (shares and mining shares) forfeited to
the Reich . . . on account of the decree of 25 November 1941." The securities were to be delivered to
the Prussian State Bank. " The Prussian State Bank
(Seehandlung) will sell the securities for the Oberfinanzpraesident Berlin." (NG-5067, Exh. 2429, Bk.
75). It was the same procedure as already applied
in pursuance of the "Decree concerning the Fine of
Atonement of 12 November 1938.

187

-93-

On 23 December 1941 a meeting was held in the Ministry of Finance, under the chairmanship of Mayer, to discuss the setting up of proper accounts for the confiscated property. The corresponding notes of Dr. Maedel on this meeting reveal that a new subdivision account was created, called Plan XVII, into which the proceeds from the sale of the securities were to be deposited. (NG-5001, Exh. 2431; Bk. 75).

On 27 February 1942 Maas issued new regulations of competence concerning the administration and utilization of confiscated property, putting the District Finance Presidents in charge of the administration and realization of confiscated real estate. (NG-4903, Exh. 2432, Bk. 75)

188

On 21 April 1942 Ministerial Dirigent Bayrhoffer by order of the Minister of Finance sent a letter to the Reichsbank and agreed that securities confiscated from Jewish persons were to be deposited at the Reichsbank "in order to simplify the administration." Simultaneously Bayrhoffer suggested:

> "To also deliver the securities fallen
> to the Reich as booty to a special
> deposit of the German Reichsbank after
> they have been screened at the Reich
> Main Cashier Office. In this instance
> foreign securities of more than 25
> different countries are concerned. . ."
> (NG-5072, Exh. 2437, Bk. 75)

As to confiscated mortgage-bonds and similar bonds, deposited with mortgage banks, Bayrhoffer in his letter to Locational Group Private Mortgage Bank, dated 19 May 1942, gave his consent that those bonds may be transferred to the banks at the current rate (NG-5071, Exh. 2439, Bk. 75), and in his letter

of 19 May 1942 declared his willingness to grant
the same privilege to other banks upon individual
application.(NG-5062, Exh. 2440, Bk. 75)   The
same information was given to the Bavarian State
Bank and to the Bank of Baden on 4 April 1942 and
16 May 1942. (NG-5057, Exh. 2435, Bk. 75 and NG-
5070, Exh. 2441, Bk. 75)

More definite distinctions with regard to
securities were made in a letter which Patzer, by
order of the Ministry of Finance, sent to the Oberfinanzpraesident of Cologne on 11 May 1942. According to this letter confiscated shares, mining shares
and colonial shares were to be delivered to the
Prussian State Bank, whereas all other securities,
i.e. bonds, etc., should go to the Reich Main
Pay Office. (NG-5059, Exh. 2438, Bk. 75). The
same Patzer stressed in his letter to the Finance
Office Aachen of 14 September 1942 that only shares
confiscated by virtue of the 11th Decree were to
be delivered to the Prussian State Bank, but
securities "fallen to the Reich for other reasons"
to the Reichsbank. (NG-5000, Exh. 2446, Bk. 75).
In other words, the Ministry of Finance in utilizing confiscated Jewish property made use of its
subordinate Oberfinanzpraesidents, the Reich Main
Pay Office and the Finance Offices as well as of
the Prussian State Bank, the Reichsbank, the Bavarian State Bank, the Bank of Baden, mortgage banks
and other financial institutes. However, all
these agencies acted only as organs of the Ministry
of Finance and upon its directives.

189

It is a foregone conclusion that all proceeds from the sale of confiscated securities had to be handed over to the Reich Main Pay Office as the instructions by Patzer and Bayrhoffer, dated 24 June 1942, 1 September 1942 and 26 September 1942 indicate. They also indicate to which budgetary account the proceeds were to be transferred. (NG-4998, Exh. 2443, Bk. 75; NG-5056, Exh. 2445, Bk. 75; NG-4997, Exh. 2448, Bk. 75). As the money was delivered to the Reich Main Pay Office by order of the Ministry of Finance there can be no doubt that it came under the jurisdiction of the Finance Ministry.

The aforementioned directives applied also to the Protectorate. In its letters to the Reichs Protector, dated 16 March 1942 and 8 July 1942, the Finance Ministry agreed that the Protectorate securities with fixed interest which were to be forfeited to the Reich could be utilized by the Reich Protector. The letter of 8 July 1942 says:

> "The proceeds from the sale of these securities are to be transferred to the Pay Department of the German Treasury." (The latter office was the Reichshauptkasse, usually translated "Reich Main Pay Office") (NG-5058, Exh. 2433, Bk. 75; NG-5060, Exh. 2434, Bk. 75)

In this connection the case of the Warsaw ghetto is relevant. The Reichsfuehrer SS had applied to the Finance Ministry for allocations of 150 and 40 million RM to be used for the demolition of the ghetto. In his answer of 15 June 1944, KROSIGK stated he could not yet make a decision with regard to the sums in question, "but I am willing to make

-96-

now the necessary installments upon request."
According to a note on the margin of the draft of
the letter the following paragraph was added:

> "If the demolition should still be
> necessary, I request that, in order
> to cover the cost, you first utilize
> the values represented by goods
> found in the ghetto or inform me
> how the money and goods, available
> in considerable quantities are to
> be utilized or in the meantime have
> been utilized."

Incidentally, in this letter von KROSIGK also
informed the Reichsfuehrer SS that he would supply
the Waffen SS in the future in accordance with the
ruling arrived at in a conference of 28 March 1944
"which provides for an operating fund averaging
145 million RM per month for the fiscal year 1944.

To this letter the Reichsfuehrer SS answered
on 25 August 1944 that the demolition of the ghetto
has been suspended for some time and stated:

> "The movable property in Jewish
> hands - inasmuch as this was con-
> fiscated by the Waffen SS offices in
> the course of the resettlement opera-
> tions - was realized and the proceeds
> paid into the Reichshauptkasse in
> favor of the Reich Finance Minister."
> (NG-5561, Exh. 3916, Bk. 212)

191

This is also confirmed by the secret memorandum by Ministerial Councillor Dr. Gossel for
Patzer, dated 7 September 1944. (NG-4094, Exh.
2451, Bk. 75). The memorandum, furthermore, gives
a hint that the proceeds were probably transferred
to the "Account Max Heiliger."

Max Heiliger was apparently a fictitious name.
The invention to be saluted by "Heil Hitler" was left
to the "Fuehrer", but no German carried the name

"Heiliger" which means "Saint". A memorandum by
Dr. Maedel, dated 16 November 1944, gives more
details on this "Account Max Heiliger". It shows
that the sums transferred to that account were
handled by Section Maedel of the Finance Ministry,
and the amounts were "transferred to the account
of the single plan XVII, Chapter 7, Title 3, paragraph A". (NG-4097, Exh. 2450, Bk. 75) The letter
of the Chief of the SS Main Economic Administration
Office to the Minister of Finance, dated 24 July
1944, finally reveals that not only the proceeds
of goods captured in the Warsaw ghetto, but also
cash amounts and the proceeds from the sale of
securities, bonds, foreign currency, jewelery and
items of all kinds made of precious metals, confiscated in the concentration camps "for the benefit
of the Reich" were paid to the "Account Max Heiliger."
The aforementioned letter states:

> "It is impossible to enclose a list
> because of the vast quantity involved.
> The valuables accumulate in concentra-
> tion camps. Reference is made to the
> fact that in this matter discussions
> have already repeatedly taken place
> with the Deputy of the Reich Minister
> of Finance (RFM)",

and it concludes:

> "The proceeds will be transferred to
> the national Treasury and be credited
> to the Reich Minister of Finance,
> special account 'Max Heiliger'."
> (NG-4096, Exh. 2499, Bk. 75)

This account is also mentioned in the affidavit
of Reichsbank official Thoms., dated 8 May 1946.
This statement describes the handling of valuables
delivered by the SS to the Reichsbank. Those
deliveries, coming from Jewish confiscations, were

made by an SS man by the name of Melmer. "The
question was discussed whether Melmer should appear
in uniform or civilian clothes, and (Brigadefuehrer)
Frank decided it was better that Melmer appear out
of uniform." Another part of the statement reads:
"It was the tenth delivery in November 1942 that
dental gold appeared. The quantity of the dental
gold became unusually great." Finally (paragraph
14 of the affidavit) states:

> "Included in the first statement sent
> by the Reichsbank and signed by me,
> to Melmer was a question concerning
> the name of the account to which the
> proceeds should be credited. In answer
> to that I was orally advised by Melmer
> that the proceeds should be credited
> to the account 'Max Heiliger'. I
> confirmed this on the telephone with
> Rechnungsdirektor Patzer of the
> Ministry of Finance, and in my second
> statement to Melmer, dated 16 November
> 1942, I confirmed the oral conversa-
> tion." (3951-PS, Exh. 1909, Bk. 151)

The defendant KROSIGK testified (Tr. p. 23329) that
he never heard of the account "Max Heiliger" before
this trial took place. The Tribunal sought to
clarify this matter.

> "Q. (By Judge Maguire): Before we
> take this up, what would be the
> occasion of Melmer or the affiant
> Thoms calling up the Finance Ministry
> at all with respect to this matter?
> Was it because it was an unusual
> proposition that funds should be
> placed under the name of an indivi-
> dual like Max Heiliger which were,
> in fact, funds of the SS or funds
> of some other agency – some other
> Reich agency?
>
> A. Your Honor, I don't know anything
> about that. I myself also have to
> rely on conjectures. I can't rely
> only on anything else, because I
> don't know this account at all, and,
> as a result of that, I wouldn't be
> able to give you the reason why
> Thoms called up at all on that
> occasion. It was not necessary,
> but I assume that it was in view of

this being an unusual account that
he called up in order to inquire
whether we perhaps might know anything about it; that's a conjecture
of mine.

Q. Well, wouldn't it be a rather
unusual thing for a Reich agency to
make a deposit in the Reichsbank
under the name of an individual
rather than pay it into the bank
or for the credit of the Reich Main
Pay Office? One gets the impression
from reading this document that it
was rather an unusual way of handling
matters. We have what appears to be
a fictitious account, at least an
account by the name of a fictitious
person and not by the name of the
agency which was interested in the
matter. I am a little puzzled
about it, and I thought perhaps
that from the matter of your greater
knowledge you would be able to tell
us about why they had it that way or
why they would call up the Minister
of Finance." (Tr. p. 23332-23333)

As a matter of fact, it is more than puzzling

that KROSIGK professes such ignorance. It certainly

was not an account of minor importance. All proceeds

from the sale of confiscated goods taken from the

Warsaw ghetto as well as from the concentration

camps were paid to that account, e.g. proceeds from

the sale of movable property, securities, bonds,

foreign currency, jewelry , not to speak of the

dental gold (the quantity of which "became unusually

great.") So large were the sums that the account

had to be "wound up from time to time" (Exh. 2450,

supra) and transferred to single budget plan

established ad hoc. The defendant Puhl, vice presi-

dent of the Reichsbank, as well as Reichsbank council-

lor Thoms knew about it. Ministerial councillor

Dr. Gossel, Rechnungsdirektor Patzer (all KROSIGK's

subordinates) knew about it. Yet KROSIGK remained

in the dark? The puzzle here seems to be one of

convenience only.

The handling of property stolen from the Rothschild family of Paris is significant. Their jewels,
gold and paintings were seized after the invasion
of France. According to the note of Ministerial
Councillor Galleiske, dated 21 April 1941, two boxes
were destined for the Ministry of Finance. Galleiske's
note, reproducing a telephone communication from the
Foreign Currency Protection Bureau (Devisenschutz-
kommando) in France, which had seized the property:

> "The contents of the two cases is not
> yet known. They are said to contain
> gold and jewels. The Reich Marshal
> (i.e. Goering) has personally discussed
> the matter with the Minister of Finance."
> (NG-4091, Exh. 2426, Bk. 75)

KROSIGK tells us that he was not eager to receive
the jewels. A memorandum of Mayer shows that KROSIGK
objected to Goering's plan because he could not understand why the Ministry of Finance should be entrusted
with the disposal of the Rothschild valuables. However, it sheds an interesting light on KROSIGK's
activities. Mayer in his memorandum states that
Goering, with regard to KROSIGK's objections:

> "retorted that, after all the RFM,
> owing to his experience concerning
> the disposal of money and jewelry
> belonging to Jews, would know best
> how to realize these assets."
> (NG-4063, Exh. 2427, Bk. 75)

Notwithstanding his uneasiness about this theft
business, KROSIGK, when the valuables were finally
realized, did not hesitate to accept the proceeds
"in the amount of 1.8 million marks" (Tr.p. 23318).
As explanation for his act of concealing stolen
goods he offered, under direct examination, the
following excuse:

-101-

"... First of all, it was actually not
possible for the Reich Main Pay Office
to refuse to take in this sum of money,
because it would have been a very simple
thing for Goering to issue a directive
instructing the Pay Office to take in
this money. If I had been the reason
for any refusal to take in the money,
then this money would have remained
in the possession of people who under
no circumstances were authorized to
dispose of it. That is the explanation for the settlement that was
finally reacted, in actual fact."
(Tr. p. 23319)

Thereupon the Tribunal inquired:

"Presiding Judge Maguire: Before we
go to another subject, I would like
to ask the witness a question. With
regard to these Rothschild jewels
and the proceeds from their disposition,
was there any question in your mind
at that time that both the jewels were
stolen and that the proceeds were
the result of the disposition of stolen
goods?

The witness: Your Honor, in view of
the fact that I turned down the handling
of the utilization of these jewels -
in view of that it can be seen I
entertained the suspicion that these
jewels had not been acquired on the
basis of a regular legal title.

Presiding Judge Maguire: Well, that
being the fact - I had assumed that
that was what your original position
was - then how would you justify
having the money paid into the Reich
Main Pay Office from the hands of the
people who had obtained the stolen
goods?

The witness: Your Honor, it was a
difficult thing to leave these funds
in the hands of people who, on their
part, had obtained these jewels, having
to entertain the suspicion as to the
illegality of their holdings. Much
rather, these people had had these
jewels turned over to them from a
Reich agency, and they wanted to pay
for them in return." (Tr.pp.23320-23321)

This testimony reveals two things. First KROSIGK

knew that the valuables were stolen from the Roth-

schilds. The above mentioned note of Gallciske

explicitly states: "Among the property seized

are paintings and six large cases." (NG-4091, Exh.

-102-

2426, Bk. 75). Second, knowing the valuables were stolen KROSIGK accepted the proceeds from their sale in order not to leave them in the hands of the thieves. Such a defense is naive.

Goering was right when he pointed to KROSIGK's experience in disposing of money and goods belonging to Jews. KROSIGK had gathered this experience throughout the years in depriving the Jews of their property. As far back as 1938 he was not only concerned with exacting the "Fine of Atonement" but was also taken into consultation when the Ministry of Interior elaborated its plans for the so-called Aryanization of trade and industry, i.e. the elimination of all "non-Aryans" from German-owned or controlled enterprises. On 14 July 1938 the Ministry of Interior submitted to KROSIGK proposals "based on the political demand that the Jewish influence, indeed any activities on the part of the Jews in German industrial life should be eliminated as soon as possible." This goal was to be reached through compulsory transfer of Jewish commercial enterprises into "Aryan hands" in such a way "that the compensation actually paid to the Jews will, as a rule, constitute only a small fraction of the actual value of property." This appears in a memorandum by one of KROSIGK's subordinates commenting on the plan of the Ministry of Interior. (NG-4031, Exh. 2423, Bk. 75). The record is replete with such evidence. KROSIGK's alleged misgivings are unconvincing. His guilt has been established.

Von KROSIGK's further activities with regard to the confiscation of property of the Jews and their deportation to the East will be discussed later.

-103-

Special attention is made, once again to the "final solution" decree co-signed by KROSIGK. The 13th Decree to the Reich Citizenship Law, dated 1 July 1943, deprived all Jews in Germany of judicial process and placed them at the mercy of Himmler's Gestapo. It further provided for the confiscation of property of persons of Jewish extraction by the Reich after their death. (1422-PS, Exh. 2456, Bk. 75). Practically all Jews were deprived of their rights, and Himmler's gang was free "to liquidate" them prior to the enactment of this decree. However, they could not be sentenced without judicial process. The decree abolished all such legal proceedings. It became open season on the Jews.

Questioned under direct examination whether he had no misgivings about signing this decree, KROSIGK came up with an astounding answer.

> ". . . I was convinced that the
> official promulgation would guarantee
> greater protection under the law
> than if the police as heretofore
> handled the matter more or less
> anonymously." (Tr. p. 23345)

The protection referred to here has been brought home to the world. Six million Jews were liquidated by the Third Reich. For such unprecedented crime, KROSIGK bears a major responsibility. His defense of good character and reputation does not refute the facts. Nothing can be said in mitigation.

B. RACIAL PERSECUTION AND EXTERMINATION

Crimes against humanity, as defined in Countrol Council Law
No. 10, are more than mere isolated cases of atrocities or persecutions. The evidence in the present case conclusively establishes the adoption and application of systematic, governmentally
organized and approved measures, amounting to atrocities and offenses of the kind embraced by Control Council Law No. 10 and
committed against "populations", and involving persecution on
racial grounds. These measures, when carried out against citizens in occupied territory, constituted war crimes and crimes
against humanity. When enforced in the Alt Reich against German
nationals, they constituted crimes against humanity. That LAMMERS
approved of and advocated the extension of the scheme of racial
persecution of Jewish citizens of non-German nationality is amply
sustained by the evidence. To quote one example only, in a letter
that he forwarded to Rudolf Hess in July 1938, he expressed his
views as follows:

> "On principal, Jews of foreign nationality
> should be treated as Jews most certainly,
> as the Jewish problem, being a racial pro-
> blem, is independent of nationality. There-
> fore, the Ministry for Foreign Affairs, in
> answer to protests by foreign states, always
> maintained the principal that Jews of foreign
> nationality should be subject to German ra-
> cial legislation just as well as German Jew-
> ish nationals..." (Exh. 1527, NG-1526, Bk.
> 76, p. 1).

This letter referred to the treatment of Czechoslovakian Jews.

LAMMERS is charged with participating in the carrying out of
a governmental plan and program for the persecution and extermination of Jews and Poles, a plan which transcended territorial
borders as well as the boundaries of primitive human decency,
and which involved the commission of crimes unprecedented in
their variety, multitude, and magnitude - ill-treatment, deportation, and genocide being the most serious ones. It is impossible

Doc. 10

199

-99-

indeed to separate and categorize the various phases of the scheme because they were closely inter-connected and they were all indispensible for the achievement of the final aim: the legislation concerning the degradation and despoiling of the Jewish population in and outside of Germany was the prelude for their segregation in ghettos. Once this aim was achieved, they could easily be deported to concentration camps in the East and there the gas chambers and furnaces set the final point to the solution of the problem.

The evidence which we shall review; namely, the minutes of the so-called State Secretary meetings, shows the representatives of the Supreme Reich agencies plotting, formulating, and implementing the vicious scheme in perfect teamwork. LAMMERS was one of them and his participation was conscious, knowing, and willing. His contribution to the formulation of the criminal plan and the discriminatory laws in its execution form the subject matter of war crimes and crimes against humanity with which he is charged.

200

The material facts which must be proved are: (1) the fact of the great pattern or plan of racial persecution and extermination, and, (2) the specific conduct of LAMMERS in furtherance of the plan. He who persuades another to commit murder, he who furnishes the lethal weapon for the purpose, and he who pulls the trigger are all principals in or accessories to the crime.

We turn first to the evidence which establishes that LAMMERS, contrary to his protestations and denials (tr.pp. 21620-22618), had full knowledge of the various phases of the criminal plan.

(a) LAMMERS had to admit in cross-examination that:

"The fact that individual cases occurred here and there, the shooting of Jews in war time in some towns or other, that I read something about that and heard something about that, that is very easily possible. I couldn't say no or deny it." (tr.p. 22635).

(b) Through his position and functions in the Reich Government and in the SS (See Introduction and Count VIII),he had free access to all confidential matters on highest government level, though it is stressed that the extermination program was not a closely guarded secret but an openly professed government plan.

(c) The program of the Nazi Party, of which he became a member in 1932, provided as follows:

> "Only a member of the race can be a citizen; a member of the race can only be one who is of German blood, without consideration of confession; consequently no Jew can be a member of the race." (tr.p. 22109).

(d) The following findings of fact of the International Military Tribunal demonstrate the development of the governmental plan of discrimination of Jews from 1933 to 1939, during the period LAMMERS held highest government office in the Third Reich:

> "With the seizure of power, the persecution of the Jews was intensified. A series of discriminatory laws was passed, which limited the offices and professions permitted to Jews; and restrictions were placed on their family life and their rights of citizenship. By the autumn of 1938, the Nazi policy towards the Jews had reached the stage where it was directed towards the complete exclusion of Jews from German life. Pogroms were organized, which included the burning and demolishing of synagogues, the looting of Jewish businesses, and the arrest of prominent Jewish business men. A collective fine of 1 billion marks was imposed on the Jews, the seizure of Jewish assets was authorized, and the movement of Jews was restricted by regulations to certain specified districts and hours. The creation of ghettos was carried out on an extensive scale, and by an order of the Security Police Jews were compelled to wear a yellow star to be worn on the breast and back." (Trial of Major War Criminals, Vol. I, pp. 248/49).

(e) In January 1939 Hitler declared in a speech to the Reichstag that:

> "If international Jewry in and outside Europe should succeed in plunging the peoples of the world once again into a world war, then the result would be... the annihilation of the Jewish race in Europe." (Exh. 3906, 2360(A)-PS, Bk. 211 B, p. 68).

LAMMERS was sitting, at that occasion, next to Hitler. (tr.p.

22634). On 13 December 1940 Kritzinger, LAMMERS' State Secretary,

ordered in a Reich Chancellory memorandum that:

> "Apart from this it must be asked whether, in
> view of the fact that the Jews will have dis-
> appeared from Germany in the near future, it
> is still worthwhile to accord them a special
> legal status. They are anyhow no Reich citi-
> zens...

> "It appears to me essential and right that the
> Jews, when losing their domicile in the Reich
> by emmigration or expulsion also loses their
> German citizenship. But for this purpose we
> only need an amendment to the citizenship law."
> (Exh. 1533, NG-2610, Bk. 76, p. 45, emphasis
> provided).

Some days before LAMMERS had notified von Schirach, the Reich

Governor in Austria that:

> "As Reichsleiter Bormann informs me, the Fueh-
> rer has decided after receipt of one of the
> reports made bv you, that the 60,000 Jews,
> still residing in the Reichsgau Vienna, will
> be deported most rapidly, that is still dur-
> ing the war, to the General Government because
> of the housing shortage prevalent in Vienna.
> I have informed the Governor General in Cra-
> cow as well as the Reichsfuehrer SS about this
> decision of the Fuehrer, and I request you also
> to take cognizance of it." (Exh. 1532, 1950-PS,
> Bk. 76, p. 44).

On 28 March 1940 LAMMERS wrote to Himmler that:

> "...I am pleased to send you herewith a photo-
> stat of an edition of 'deportation is being
> continued' which was sent to me anonimously."

The enclosed report headed, "Deportation is Being Continued -

The Death March from Lublin - Deaths from Freezing - Goering's

Decision Appealed To", reads in part as follows:

> "In spite of the objections of the Government
> General to a hasty and unplanned continuation
> of the deportation of Jewish German nationals
> to Eastern Poland this is being continued at
> the order of the Reichsfuehrer SS.

> "On 12 March 1940, 160 more Jews were evacuated
> from Schneidemuehl in a freightcar to the Lub-
> lin district. Additional transports are re-
> ported in Lublin. The deported persons had to
> leave their entire property behind. They were
> not allowed to take even a suitcase with them.
> The women had to give up their handbags before
> the trips. Some persons had their overcoats

taken away from them, these being men and women who had tried to put on several coats or suits of underwear over each other as a protection against the cold. They were not allowed to take one cent in cash with them, not even the 20 zloty which those deported from Stettin were allowed. Nor were they permitted to take food, beds, household articles (cooking pots, etc.) with them. Upon their arrival in Lublin the deportees only had with them what they wore on their bodies...

"Men, women and children had to march from Lublin to these villages on foot in a temperature of 22 degrees (centigrade) along country roads deeply covered with snow. Shocking things occured during this march. Of the approximately 1200 persons deported from Stettin 72 persons, including men and women up to 86 years old, were left lying on the march, which lasted more than 14 hours. The greater part of these people froze to death. Among them was a mother who was carrying her three-year old child in her arms, tried to protect it from the cold with her clothes and was left lying in this position after inhuman hardships. Furthermore, the body of a child about five years old was found in a half frozen condition. It carried a cardboard sign around its neck with the name 'Renate Alexander from Hammerstein in Pomerania'. It appeared that this child was deported with the others while visiting relatives in Germany. This child had to have its hands and feet amputated in the Lublin hospital. After the transport the corpses were collected on sleds along the country road and brought to the Jewish cemeteries in Piaski and Lublin.

"...Since there were no additional quarters available anywhere the greater part of the deportees, on the contrary, had to be lodged in stables, sheds, etc., and since besides this there is no food except black bread and the sanitary conditions are desperate, numerous persons are dying every day, especially old people and children. Up to 12 March the death rate among the Jews deported from Stettin alone increased to a total of 230..." (Exh. 1529, NG-2490, Bk. 76, pp. 8/9, emphasis provided).

203

It deserves special attention that the same LAMMERS testified in

this Tribunal that he only "found out through the IMT Judgment"

and through documents submitted to him in Nurnberg that "at the

time of Wannsee meeting of 20 January 1942 the evacuation of

Jews was already in progress". (tr.p. 21625, emphasis provided).

In cross-examination, he expounded again a different story:

> "Q. ...Did Hitler, let us say in 1941, give
> you any information about his view that no
> Jews would be left in Germany after the war?
>
> "A. I can't remember that for certain but I
> heard, and I suppose he occasionally said
> that in conversation, that nearly all Jews
> would have to get out of Germany..." (tr.p.
> 22627).

(f) LAMMERS assured this Court that he "was never a violent
anti-Semite nor did I ever permit myself to be affected by racial
hatred". (tr.p. 21592). However, he wrote in the official Prague
Archives for Law, Administration, and Economy, in March 1944, that
"in the life and death struggle against the plutocrat - Bolshevist
powers lead by world Jewry this test has lasted almost five years".
(Exh. 3905, NG-1633, Bk. 211 B, p. 62; tr.p. 22633).

(g) In May 1941 LAMMERS informed Bormann:

> "For your own confidential information I take
> the liberty of adding the following: The
> reason why the Fuehrer rejected the legisla-
> tion proposed by the Reich Minister of the
> Interior, was chiefly that he is of the
> opinion that after the war there would not
> be any Jews left in Germany any way and that
> therefore it is not necessary to issue now a
> regulation which would be difficult to en-
> force, which would tie up personnel, and
> which would not bring about a solution in
> principal." (Exh. 3902, NG-1123, Bk. 211 B,
> p. 42, tr.p. 22627).

In September 1948 he saw fit to testify that "in the summer or
fall of 1942" he was alarmed over the "rumors about evacuation".
(tr.p. 21607). He reported to the Fuehrer for the third time.
Thereafter, his qualms dispelled.

(h) A number of policy proclaiming speeches by Hitler and
Goering, which were made publicly before thousands of people,
broadcasted by radio to Germany and the whole world and published in many millions of newspaper copies, further rebuts
LAMMERS' statement that he had no knowledge of the extermination
program against Jews. On 30 January 1942, 10 days after the

204

so-called Wannsee conference (Exh. 1458, NG-2586 M, Bk. 59, p. 144), Hitler publicly reiterated, with unmistakable candor, his intention to annihilate the European Jews:

> "I have already declared on September 1, 1939, in the German Reichstag, and I am careful today not to make premature predictions - when I say today that this war will not turn out the way the Jews think it will, that the European aryan peoples will not be wiped out, but the result of this war will be the annihilation of Jewry." (Exh. 3906, 2360(B)-PS, Bk. 211 C, p. 1).

Yet, when LAMMERS was, at about the same time or thereafter, permitted to interview his Fuehrer and to elicit from him what "final solution" meant in fact, the Fuehrer declined to trust his Minister with the same straight forward information he had given in full public on 30 January 1942:

> "However the Fuehrer refused to discuss these matters with me." (tr.p. 21602).

And whereas the Fuehrer had made no bones whatsoever about the fact that the Jews were being exterminated, an atmosphere of utmost secrecy allegedly prevailed in the Reich Chancellory and it went so far that LAMMERS allegedly ordered his officials "to refrain from making any comments on this matter, if it should ever crop up in the Reich Chancellory" and he further directed them "that if invitations should be received at any conferences for any of my officials, he was to attend only in the capacity of a listening post without making any statements". (tr.p. 21602).

205

While LAMMERS was half-way through with his alleged five "reports" to Hitler and the three discussions with Himmler on his search for the real meaning of "final solution" of the Jewish problem, a remarkable event occurred. "Some weeks" after the second meeting of the State Secretaries of March 1942, LAMMERS was able to see the Fuehrer. Again Hitler was brisk at the beginning but "finally he said, pretty clearly that he wished than an end might be put to all these Jewish affairs, once and for all.... He added that after the war he would make

a final decision as to where the Jews were to go." And there
would be enough room in the East or other places where they could
be taken. (tr.p. 21604). LAMMERS allegedly hurried to inform
Goering, Frick, the RSHA, and a number of other agencies of the
Fuehrer's decision and the gentlemen in the Reich Chancellory
"interpreted it as a definite victory over the RSHA". (tr.p.
21605) - a rather nebulous statement considering that there is
no trace in LAMMERS' testimony of an alleged feud over the issue
of the final solution between the Reich Chancellory and the RSHA.
Hitler's alleged decision, designated by the Defense as "stop
order" (tr.p. 21106) is nowhere supported by the evidence which
shows, on the contrary, that nothing was stopped and that the
implementation of the final solution was being continued by
all departments with undiminished intensity. Even LAMMERS
conceded that. (tr.pp. 21606 ff.). It is, consequently, safe
to assume that LAMMERS' efforts to provide some alibi rather
than the reproduction of the historical truth gave birth to the
myth of the so-called "stop order". Be it as it may, "only
after the collapse has it become clear to me that both the
Fuehrer...and Himmler...were deliberately lying to me and
were putting me off with false statements...I at that time
had to believe what he said and held it to be binding". (tr.
pp. 21618/19). It is deplorable that LAMMERS did not always
extend the same credulity to his Fuehrer, who certainly did not
lie to the world on 30 September 1942 (a couple of months after
the alleged "stop order") when declaring:

> "On the first of September 1939 I made two
> statements in the Reichstag session:...and
> secondly, that if the Jews should start an
> international world war for the wiping out
> of the aryan peoples of Europe, then the
> aryan peoples would not be wiped out, but
> Jewry.... The Jews have laughed at one time
> even in Germany over my prophecies, I do
> not know whether they are laughing still
> today or whether their laughing has already
> ceased. But I can also now make one certain
> statement: their laughing is going to come
> to an end everywhere, and I am going to be
> right also with these prophecies." (Exh.
> 3906, 2360(C)-PS, Bk. 211 C, p. 2).

206

In February 1943 Hitler publicly pronounced:

> "This fight will also not, for this reason,
> as they are intending, end with the des-
> truction of the aryan people but this war
> will find its end with the annihilation of
> Jewry in Europe." (Exh. 3906, 2360(D)-PS,
> Bk. 211 C, p. 3).

LAMMERS commented, with respect to Hitler's speeches, that "the word extermination is one the Fuehrer used a lot in various speeches. The question is how he meant it." (tr.p. 22633). As far as our knowledge of the German language goes, we can but say its meaning is an unambiguous as it is in the English.

At about the same time Goebbels said, in a speech in the Berlin Sportpalast, that no protests against the Jewish perse- cution "can prevent us from doing the necessary. Germany has no intention to yield to this threat, but intends to counteract it at the right time, and, if necessary, with the most radical counter-measures." (Exh. 3906, 2360(E)-PS, Bk. 211 C, p. 4).

(i) On 16 July 1943 the protestant Bishop Wurm warned Hitler and the members of the Reich Cabinet in a letter ad- dressed to the Reich Chancellory that the so-called privileged non-aryans were "in a mortal danger, now that the (other) non- aryans have already been eliminated to a large extent in the areas which are under the power of Germany". (Exh. C-241, NG- 5874(A), Bk. 211 C, p. 5). Towards the end of 1943 he repeated his protests against the mass killings of Jews with the follow- ing words:

> "For religious and ethical reasons, I have
> to state, in agreement with the judgment
> of all German people who subscribe posi-
> tively to Christianity, that we as Chris-
> tians regard the annihilation policy
> against Jewry as a grave injustice which
> is also very dangerous for German people."
> (Exh. C-241, NG-5874(A), Supra).

LAMMERS testified, relative to the receipt of letters from Bishop Wurm, as follows:

> "Q. ...How many letters did you receive

207

from Catholic or Protestant churchmen saying
that the killing of the Jews in the East was
not in the German national interest?

"A. I can't remember having received such
letters.

"Q. Don't you remember that the Bishop of
Wuerttemberg, Dr. Wurm, repeatedly wrote you
such letters that it was a scandal for Germany and that all one was doing was to pour
grist into the mill of war agitator Roosevelt if it didn't stop?

"A. I know that I got letters from Wurm which
I deliberately did not pass on in order to
save him from criminal proceedings before the
Peoples' Court which the Ministry of Justice
were already preparing. As for the actual
detailed contents of his complaints, I can
only comment on those if you submit them to
me." (tr.pp. 22630/631).

(j) Two letters which were received in March 1943 by the

Reich Chancellory and initialled by LAMMERS (tr.p. 22631) were

very apt to give LAMMERS an accurate idea of the realities of

the final solution of the Jewish question in Poland - far from

Berlin conference rooms. One of the writers was a certain

Seidenglanz, an eye witness of such occurrences; the other one

explained why he had signed his communication only with his

initials:

"Because for the time being, I would not like
to have anything to do with the noble Gestapo..."

We quote from these two letters:

"...Only lately, in the morning, when the Jews
left the camp and were on their way to work,
many Jews were seized and,--, well, today
these Jews can no longer go to work. We are
lacking so many workers, and I am of the firm
conviction that the Fuehrer does not know
what is going on here, for these men, too,
have filled their working places, which are
now empty.

. . . .

"Third: A Polish policeman I know asked me
whether I were not yet ashamed to be a racial
German. At last he had come to know German
Kultur. The Germans would not have any reason to complain if they were treated afterwards, he meant after this war, according to
German Kultur. It cannot be described what
he saw when the Jewish ghettos were dissolved.

"The Gestapo and the German Police he called
beasts, animals in the shape of men, and
something much worse. He meant that a proper word for it would have to be found only.
The Jews were being exterminated, children,
also of the most tender age, were taken
away from their mothers, even when still
being nursed, thrown on the floor and their
heads are being bashed in by the boot heels.
If any mother objected to that only mildly,
she would be slain with the rifle butts,
the others would be segregated approximately according to age and sex, as if
they were being taken away to work, but
instead they were being removed to a ra-
vine outside the town. There they were
being forced to undress, and then slain
with the rifle butts, hardly any use was
being made of shotguns, apparently for
the sake of thrift.

"Those who were half or fully slain were
being thrown into prepared pits, quick
lime was being strewn on them. When the
lime started to steam in the flowing blood
screams and sobs of the partly slain people were still to be heard. Like that
hundreds of thousands of all ages were
being sent to the next world. The question now is, was the order given like that
from above, or whether the Gestapo men
want to excel one another in bestiality.
However, that may be, the Polish people
come to know a fine Kultur, as he said,
and they hope to be able to use this on
the German people. Whoever lives among
the Poles and wants to remain here after
the war, sees what danger can result from
this for a racial German." (Exh. 3904,
NG-1903, Bk. 211 B, p. 56; tr.p. 22631).

209

(k) That LAMMERS' participation in the scheme of racial

persecution and extermination was prompted by solid ideological

reasons becomes evident from a statement which he made on the

witness stand:

"...I do, however, realize that the Jews
bear considerable part of the guilt in
all the wars of the world." (tr.p. 22633).

This ennunciation is closely reminiscent of Hitler's views as

voiced on 31 January 1939. (Exh. 3906, 2360(A)-PS, Supra).

The conclusions to be drawn from the aforementioned evi-

dence shall best be expressed in words of Tribunal III in the

Case against the officials of the Ministry of Justice:

"A large proportion of all of the Jews in Germany were transported to the East. Millions of persons disappeared from Germany and the occupied territory without a trace. They were herded into concentration camps within and without Germany. Thousands of soldiers and members of the Gestapo and SS must have been instrumental in the processes of deportation, torture, and extermination. The mere task of disposal of mountainous piles of corpses, (evidence of which we have seen), became a serious problem and the subject of disagreement between the various organizations involved. The thousands of Germans who took part in the atrocities must have returned from time to time to their homes in the Reich. The atrocities were of a magnitude unprecedented in the history of the world. Are we to believe that no whisper reached the ears of the public or of those officials who were most concerned? Did the defendants think that the nation-wide pogrom of November 1938, officially directed from Berlin, and Hitler's announcement to the Reichstag threatening the obliteration of the Jewish race in Europe were unrelated? At least they cannot plead ignorance concerning the decrees which were published in their official organ The Reichsgesetzblatt'. Therefore, they knew that Jews were to be punished by the police in Germany and in Bohemia and Moravia. They knew that the property of Jews was confiscated on death of the owner. They knew that the law against Poles and Jews had been extended to occupied territories and they knew that the Chief of the Security Police was the official authorized to determine whether or not Jewish property was subject to confiscation. They could hardly be ignorant of the fact that the infamous law against Poles and Jews of 4 December 1941 directed the Reich Minister of Justice himself, together with the Minister of the Interior, to issue legal and administrative regulations for 'implementation of the decree'. They read 'The Stuermer'. They listened to the radio. They received and sent directives. They heard and delivered lectures. This Tribunal is not so gullible as to believe these defendants so stupid that they did not know what was going on. One man can keep a secret, two men may, but thousands never." (Tribunal III, Case III, Opinion and Judgment, tr.pp. 10782-784).

The evidence heretofore reviewed reveals the pattern and plan of racial persecution, LAMMERS' knowledge of the outlines thereof, in all its immensity, and his taking a consenting part in the crimes perpetrated in its execution.

210

We shall now discuss evidence which we believe proves, beyond reasonable doubt, LAMMERS' active and conscious participation in the plan.

211

1. MISCELLANEOUS ANTI-JEWISH LEGISLATION AND THE FORMULATION OF
THE 11th ORDINANCE TO THE REICH CITIZENSHIP LAW

On 31 August 1940 the Reich Chancellory received a communication from the Minister of the Interior with the request to obtain a Fuehrer decision concerning the enforcement of anti-Jewish
matters in Luxembourg. (Exh. 1530, NG-2297, Bk. 76, p. 11). As
indicated in a file note of the Reich Chancellory, Hitler authorized the immediate enforcement of anti-Jewish measures there.
(Ibid, p. 12). Three decrees were passed by which the Nurnberg
Laws and other discriminatory legislation was extended to occupied Luxembourg. (Ibid, pp. 16-22). The introduction of these
laws was obviously violative of the Hague Regulations.

In April 1940 the Reich Minister for Labor forwarded to
LAMMERS, as member of the Ministerial Council for the Defense
of the Reich, a draft for a law excluding Jewish workers from
the benefits of the German labor legislation. (Exh. 1531, NG-
1143, Bk. 76, p. 24). LAMMERS circulated this draft to the
Reich agencies concerned and a conference was held thereafter
on 8 January 1941 at which a representative of the Reich Chancellory was present. (Ibid, p. 39). The following agreement was
reached:

> "1. Jews are obliged to accept work to which
> they are directed by the Labor Offices.
>
> "2. The working conditions governing the Jews
> are not labor-regulations in the sense of the
> rules existing for the German worker. The
> Reich Labor Minister is authorized to regulate
> present and former working conditions for Jews,
> and, if necessary, to change the present laws."
> (Ibid, p. 41)

In December 1940 preparations were started for a legislation which lead up to depriving the Jews of their citizenship
and to confiscating their property. On 11 December 1940 the
Reich Chancellory received an invitation by the Ministry of
the Interior to attend a conference on a proposed draft for

the 10th ordinance implementing the law concerning Reich citizenship. The letter stated that:

> "In the course of ordering the affairs of citizenship in connection with the population of the incorporated Eastern territories, it has become necessary to exclude on principal the part of the population which is of alien stock from German citizenship..." (Exh. 1533, NG-2610, Bk. 76, p. 45).

Enclosed with the defendant Stuckart's letter was a draft which can be found on page 49 of document book 76. A memorandum of 15 December 1940, initialled by Kritzinger, discloses that a copy of this draft was submitted to LAMMERS and it goes on to say that no special legislation appears to be necessary, as the Jews will disappear anyway in the near future from Germany either by emigration or by expulsion. (Ibid). On 28 December 1940 LAMMERS informed the Minister of the Interior to this effect, (Ibid, p. 51). Another memorandum from the Reich Chancellory records, on 30 January 1941, that the Ministry of the Interior, in agreement with the other parties concerned, suggested that all Jews of German citizenship be declared stateless. The attitude of the Reich Chancellory is expressed in the remark that "there should be no scruples against the suggestion of the Minister of the Interior". (Exh. 1534, NG-300, Bk. 76, p. 57). Numerous conferences were held in the months to follow, drafts were formulated and re-formulated and a continuous exchange of opinions between parties concerned took place, all with the co-operation of the Reich Chancellory. (Ibid, pp. 58-87). A revised draft was elaborated by the Ministry of Justice in conjunction with the Reich Chancellory. (Exh. 3902, NG-1123, Bk. 211 B, Supra). Yet Hitler remained reserved and was reluctant to deprive the German Jews of their citizenship. LAMMERS was, of course, well informed of the motives which prompted the negative attitude of the Fuehrer. In three letters to Frick, Schlegelberger, and Bormann, he conveyed Hitler's decision but he was careful not to impart to them the same amount of

213

-113-

information. He told Frick and Schlegelberger that:

> "The Fuehrer does not feel that a regulation
> to the extent proposed by the Reich Minister
> of Interior is necessary at the present time.
> The Fuehrer rather believes that a regulation
> would be sufficient which would deprive those
> Jews who reside abroad of their German citi-
> zenship and which would declare their fortune
> as forfeited to the Reich..." (Ibid).

Feeling that his associate Bormann was entitled to a more detailed

explanation, LAMMERS told him "for his confidential information"

that, according to Hitler's views, legislation against German

Jews was superfluous because none of them would be left in Ger-

many after the war. (Ibid).

On 7 July 1941 the Reich Minister of the Interior invited

LAMMERS and the representatives of other Supreme Reich agencies

to a conference concerning the draft for the 11th decree of the

Reich Citizenship Law. (Exh. 1536, NG-2499, Bk. 76, p. 88).

Final details of the decree were thrashed out at this confer-

ence which was attended by a representative of the Reich Chan-

cellory (Ibid, p. 96) and, on 26 October 1941, the Reich Chan-

cellory received the final draft. (Ibid, p. 98). The 11th

regulation of the Reich Citizenship Law was promulgated in the

Reichs Gesetzblatt on 25 November 1941 and it decreed the loss

of citizenship by German Jews who were residing abroad and

simultaneously the confiscation of their property by the Reich.

Section 12 made it applicable to the Protectorate of Bohemia

and Moravia and to the annexed Eastern territories. (Ibid,

pp. 99-102). The ordinance for the execution of the 11th decree

to the Reich Citizenship Law, which was received and initialled

by LAMMERS, gives a conclusive explanation why the Nazi legis-

lators did not deem it necessary to deprive German Jews of their

nationality:

> "...(1) The loss of citizenship and the for-
> feiture of property refers also to such Jews
> coming under this decree, who have their per-
> manent place of residence, or who will reside

later on, in territories occupied by German
troops or such territories which are under
German administration, especially also in
the Government General or in the Reich Com-
missariate Ostland and the Ukraine.

"(2) The publication of this ordinance shall
be avoided..." (Ibid, p. 103, emphasis provided).

A similar decree was passed for the Protectorate of Bohemia and

Moravia after its draft had been circulated to the Reich Chancel-

lery and other Reich authorities. (Exh. 1547, NG-1112, Bk. 76,

p. 280; see also 1942, RGBl, I, p. 627).

2. THE DECREE OF 4 DECEMBER 1941 "CONCERNING THE ORGANIZATION AND CRIMINAL JURISDICTION AGAINST POLES AND JEWS IN THE INCORPORATED EASTERN TERRITORIES"

In February 1940 the Plenipotentiary General for the Reich Administration submitted to LAMMERS, as a member of the Council of Ministers for the Reich Defense, a draft for a "law for the combating of acts of violence in the incorporated Eastern territories" which, according to a file note of the Reich Chancellery, was to be made applicable only to Poles and Jews. (Exh. 1528, NG-944, Bk. 76, p. 3). LAMMERS forwarded this draft to Goering for his information and comment, stating that "it would have been most welcomed if the law had been issued in the Incorporated Eastern Territories in October (1939)". (Ibid, p. 5).

In the fall and winter of 1939 an extensive correspondence and frequent discussions were being conducted between LAMMERS, Hess, and Schlegelberger. It was generally agreed that discriminatory legislation should be enacted in the incorporated territories. (Exh. 1567, NG-229, Bk. 77, p. 24).

On 9 October 1940 the Minister of Justice invited LAMMERS to a discussion on the question of passing a special penal legislation for Poles and Jews. (Exh. 1568, NG-127, Bk. 77, p. 38). Enclosed with this invitation was a letter from the Chief of the Security Police and the SD stressing the desirability of the issuance of a special penal code for the Poles in the incorporated territories, with this addition:

> "The criminal code which has to be created
> for the Poles, must be much more severe in
> its criminal tenor as well as in the form
> of its prescribed application, than it is
> necessary for the criminal law valid for
> the Germans." (Ibid, p. 39).

A memorandum of the Reich Chancellery, dated 26 November 1940, states that the Deputy of the Fuehrer suggested to "create a special penal code and a special law of criminal procedure for Poles. The dominating principle of a penal code must be to deter by fear and there must be a possibility of pronouncing a sentence of corporal punishment. The law of criminal procedure must not allow for obstruction; here the deputy of the Fuehrer is in favor of police court martials rather than legal courts." (Ibid, p. 41).

A file note of the Reich Chancellery, dated 22 April 1941, and bearing LAMMERS' initial, reveals that the finished draft for the proposed decree was forwarded to LAMMERS by the Minister of Justice. It further states that:

> "The draft establishes a draconic special criminal law for Poles and Jews, giving a wide range for the interpretations of the facts of the case, with the death penalty applicable throughout. The conditions of imprisonment are also much more severe than provided for in the German criminal law... Provisions of criminal law, which might be used to obstruct the procedure, have been eliminated (the opportunity of the defendant for an appeal, compulsory indictment, the challenge of a judge, compare also article XII, S. 2)." (Exh. 1572, NG-130, Bk. 77, p. 52).

Another file note of the Reich Chancellery records, on 27 May 1941, that the Reichsfuehrer SS agrees to the special penal code for Poles but asks "for Police drumhead courts martial jurisdiction and requests that this be presented to the Fuehrer when the Reich Minister (LAMMERS) makes his intended report". Drumhead courts martial had been, as it is further pointed out, proposed in the draft of a decree of the Ministerial Council on 21 February 1940, but postponed at the time following Goering's objections. (Exh. 1573, NG-136, Bk. 77, p. 54).

On 27 May 1941 LAMMERS informed Schlegelberger that after the assassination of a German policeman in a Polish village, Reichsstatthalter Greiser gave the order to execute not only the culprits but twelve hostages on the spot and under the eyes of the entire native village population. In view of these sabotage acts, the Fuehrer decided that Greiser be given authority to set up the drumhead courts martial and to exercise the right of clemency concerning Poles who would be sentenced by such courts. LAMMERS then went on to say:

"I beg to inform you of these decisions taken
by the Fuehrer and to ask you to take the
necessary steps to put then into practice
everything necessary for their execution
without delay. I leave it to you to consider whether it is advisable to include
this ruling on the basis of the above-mentioned decisions of the Fuehrer, in whole
or in part, in the draft of the decree
which you have prepared concerning the
administration of criminal law against
the Poles and Jews in the incorporated
Eastern territories and in the territory
of the former free city of Danzig. I
ask you to report to the Fuehrer, for my
attention, on the measure you have taken."
(Ibid, p. 54; Exh. 1427, NG-139, Bk. 72 H,
p. 1).

In accordance with and based on LAMMERS' suggestion, the Minister

of Justice and Gauleiter Greiser reached complete agreement on the

establishment of summary courts martial and on the delegation of

the right to grant clemency. A letter from the Reich Minister of

Justice to Gauleiter Greiser reads, in part, as follows:

"The letter written to me on 27 May 1941 by
the Reich Minister and Chief of the Reich
Chancellory formed the basis of our discussion of the first two points. I enclose a
copy for your information, in accordance
with your wishes.

"As regards the establishment of summary
courts martial, we were in complete agreement that the best way to incorporate the
Fuehrer's decision in the proposed Polish
penal law is to insert the following decree
into this law:

'The Reich Governor may, with the approval of the Reich Minister of Justice decree that in individual districts of the incorporated Eastern
territories, including the territory
of the former Free City of Danzig,
Poles accused of committing serious
excesses against Germans or of other
grave offenses which seriously jeop-
ardize the work of German reconstruction, may, until further notice, be
dealt with by summary court martial
instead of by special court.

'The penalties pronounced by the summary courts martial will be death or
concentration camp.

'The Reich Governor will make further
arrangement regarding personnel and
procedure of the summary courts martial.'" (Exh. 1838, NG-135, Bk. 74,
p. 24).

-118-

It should be noted that this provision was incorporated in the final decree against Jews and Poles. (Exh. 1576, NG-1641, Bk. 77, p. 78; Section XIII, p. 81, Infra).

The foregoing explodes LAMMERS' story that he did not object to the decree against Jews and Poles - neither when he reported on it to Hitler nor when it was discussed in the Ministerial Council - because he allegedly was afraid that Hitler might supplant this decree by a more rigorous court martial procedure. (tr.pp. 21757/758; 22602/603). This defense is untenable because:

(a) Courts martial existed in the incorporated territories since May 1941.

(b) It was LAMMERS who suggested to Schlegelberger to include the drumhead courts martial into the proposed final decree.

(c) The final decree expressly provided for drumhead courts martial jurisdiction which existed side by side with the jurisdiction of the special courts. Consequently, there was no point and no need for LAMMERS to prevent Hitler from instituting courts martial. The reason why LAMMERS abstained from raising objections is near at hand: he was in complete accord with the proposed legislation and, more than that, he had been instrumental in bringing it about.

The decree was then passed by the Ministerial Council for the Defense of the Reich - of which LAMMERS was a member - and co-signed by him. (tr.p. 21758).

The decree of 4 December 1941 "concerning the Organization and Criminal Jurisdiction against Poles and Jews in the Incorporated Eastern Territories" (Exh. 1576, NG-1641, Supra) was the subject of detailed comment and analysis in the finding of Tribunal III in the case of the United States of America vs. Joseph Altstoetter, et al. We propose to follow closely in our argument the findings of fact and law of this Tribunal insofar as they are

219

based on evidence which was also introduced against LAMMERS.* This

Tribunal found that the aforementioned decree "marks perhaps the

extreme limit to which the Nazi Government carried its statutory

and decretal persecution of racial and religious minorities, but

it also introduces another element of great importance. We refer

to the extension of German laws to occupied territory, to pur-

portedly annexed territory, and to territory of the so-called

Protectorates." (Case III, Opinion and Judgment, tr.p. 10664).

The law of 4 December 1941 against Poles and Jews applied to the

incorporated territories. These territories were seized in the

course of a criminal aggressive war but, aside from that fact,

the purported annexation was premature and invalid under the

laws and customs of war. Sir Arnold D. MacNair expressed the

principle in the following words:

> "A purported incorporation of occupied terri-
> tories by a military occupant into his own
> kingdom during the war is illegal and ought
> not to receive any recognition..." (Legal
> Facts of War (2nd Edition), (Cambridge,
> 1944), p. 320, Note).

The so-called annexed territories in Poland were in reality nothing

more than territories under belligerent occupation of the military

forces of Germany. The extension to and application in these ter-

ritories of the discriminatory law against Poles and Jews was in

furtherance of the avowed purpose of racial persecution and ex-

termination. It is noted that Article XIV of the decree under

discussion makes it also applicable to acts of Poles and Jews

within any part of the German Reich, if, on 1 September 1939,

they were domiciled within the former Polish state. Tribunal

III found that "this section was repeatedly employed by the

courts in the prosecution of Poles". (Case III, Opinion and

Judgment, tr.p. 10666). In the passing and enforcement of that

- - - - - -

* Reference is made to the following pages of the Opinion in
Case III which we ask this Tribunal to take judicial notice
of: tr.pp. 10664/665/666/673/674/708/709/765/770/777/790/
792.

law,.the following provisions of the Hague Convention were violated:

"Until a more complete code of laws of war
has been issued,.the high contracting parties deem it expedient to declare that in
cases not included in regulations adopted
by them the inhabitants and belligerants
remain under the protection and the rule
of the principles of law of nations as
they result from the usages established
among civilized populations,.from the
laws of humanity, and from the dictates
of public conscience.

"Article 43 - The authority of the legiti-
mate power having in fact passed into the
hands of the occupant,.the latter shall
take all the measures in his power to restore and insure as far as possible public order and safety while respecting,.
unless absolutely prevented, the laws
in force in the country."

It constituted,.in addition, a violation of Articles 23 and 46 of

the Hague Regulations.

The decree provides, in part, as follows:

"(1) Poles and Jews in the incorporated Eastern territories, are to conduct themselves in
conformity with the German laws and with the
regulations introduced for them by the German
authorities. They are to abstain from any
conduct liable to prejudice the sovereignty
of the German Reich or the prestige of the
German people.

"(2) The death penalty shall be imposed on
any Pole or Jew if he commits an act of violence against a German on account of his being
of German blood.

"(3) A Pole or Jew shall be sentenced to
death, or in less serious cases to imprisonment, if he manifests anti-German sentiments
by malicious activities or incitement, particularly by making anti-German utterances, or by
removing or defacing official notices of German authorities or offices, or if he, by his
conduct, lowers orprejudices the prestige or
the wellbeing of the German Reich or the German people.

"(4) The death penalty, or in less serious
cases imprisonment, shall be imposed on any
Jew or Pole:

. . . . . .

"3.--If he urges or incites to disobedience to
any decree or regulation issued by the German
authorities;

221

-121-

"4.--If he conspires to commit an act punishable under sub-sections (2), (3) and (4), paragraphs 1 to 3, or if he seriously contemplates the carrying out of such an act, or if he offers himself to commit such an act, or accepts such an offer, or if he obtains credible information of such act, or of the intention of committing it, and fails to notify the authorities or any person threatened thereby at a time when danger can still be averted.

"II.--Punishment shall also be imposed on Poles or Jews if they act contrary to German criminal law or commit any act for which they deserve punishment in accordance with the fundamental principles of German criminal law and in view of the interests of the State in the incorporated Eastern territories.

"III.--(2) The death sentence shall be imposed in all cases where it is prescribed by law. Moreover, in those cases where the law does not provide for the death sentence, it may and shall be imposed if the offense points to particularly objectionable motives or is particularly grave for other reasons; the death sentence may also be passed upon juvenile offenders...

"IV. The State Prosecutor shall prosecute a Pole or a Jew if he considers that punishment is in the public interest.

"V. (1) Poles and Jews shall be tried by a special court or by the district judge.

"VI. (1) Every sentence will be enforced without delay. The State Prosecutor may, however, appeal from the sentence of a district judge to the court of appeal. The appeal has to be lodged within two weeks.

"(2) The right to lodge complaints which are to be heard by the court of appeal is reserved exclusively to the State Prosecutor.

"VII. Poles and Jews cannot challenge a German judge on account of alleged partiality.

"VIII. *** (2) During the preliminary inquiry, the State Prosecutor may order the arrest and any other coercive measures permissible.

"IX. Poles and Jews are not sworn in as witnesses in criminal proceedings. If the unsworn deposition made by them before the court is found false, the provisions as prescribed for perjury and false statements shall be applied accordingly.

"X. (1) Only the State Prosecutor may apply for the reopening of a case. In a case tried before a special court, the decision concerning an application for the reopening of the proceedings rests with this court.

222

"(2) The right to lodge a plea of nullity rests with the State Prosecutor-General. The decision on the plea rests with the court of appeal.

"XI. Poles and Jews are not entitled to act as prosecutors either in a principal or a subsidiary capacity.

"XII. The court and the State Prosecutor shall conduct proceedings within their discretion and according to the principles of the German Law of Procedure. They may, however, deviate from the provisions of the German law on the organization of courts and on criminal procedure, whenever this may appear to them advisable for the rapid and more efficient conduct of proceedings.

. . . .

"XV. Within the meaning of this Decree, the term 'Poles' includes 'Schutzangehoerige' or those who are stateless." (Case III, Opinion and Judgment, tr.pp. 10664/665; 10673/674). (Exh. 1576, NG-1641, Supra, emphasis provided; RGB1, 1941, I, p. 759).

Tribunal III also held that:

"In the year 1942, 61,835 persons were convicted under the law against Poles and Jews. This figure includes persons convicted in the incorporated Eastern territories, and also convictions for crimes committed in 'other districts of the German Reich by Jews and Poles who on 1 September 1939 had their residence or permanent place of abode in territory of the former Polish state'. These figures, of course do not include any cases in which Jews were convicted of other crimes in which the law of 4 December 1941 was not involved." (Case III, Opinion and Judgment, tr.p. 10781).

On 26 January 1941 the Governor of the Province of Upper Silesia wrote to LAMMERS:

"Dear Reich Minister:

"The decree of 4 December 1941, (Reich Law Gazette I, p. 759), concerning penal measures against Poles and Jews in the incorporated Eastern territories aims at punishing quickly and effectively criminal acts committed by Poles and Jews within the incorporated Eastern territories. Its success, however, is doubtful as long as it is necessary to obtain a decision from the Reich Minister of Justice to grant amnesties to Poles and Jews sentenced to death. In view of the peculiar criminal and political situation in Upper Silesia, which is marked by the growing Polish resistance movement, such delays - especially in war-time - are intolerable.

223

"I therefore request you to take steps to
have transferred to me the power of grant-
ing amnesties - at least for the duration
of the war - to Poles and Jews within the
province of Upper Silesia who have been
legally sentenced to death.

"I should like to point out especially that
according to an article in the periodical
'Deutsches Recht', 1941, (p. 2472), the
Gauleiter and Reichsstatthalter in the
Reichsgau Wartheland has already been
granted similar powers." (Exh. 1581,
NG-128, Bk. 77, p. 92).

A number of documents prove that LAMMERS was also implicated
in the legislation which secured the "success" of the decree of
4 December 1941 by delegating the clemency right to the local Gauleiters in the incorporated territories. (Exh. 1578, NG-137, Bk.
77, p. 86; Exh. 1580, NG-129, Bk. 77, p. 90; and, Exh. 1839, NG-
126, Bk. 74, p. 29).

224

3. THE "FINAL SOLUTION OF THE JEWISH PROBLEM"

In the fall of 1941, some months prior to the conferences of the State Secretaries at which the representatives of the governing agencies of the Third Reich - including the Reich Chancellery - shaped the policy of extermination of Jews and confronted the half-Jews with the alternative of sterilization or deportation to concentration camps in the East, LAMMERS discussed with Dr. Gross, from the NSDAP Racial Political Office, for one and one-half hours the racial and biological aspects of the Jewish problem. Dr. Gross emphasized the necessity to sterilize half-Jews and to maintain some kind of clear distinction between one-quarter-Jews and Germans. "Reich Minister LAMMERS gave ear to both ideas and declared himself positively in favor of the proposal to sterilize persons of mixed blood of the first degree...". LAMMERS further stated that:

> "...It was possible that the Fuehrer might be
> willing to introduce some statutory settlement
> while the war was still on. He, Lammers,
> would welcome such a measure, as it seemed not
> to the purpose to go on working through many
> long years on the lines of former practice, if
> future development should follow the lines in-
> herent in the new proposals. He would there-
> fore even if the Fuehrer were to postpone the
> statutory settlement for the time being, in
> any case have the principles of the new direc-
> tive proclaimed and would then consider it
> correct for the practice of the administration
> and handling of mixed race questions to be
> settled even now in accordance with the mean-
> ing of the new directive, independently of
> when the statutory regulation should even-
> tually be made." (Exh. 1542, NG-978, Bk. 76,
> pp. 152/53).

In cross-examination LAMMERS appeared to have adopted a consider-ably more liberal approach to the racial problem:

> "Q. Tell me, is it correct to say that the
> national socialist regime was in the first
> line against foreign Jews, then against Ger-
> man Jews, and then half-Jews, and then
> quarter-Jews - who still had a certain
> vlue, is that correct in this sequence?
>
> "A. Well, I heard of people who stood up
> for this sequence, but I can't say more
> than that. It was certainly not set up
> officially." (tr.p. 22626).

On 20 January 1942 the infamous Wannsee Conference took place
at which the State Secretaries or representatives of the Ministers
concerned attended. According to the official minutes of this conference, "the following persons took part in the discussion about
the final solution of the Jewish question":

> The State Secretaries of the Reich Ministry of the In-
> terior (the defendant Stuckart), the Reich Ministry of
> Justice, an Under-Secretary of the Foreign Office, a
> State Secretary of the Plenipotentiary General for the
> Four Year Plan, representatives of the Reich Ministry
> for the Occupied Eastern Territories, of the Office of
> Government General, of the Party Chancellery, and Mini-
> sterial Director Kritzinger for the Reich Chancellery;
> further participants were the Commanders of the Secur-
> ity Police and the SD in the Government General and of
> the Reich Commissariate "Eastland", SS Gruppenfuehrer
> Hoffmann for the SS Race and Settlement Main Office,
> and SS Gruppenfuehrer Mueller and SS Obersturmbann-
> fuehrer Eichmann for the RSHA. (Emphasis provided).

It was the same Eichmann whose name the Opinion of the International
Military Tribunal mentioned in the following context:

> "In the summer of 1941, however, plans were
> made for the 'final solution' of the Jewish
> question in Europe. This 'final solution'
> meant the extermination of the Jews, which
> early in 1939 had threatened would be one
> of the consequences of an outbreak of war
> and a special section in the Gestapo under
> Adolf Eichmann, as head of Section B-4, of
> the Gestapo, was formed to carry out the
> policy." (Trial of Major War Criminals,
> Vol. I, p. 250).

The agenda of the conference of 20 January 1942 was a gruesome
one: to formulate the policy and to establish the techniques of
the program for the extermination of all European Jews.

At the beginning of the discussion, SS Obergruppenfuehrer
Heydrich said that "this discussion had been called for the purpose

of clarifying fundamental questions" and that:

> "The wish of the Reichsmarshall (Goering) to
> have a draft sent to him concerning organi-
> zational, factual and material interests in
> relation to the final solution of the Jewish
> people in Europe, makes necessary an initial
> common action of all Central Offices immedi-
> ately concerned with these questions in order
> to bring their general activities into line."
> (Exh. 1544, NG-2586, Bk. 76, p. 157).

Then he was looking back to things accomplished and pointed out

that, in spite of many difficulties, 537,000 Jews had been sent

out of the country, between the days of the seizure of power and

the deadline on 31 October 1941, 36,000 of them from Germany pro-

per, 147,000 from Austria, and 30,000 from the Protectorate of

Bohemia and Moravia. (Ibid, p. 159). He concluded with this

observation:

> "In the meantime the Reich Fuehrer SS and Chief
> of the German Police had prohibited emigration
> of Jews for reasons of the dangers of an emi-
> gration during war-time and consideration of
> the possibilities in the East." (Ibid, p. 160).

In the second part of his introductory observations (Ibid, pp. 160-

64), Heydrich was looking forward to things to be achieved:

> "Another possible solution of the problem has
> now taken the place of emigration, i.e. the
> evacuation of the Jews to the East, the Fueh-
> rer having agreed to this plan." (Ibid, p.
> 160).*

He went on to point out that approximately eleven million Jews

would be involved in the final solution of the European problem

and acquainted his confederates with the underlying statistical

data. (Ibid, p. 161). And, thereafter, he became most explicit

as to the methods and objectives of the scheme for genocide in

preparation:

> "Under proper guidance the Jews are now to
> be allocated for labor to the East in the
> course of the final solution. Able-bodied
> Jews will be taken in large labor columns
> to these districts for work on roads, sep-
> arated according to sexes, in the course
> of which action a great part will undoubtedly
> be eliminated by natural causes.

- - - -

* Translation on page 160 of document book 76 should be changed
  to read: "...the Fuehrer having agreed to this plan".

227

"The possible final remnant will, as it must
undoubtedly consist of the toughest, have to
be treated accordingly, as it is the product
of natural selection, and would, if liberated,
act as a bud cell of a Jewish reconstruction
(see historical experience)." (Ibid, pp.
162/63).

From this moment on each of the attendants plainly knew that
the final solution of the Jewish problem meant genocide and extermination. None of those present declined his cooperation in
a scheme so shocking and revolting. On the contrary. There was
perfect harmony and they proceeded after Heydrich's introduction
to discuss the circle of those who were to be marked down for
extermination. There was already some material on hand on which
this discussion could be based:

"The chief of the Security Police and the SD
first discussed, with reference to a letter
from the Chief of the Reich Chancellory, the
following points theoretically...." (Ibid,
p. 165).

228 The items discussed and a compilation thereof can be found on
pages 165 to 171 and 249 to 253 of document NG-2486 in document
book 76. In short, the following outline of the scheme was
shaped: so-called full Jews were eligible without exception
for the "final solution". Half-Jews were to receive in principal the same treatment except those who, after having undergone
sterilization, were to be permitted to stay in the Reich.
Quarter-Jews were to be treated as persons of German blood save
certain categories who were to be equally subject to the "final
solution".

Heydrich adjourned the conference "with the request to the
persons present...that they render him appropriate assistance
in the carrying out of the tasks involved in the solution".
(Ibid, p. 170).

The program of the "final solution" was elaborated and further
developed in another inter-departmental conference on 6 March 1942.

Referat IV B 4 of the RSHA (Eichmann's Department) acted as host

(Ibid, p. 195) and Dr. Boley represented the Reich Chancellery.

The top secret minutes of this conference (the document in evi-

dence on pages 195-204 being the third out of a total of 20 copies)

states .that:

> "There existed also unanimity on the necessity
> of not making any exceptions among the persons
> of mixed blood (first degree)." (Ibid, p. 197).

That the representative of the Reich Chancellery was not a mere

"listening post", as LAMMERS claimed in his testimony (tr.p. 21602),

appears from the following part of the records:

> "1. According to information given by the repre-
> sentative of the Reich Chancellery, one of the
> very highest authorities expressed the opinion,
> in connection with the discussion on the ques-
> tion of persons of mixed blood in the Wehrmacht,
> that it would be necessary to divide up the per-
> sons of mixed blood into Jews and Germans, and
> that it was unwarrantable under all circumstances
> to have the persons of mixed blood permanently
> existing as a third small race. This require-
> ment would not be met by the means of sterili-
> zing all persons of mixed blood and permitting
> them to remain in the Reich territory.

> "2. The examination of every individual of
> mixed blood which was suggested by the working
> group (Arbeitskreis) and which, by the way, is
> also considered necessary by the highest author-
> ities, according to information given by the
> representative of the Reich Chancellery, would
> only require administrative expenditure for one
> isolated process. The selection would be facil-
> itated by the numerous records already in exist-
> ence concerning the individual person of mixed
> blood. When the selection had been carried
> through, however, only a relatively small part
> of the persons of mixed blood would remain in
> the Reich, and for these the restrictions would
> not have to be maintained. This procedure, con-
> trary to the suggestion of a uniform general
> sterilization, would make all future administra-
> tive work unnecessary. The only matter which
> might have to be dealt with would be the volun-
> tary sterilization of the remaining persons of
> mixed blood in return for the act of clemency
> permitting them to stay in the Reich." (Ibid,
> pp. 200/01, emphasis provided).

The minutes concluded by stating:

> "The above result of the conference is to be
> submitted to the agencies concerned, and they
> are to give their final opinion on it within
> two weeks.

229

"When they have pronounced their opinion, a
further conference, if necessary, will take
place at the Reich Security Main Office, in
order to determine the final formulation."
(Ibid, p. 204).

On 12 March 1942 Dr. Schlegelberger, the acting Reich Minister of

Justice, wrote to LAMMERS:

"I am just being informed by my advisor about
the result of the meeting of March 6 regarding the treatment of Jews and descendants of
mixed marriages. I am now expecting the official transcript. According to the report
of my advisor, decisions seem to be underway
which I am constrained to consider absolutely
impossible for the most part. Since the result of these discussions are to constitute
the basis for the decision of the Fuehrer,
and since one of the advisors from your
Ministry participated likewise in these discussions, I urgently desire to discuss this
matter with you on time. As soon as I have
received the transcript of the meeting, I
shall take the liberty in calling you to
ask you if and when a discussion may take
place." (Exh. 1545, 4055-PS, Bk. 76, p. 275).

Dr. Schlegelberger's objections were merely directed against some

technicalities of comparatively minor importance concerning the

treatment of quarter-Jews. (Ibid, pp. 276-78). The discussions

of the prepared measures against half-Jews were being conducted

after this conference between the Ministry of the Interior and

Himmler, and LAMMERS was kept informed on the developments.

(Exh. 1545, NG-2982, Bk. 76, p. 287).

On 27 October 1942 a third conference concerning the final

solution of the Jewish problem took place in Eichmann's division

in the RSHA and he again attended in person. (Ibid, p. 213).

The secret minutes of the conference show that the Reich Chan-

cellery was again represented by Dr. Boley. The scheme of

elegibility for the "final solution" was completed at this oc-

casion and the result of the conference can be found on pages

216 to 220 of document book 76. There it is stated, among other

things, that:

"When giving this choice, it serves a better
purpose to depict deportation as the more
severe measure in comparison to sterilization.

"Thus, the aim should be that in the few cases where an exception - though generally not provided for - has to be made, the possibility of compulsory sterilization should still exist. For this reason sterilization is to be considered a gracious favor, which will be recognized as such and obtain the required results to the effect that the number of applications for release from those prescribed measures is likely not to be very large. As it can be assumed that almost all persons of mixed blood of the first degree will decide on the lesser evil of sterilization, the choice for the required sterilization stands out clearly as a primary feature." (Exh. 1544, NG-2586, Supra, pp. 216/17).

Abstaining from further argument on the question of sterilization of half-Jews, we quote the words in which another judicial finding commented on LAMMERS' part in the scheme of the program of sterilization:

"He (LAMMERS) testified further that the half-Jews were not subject to any compulsion. He was apparently of the opinion that a person was a free agent if he had a choice between sterilization and deportation to a concentration camp." (Tribunal III, Case III, Opinion and Judgment, tr.p. 10777).

231

The formulation of the extermination program coincided with the launching of a propaganda drive for the spiritual indoctrination of the NSDAP with the issues involved. On 5 July 1942 LAMMERS circulated to the highest Reich authorities and other offices which were directly subordinate to Hitler, a Fuehrer order entrusting Reichsleiter Rosenberg with the supervision of:

"...the total spiritual and philosophical indoctrination and education of the NSDAP in the spiritual battle against Jews and free Masons as well as against the affiliated philosophical opponents of national socialism who are the cause of the present war." (Exh. 1546, 154-PS, Bk. 76, p. 279).

In conclusion of this letter, LAMMERS said:

"I inform you of this order of the Fuehrer and request you to support Reichsleiter Rosenberg in the fulfillment of his task." (Ibid).

For further evidence showing LAMMERS' knowledge of and connection with the racial discrimination and persecution, see Exh.

1537, NG-2620, Bk. 76, p. 104; Exh. 1552, NG-1292, Bk. 76, p. 332 (initialled by him); Exh. 1555, NG-1063, Bk. 76, p. 355; and, Exh. 1556, NG-998, Bk. 76, p. 357.

The following findings of fact of the International Military Tribunal will show that the extermination program, as conceived by its spiritual authors and legislators, was strictly adhered to and ruthlessly carried out:

> "Adolf Eichmann, who had been put in charge of this program by Hitler, has estimated that the policy pursued resulted in the killing of 6 million Jews, of which 4 million were killed in the extermination institutions." (Trial of Major War Criminals, Vol. I, pp. 252/53).

LAMMERS testified with regard to the conference of 20 January 1942:

> "If at all, Kritzinger gave me only a very short and snappy report, lasting perhaps one or two minutes about that conference. At that time I wasn't in Berlin at all. He didn't tell me anything about the killings of Jews. He wouldn't have undertaken to tell me that any way. He would have told it to the expert Ficker instead..." (tr.p. 22629).

He supplemented his story by stating that:

> "I am sure that he (Kritzinger) was invited to the conference without my knowledge; he attended it without getting instructions from me, (which I could not give him) and I am convinced that he will not have made any statements on my behalf." (tr.p. 21602).

The blame is thus shuttled on a subordinate official who, today, is dead. LAMMERS would make this Tribunal believe that Kritzinger attended a top secret policy making conference between the highest Reich authorities without authorization and without knowledge of his superior Minister and that he even refrained afterwards from reporting to him on the abhorent decisions arrived at, lest LAMMERS' feelings of decency and humanity be shocked. Such a statement constitutes not only a chain of utter impossibilities; it is blatantly contradicted by numerous authentic documents in evidence which reduce it to what it is: a fabricated self-saving statement. We submit that it is established by the foregoing evidence that LAMMERS, as member of the immediate circle, had knowledge of the extermination program even before the conference of 20 January 1942 and that he was, in theory and practice, a willing and zealous participant in the scheme of racial persecution and extermination. The voluminous documentary evidence is barren even of a vestige of proof that he ever used his influential position to press for primitive human decency.

LAMMERS also stated that he improved the status of half-Jews. (tr.p. 22629). The documentary evidence proves the very opposite of his contention. Thus, for example, on 20 July 1942 he requested the Supreme Reich authorities to take further action in conformity with the Fuehrer's wish that only such persons of mixed descent be put on equal footing with aryans who had rendered special services to the national socialist regime. (Exh. 3903, NG-4819, Bk. 211 B, p. 54).

233

4. THE 13th REGULATION UNDER THE REICH CITIZENSHIP LAW *

In August 1942 the question of restricting legal rights for
Jews in criminal cases came up. Between 3 August and 21 August
1942 joint preparations for such a legislation were well under
way - the Reich Chancellery, the Party Chancellery, the Ministry
of the Interior, the Ministry for Public Enlightenment and Propaganda, and the Foreign Office participating therein. (Exh. 1551,
NG-151, Bk. 76, pp. 301-311). By 21 August 1942 two drafts were
compiled by the Ministry of Interior and the Ministry for Propaganda and LAMMERS forwarded them to the Plenipotentiary General
for the Administration of the Reich with the following suggestion:

> "I may leave it to you as Plenipotentiary Gen-
> eral for the Administration of the Reich to
> see to it that the different drafts be coor-
> dinated and that the decree be submitted to
> the Ministerial Council for the Defense of
> the Reich. I sent a copy of this letter to
> the President of the Ministerial Council for
> the Defense of the Reich, the Reich Minister
> of Justice and the Reich Minister for Public
> Enlightenment and Propaganda." (Ibid, p. 311).

LAMMERS testified that he had to do this "in order to get things
coordinated". (tr.p. 22605). On 18 September 1942 a conference
was held among Thierack, Himmler, Bormann, and others. Thierack's
notes of the conference disclose that the subjects of discussion
included "special treatment" at the hand of the Police in cases
where judicial sentences were not severe enough. Among other
points agreed upon were the following:

> "The Reich Minister of Justice will decide
> whether and when special treatment at the
> hands of the Police is to be applied...

> "The delivery of anti-social elements from
> the execution of their sentences to the
> Reichsfuehrer of the SS to be worked to
> death... It is agreed that in consider-
> ation of the intended aims of the govern-
> ment for clearing up of the Eastern pro-
> blems, in future Jews, Poles, Gypsies,
> Russians and Ukrainians are no longer to
> be judged by the ordinary courts, so far

- - - -

* This ordinance was held to be illegal by Tribunal III in Case
III against the leading officials of the Ministry of Justice.
It was extensively discussed in its Opinion on pages 10666/667
763/764/768 and we are referring to these pertinent sections
for judicial notice.

234

as punishable offenses are concerned but are
to be dealt with by the Reichsfuehrer SS..."
(Exh. 1591, 654-PS, Bk. 77, p. 157).

Thierack's pencil note to paragraph one on the first page of the

photostatic copy states:

"Dr. Lammers informed." (Ibid; tr.p. 21784).

Three different versions of LAMMERS' testimony on the sub-

ject of his knowledge of this agreement are available in the record:

(a) "A. As I know now only after the serving
of the indictment and having seen the
documents, the new Minister of Justice,
shortly after his taking office, reached
a definite agreement with Himmler according to which criminal procédure a-.
gainst Poles and Jews was to be removed
from regular judicial procedure and was
to be taken care of by the police, but
the documents here show with respect to
me that apparently quite deliberately I
was not allowed to participate in this,
but that it had been kept secret from
me." (tr.p. 21783).

(b) "...but I can only remark with respect to
that, that I was not informed that this
discussion had taken place by the Reich
Minister of Justice nor by any ministries
involved, but only by my specialist
Reichskabinettsrat Dr. Ficker who reported to me on the fact that the discussion took place, without entering into the contents of that discussion in
any way; and, this document is in my
document book as NG-059, with Lammers'
Exhibit No. 24; Book III, page 6."
(tr.pp. 21784/85).

(c) "Q. You were aware of the agreement between Thierack and Himmler to turn Jews
over to the Police.

"A. I myself did not receive this agreement. The notes made by Thierack never
came to me. However in the fall of 1942
he applied to have the matter regulated
on the basis of a justice reform decree
of 20 August 1942. I refused. On that
occasion he mentioned an agreement with
Himmler. So in the fall I did learn
that something of the kind was pending
and he attached importance to having a
legal foundation for it." (tr.p. 22606).

On 29 September 1942 Frick notified the ministers concerned,

including the Reich Chancellery, that:

235

"On the basis of a discussion on 25 September
1942 between the officials in charge, a new
draft of an ordinance concerning the restrictions imposed on Jews in the proceedings before the administrative agencies or courts
has been drawn up under the title of 'Ordinance concerning Legal Restrictions to be imposed on Jews'. Please let me know as soon
as possible your opinion about the enclosed
new formulation.

"If no reply has been received by 14 October
your consent will be taken for granted."
(Exh. 1551, NG-151, Supra, p. 315).

On 13 October 1942 the Reich Minister of Justice wrote to Reichs-

leiter Bormann, in part, as follows:

"With a view to freeing the German people of
Poles, Russians, Jews and Gypsies and with
a view to making the Eastern territories
which have been incorporated into the Reich
available for settlement for German nationals,
I intend to turn over criminal proceedings
against Poles, Russians, Jews and Gypsies to
the Reichsfuehrer SS. In so doing I base myself on the principle that the administration
of justice can only make a small contribution
to the extermination of members of these peoples. The Justice Administration undoubtedly
pronounces very severe sentences on such persons, but that is not enough to constitute
any material contribution towards the realization of the above-mentioned aim...

"The Reichsfuehrer SS, with whom I discussed
these views, agrees with them. I also informed Herr Dr. Lammers.

"I submit this matter to you, requesting you
to let me know whether the Fuehrer approves
this view. If so, I would make my official
recommendations through Reich Minister Dr.
Lammers." (Exh. 1553, NG-558, Bk. 76, pp.
337/38).

About one month later Thierack contacted Bormann again concerning

"the handing over of criminal prosecution of Poles, Soviet Russians,

Jews and Gypsies". (Exh. 1586, NG-2927, Bk. 77, p. 137). A copy

of this letter was forwarded to LAMMERS (Ibid, p. 141) and received

by him as it appears from the file number "RK (Reich Chancellery)

11579B". (Ibid, p. 139). Thierack pointed out that the Gauleiters

of the incorporated territories and other authorities had objected

to the turning over of Poles to the Police for criminal prosecution,

chiefly on political grounds in order to avoid antagonizing the

236

Polish population. Then he went on to state:

> "In view of this attitude I think we should
> abstain from further steps in this matter,
> as far as the Poles and Russians are con-
> cerned, until the intended conference of
> the Gauleiter with the Fuehrer has taken
> place. However, there is no objection to
> handing over the criminal prosecution as
> far as Jews and gypsies are concerned, un-
> til the intended conference of the Gau-
> leiter with the Fuehrer has taken place."
> (Ibid, p. 140).

In the following months LAMMERS was continually kept informed of

developments in this matter. On 27 February 1943 one of his of-

ficials submitted to him the following report:

> "...a) Jews have, in future, to be prose-
> cuted exclusively by the Police. The ap-
> propriate provisions will be a part of the
> decree prohibiting Jews from appearing in
> court. With respect to this decree, dif-
> ficulties are caused by the suggestion
> that the heritage of all Jews should de-
> volve on the Reich. The decree is being
> prepared by the GBV (Delegate General in
> charge of Administration).
>
> "b) Poles are to be prosecuted by the courts,
> as before. The Reichsfuehrer SS is said to
> have agreed. Uniform criminal law for Poles:
> Crimes Ordinance for Poles.
>
> "c) The prosecution of Russians is still be-
> ing discussed. At present offenses of
> workers, coming from Soviet territory --
> with the exception of the Baltic countries
> -- in the Reich are punished, almost exclu-
> sively, by the Police. The Ministry for
> Eastern questions, the G.B.A. (Delegate
> General for supply of labor) and the Min-
> ister of Justice consider this as undesir-
> able, particularly with regard to the un-
> desirable arrival of further labor.
>
> "d) According to information given by the
> Party Chancellery, the Gypsies question
> has, first, to be clarified to a larger
> extent. Recent investigations have shown
> -- so it is said -- that there are racially
> valuable elements also among the Gypsies."
> (Exh. 3899, NG-2926, Bk. 211 B, p. 30).

This memorandum is initialled by LAMMERS and his closest co-con-

spirators, his subordinates - Willuhn, Killy, von Stutterheim,

Ficker, and Kritzinger - all of whom, except the late Kritzinger,

appeared before this Tribunal as Defense witnesses for LAMMERS.

237

On 3 April 1943 the Plenipotentiary General for Reich Administration forwarded to LAMMERS, "with reference to today's conference between Secretary of State Kritzinger and Secretary of State Stuckart", the drafts for an Ordinance concerning the Legal Restrictions to be imposed on the Jews and the copy of a letter from Kaltenbrunner dated 8 March 1943. (Exh. 1551, NG-151, Supra, pp. 319/21). Kaltenbrunner urged immediate passage of the proposed ordinance giving the following reasons:

> "1. Previous evacuations of Jews have been restricted to Jews who were not married to non-Jews. In consequence, the number of Jews who have remained in the interior is quite considerable. As the ordinance would also include these Jews as well, the measures it plans are not objectless.

> "2. The provisions of Article 7 of the ordinance according to which, at the death of a Jew, his fortune escheats in its entirety to the Reich, results in the accumulation of considerably less work for the state police. At the present time the procedure used by the state police in handling the confiscation of such Jewish inheritances must frequently be modified to suit each special case..." (Ibid, p. 320).

A further development is apparent from a file note prepared by State Secretary Kritzinger:

> "...On 5 April I discussed the affair with Secretary of State Klopfer. The latter is of the same opinion as myself, that with the exception, perhaps, of Articles 6 and 7 of the draft, the ordinance can be dispensed with. As regards Article 7 of the draft, Secretary of State Klopfer took my point of view that the possibility must be considered of directing the heritage of deceased Jews either in part or in its totality to their non-Jewish relatives.

> "The Reich Minister, to whom I reported on 6 April, is of the opinion that we should repair as far as possible from any settlement of the matter by an ordinance.

> "In order to help on the affair I came to an agreement with Secretary of State Klopfer and suggested to Secretary of State Stuckart that the question of the further consideration of the draft should be raised at a discussion in which, in addition to myself and him, Secretary of State Klopfer and Secretary of State Rothenberger and the Chief of the Security Police Kaltenbrunner should take part.

"Secretary of State Stuckart agreed to this
and suggested that the conference should
take place on Wednesday, 14 April, 11
o'clock." (Ibid, pp. 322/23).

On 21 April 1943 a memorandum for the files of the Reich Chancellery reports a conference of State Secretaries - suggested by
Kritzinger - on the proposed ordinance, at which Kritzinger, as
representative of the Reich Chancellery, was present. The conference came to the conclusion that certain modifications should
be made, and Kritzinger's file note says that "the regulation
would accordingly approximately take the form as shown in Appendix II". (Ibid, p. 324). This Appendix can be found on
page 325 of document book 76 and it contains the final draft
for the ordinance as formulated in the meeting of the State
Secretaries on 21 April 1943. (Ibid, p. 325). This draft was
almost completely and literally embodied into the final regulation which was promulgated under the date of 1 July 1943 and
provides:

"Article 1: (1) Criminal actions committed
by Jews shall be punished by the Police.

"(2) The provision of the Polish penal laws
of 4 December 41 (RGBl. I, p. 759) shall no
longer apply to Jews.

"Article 2: (1) The property of a Jew shall
be confiscated by the Reich after his death...

"Article 3: The Reich Minister of the Interior
with the concurrence of the participating high
authorities of the Reich shall issue the legal
and administrative provisions for the administration and enforcement of this regulation.
In doing so he shall determine to what extent
the provisions shall apply to Jewish nationals
of foreign countries."

By Article 4 it was provided that in the Protectorate of
Bohemia and Moravia the regulation shall apply where German
administration and German courts have jurisdiction. (Exh.
2456, 1422-PS, Bk. 75, p. 189). Tribunal III characterized
this decree in its Opinion in the following terms:

"There was promulgated a 13th regulation under
the Reich Citizenship Law which illustrates

the increasing severity by means of which the
government was attempting to reach a 'solution
of the Jewish problem' under the impulsion of
the progressively adverse military situation..."
(U.S. vs. Joseph Altstoetter, et al, tr.p.
10666).

LAMMERS' contention that the draft contained in document NG-151,

Book 76, page 325, is not identical with the decisions arrived

at at the meeting of the State Secretaries on 21 April, but

"some preliminary draft pending somewhere or other which you

are trying to connect up here". (tr.p. 22615) is belied by

the following facts:

(a) The photostatic copy of Kritzinger's memorandum of 21

April 1943 shows at the bottom on the left side a note, "Anl..

II" (Enc. II) in Kritzinger's handwriting. The cross reference,

"Anl. II" (Enc. II), appears again in Kritzinger's handwriting

on the attachment. (Exh. 1551, NG-151, Supra, pp. 324/25; tr.

p. 22611).

(b) Kritzinger's memorandum states that it was considered

suitable to have the regulation issued as a supplementary ordi-

nance to the Reich Citizenship Law and that the regulations

would take approximately the form as shown in Appendix II. Ac-

cordingly, on the top of the enclosure, a note can be found in

Kritzinger's handwriting: "12th ordinance for the Reich Citi-

zenship Law". (Ibid; tr.p. 22611).

(c) Originally it was intended, at that time (April 1943),

to promulgate the regulation as the 12th ordinance of the Reich

Citizenship Law. It was eventually promulgated on 1 July 1943

as the 13th ordinance, the reason being that an intervening

ordinance had meanwhile been issued as the 12th ordinance re-

lating to a different topic. (tr.pp. 22613/614; RGBl, 1943, I,

p. 286).

(d) In paragraph 2 of Kritzinger's memorandum, it is pointed

out that Article 7 (of Stuckart's draft of April 3; see p. 322,

Ibid) is to be supplemented by a regulation in the case of

240

confiscation of property, "a settlement in favor of non-Jewish heirs and legal dependents". (Ibid, p. 324). Again Article 2 of the enclosed draft contains the corresponding reference in Kritzinger's handwriting: "I would include the clause in favor of non-Jewish heirs and legal dependents". (Photostatic copy of Exh. 1551, NG-151, Supra, tr.p. 22613).

(e) Kritzinger's supplement to paragraph 2 of the draft was incorporated into the final ordinance. (Exh. 2456, 1422-PS, Supra).

(f) At the bottom right hand corner of Kritzinger's memorandum (photostatic copy of Exh. 1551, NG-151, Supra, p. 324) appears a note signed by Ficker to the effect that "OKR (Oberkriegsgerichtsrat) Feldscher is going to send the draft".

(g) Kritzinger's memorandum and its attachment form part of the official files of the Reich Chancellery. Their consecutive numbering (numbers in pencil 1508/11 and 1508/12 on top and 344549, 344550 at the bottom of each page) show, to say the least, that they were found next to each other in the files of the Reich Chancellery.

241

M I L I T A R Y   T R I B U N A L   I V

CASE NO. 11

THE UNITED STATES OF AMERICA

V.

ERNST VON WEIZSAECKER, et al.

FINAL BRIEF ON THE

CRIMINAL RESPONSIBILITY

OF

KARL RITTER

UNDER COUNT V (PERSECUTION OF JEWS)

Nurnberg

2 November 1948

Doc. 11

242

BY: Max Mandellaub
      Trial Attorney

      and

      Robert M. W. Kempner
      Director, Political
      Ministries Division

FOR: Telford Taylor
      Brigadier General, USA
      Chief of Counsel for
      War Crimes

OF COUNSEL:

      Jane Lester

TABLE OF CONTENTS

Errata Sheet inserted after this page.

243

<u>ERRATA SHEET</u>

CASE NO. XI – – Ministries Case

Please make the following correction in the Prosecution brief
entitled "FINAL BRIEF ON THE CRIMINAL RESPONSIBILITY OF KARL RITTER
UNDER COUNT V (PERSECUTION OF JEWS)":

Page 12, Line 1: (Pros.Ex.1714, NG–3354, Doc.Bk.61)

244

I. THE CHARGES UNDER COUNT V

The defendant Karl RITTER is charged under Count V of the Indictment
with the commission of War Crimes and Crimes against Humanity as defined
in Control Council Law No. 10, in that he participated in atrocities and
offenses including murder, extermination and enslavement, deportation,
imprisonment, killing of hostages, torture, persecution on political,
racial and religious grounds and other inhumane and criminal acts against
German nationals and members of the civilian populations of countries and
territories under the belligerent occupation of or otherwise controlled
by Germany.

II. POSITION OF RESPONSIBILITY AS REGARDS COUNT V

The career and positions of responsibility of the defendant RITTER
are covered in the trial brief against RITTER dealing with the charges
under Counts I and II of the Indictment.

For the purpose of analysing RITTER's criminal activities under
Count V, it is only necessary to bear in mind that, during the period
from 1941 to 1945, when the murder program for the liquidation of millions
of European Jews was developed and enforced, RITTER was the Chief of the
liaison office between the Foreign Office of Ribbentrop and his State
Secretaries von Weizsaecker and von Steengracht on the one side, and the
OKW of Keitel and Jodl on the other side. In this influential position,
the defendant RITTER played his part in the "final solution" because the
liquidation of the Jews was part of the total war program of the Third
Reich (see IMT Judgment, Vol. I, p. 249).

This program had necessarily to be enforced in closest collaboration
with the military leaders, in accordance with the logistic possibilities
permitted by the war, such as suitable areas for the killings, available
transport facilities, available manpower for execution of the program, etc.
The intimate connection of the murder of Jewry with the German fortunes
of war is again established in Exhibit 1452 (Pros. Doc. Bk. 59), where it
is pointed out that after Germany had conquered Eastern areas

> "The emigration program has now been replaced
> by the evacuation of the Jews to the East."
> (p. 88).

The document shows also that Europe should be

"combed through from the West to the East."
(p. 191 of the same document)

This shows the connection of the liquidation program with the military situation of that time, namely the winter of 1941 to 1942: France, Belgium, the Netherlands were under the German heel. Thus, the plan of deportations could be carried out in the West without any difficulties. In the South East a certain caution had to be observed in order not to endanger there a complete line-up of the satellite states against Russia. On the other hand, the Eastern territories, especially Poland, lay numb and prostrate. It was there that this ignominy against the human race could be perpetrated without restraint. There the gas chambers could be built and the victims could be driven to their death.

On account of the close inter-relation between the strategy of war and the strategy of killing the Jews, the name of the defendant RITTER recurs again, again and again in the files of the Final Solution. When problems of strategy in both fields had to be ironed out, the forceful personality of the defendant RITTER, the liaison chief between the Foreign Office and the OKW, smoothed the way with energy and dexterity.

246

III. RITTER'S FAMILIARITY WITH THE MURDER PLAN AGAINST THE JEWS

From the beginning of the Third Reich RITTER, who had many personal Jewish friends and connections, was well aware of the anti-Jewish measures of his regime.

He admitted in his direct examination

> "When I returned from Brazil (in 1938) and noticed that in the meantime the Jewish policy had become more severe, a number of my acquaintances, Jewish acquaintances—and I had many Jewish friends—about whom I asked when I came back from Brazil, were no longer there and in private circles I naturally asked about them and heard that some had emigrated, others had been sent to concentration camps, without being able to find out where they had been sent and what they were doing there. In private conversation, of course, I saw that a most regrettable deterioration in the Jewish situation had taken place, but officially I never heard anything about these matters and didn't have anything to do with them. With the word 'officially' I mean to express that I had general unofficial information. I didn't go through the world blindly. I saw things had changed but I never saw a document about these things." (Trans. p. 12200)

In his cross-examination, he said:

> "Q. Did you have any doubt as to whether, if anyone from among your Jewish friends disappeared in the Gestapo Headquarters, you would ever see him again?
>
> A. I did not say that I knew that they had disappeared in the Gestapo Headquarters. I just knew that they were no longer around. Some had emigrated and some were no longer accessible. I don't know where they were." (Trans. p. 12464)

If RITTER did not know where they were, he must have learned it sometime later because his close friend, associate, and defense witness, Wilhelm Mackeben stated under cross-examination,

> "It is, of course, natural that we talked also about Jewish questions during these conversations as it moved us considerably."

* * *

> "Q. ... First, when you were in the Field headquarters near the Russian border when did you hear for the first time there that Russians, Poles and Jews were being killed by the Einsatzgruppen?
>
> A. It's of course impossible to give you a date.
>
> Q. Approximately?
>
> A. I think for the first time I heard it approximately in the middle of 1942.

-3-

Q. Did you read the reports about these killings?

A. Yes, one or the other V.A.A. (Representatives of the Foreign Office with the army-groups) reports I did read.

Q. When you discussed this with RITTER, what did he say to you? What was his attitude toward these things?

A. What we read there, of course, was repulsive and despicable to any decent human being and both of us opposed and rejected it.

Q. Did he ever say that it was atrocious or horrible?

A. I think I can answer that in the affirmative."
(Trial Tr. p. 11738)

In addition to the specific knowledge on the part of RITTER, about the terrible fate of the Jews, he had to be and was familiar with the public pronunciamentos of his Fuehrer Adolf Hitler about the liquidation of the Jews repeated over and over again in the German Reichstag, and broadcast to Germany and the world. On January 30, 1939, Hitler made the dread proclamation that if another war came to Europe the Jews would be liquidated. In his speeches of January 30, 1942, September 30, 1942, and February 24, 1943, he solemnly warned, after war had come, that:

"their laughing is going to come to an end everywhere, and I am going to be right also with these prophecies",

and

"this war will find its end with the annihilation of Jewry in Europe." (Ex. 3906, Doc. Bk. 211)

Hitler's publicly made pronunciamentos, whose correctness the defendant RITTER could check against his own manifold experience in connection with the annihilation of the Jews, amply attest to his full knowledge.

IV. RITTER'S PARTICIPATION IN THE EXECUTION OF THE ANNIHILATION PROGRAM

The establishment, development, and enforcement of the "Final Solution" of the Jewish question under the co-auspices of the German Foreign Office is described in the trial brief against the defendant Weizsaecker, as charged under Count V of the Indictment. Said trial brief should be regarded as part of this trial brief. However, the proof for RITTER's individual responsibility will be set forth in this brief.

RITTER participated in the execution of this program throughout his four years as chief of the liaison activities between the Foreign Office and the OKW. A number of outstanding examples in point will be detailed.

In September 1942, RITTER was occupied with coordinating the German military and political measures in Croatia, which was partly under German, partly under Italian influence. He himself describes his activities in an office memorandum of September 24, 1942 (Pros. Ex. 1717, Doc. Bk. 61, p. 34). In his memorandum, which was directed toward the implementation of the German policy in Croatia, the defendant RITTER took up the Jewish question. He points out what strong-armed strategy the German represent-ative in Croatia, Minister Kasche, should follow in the Jewish question (see p. 36 in Doc. Bk. 61, Ex. 1717). There, under VI, RITTER states:

> "VI. Up to now, the Croat legislation for Jews
> has only been introduced in the Northern part of
> Croatia. Introduction of this legislation in the
> Southern part of the country has been prevented
> by Italian opposition, although the Duche had ex-
> pressed his approval of the plan also for the
> Southern part. It is necessary that the
> legislation for Jews be also introduced in the
> Southern part of Croatia. The Poglavnik is
> willing to see this done."

The program developed by the defendant RITTER worked out so well that the German representative in Croatia, Minister Kasche, was only a few weeks later able to inform the defendant RITTER and the Foreign Office that the "measures for the evacuation of the Jews" were already underway. RITTER learned on the same occasion that the program was co-ordinated with the RSHA, the Reich Main Security Office alias Gestapo. Kasche also informed RITTER and his associates cynically that the Croat finance minister

> "declared himself willing to pay the German Reich
> thirty marks for each evacuated Jew."

So, RITTER was the recipient of information that the German Reich even
insisted on the financing of its own murderous activities by the small
satellite states (Pros. Ex. 1719, NG-2367, Doc. Bk. 61, p. 39).

RITTER was kept constantly informed about the execution of the
program developed and sponsored by him, and of the pressure which it
was necessary to exert against the obstructing Italian occupational
forces in Croatia, etc. This is proven by the fact that his name appears
on the distribution list of the following secret telegrams: Pros. Ex.
1720, NG-2814, Doc. Bk. 61, p. 40 et seq.; Pros. Ex. 1722, NG-2345, Doc.
Bk. 61, p. 46 et seq.; Pros. Ex. 1723, NG-2348, Doc. Bk. 61, p. 47.

One year later, in 1943, RITTER had again to coordinate military
and civilian measures for the persecution of the Jews. This time, the
Danish Jews were his victims, when the civilian forces complained that
they could not carry out the deportation without military help. RITTER,
when asked about the Danish Jews under cross-examination, had to admit
these activities.

> "Q. In 1943, did you have anything to do with having
> the Jews evacuated from Denmark?
>
> A. Have anything to do with having the Jews taken from
> Denmark? Certainly not. I had nothing to do with these
> things. I merely recall that at one time, in connection
> with the abrogation of the military emergency condition,
> about which I had to speak with Keitel, this same
> question was discussed and worked on by others, whether,
> during this time of the military emergency period, the
> Jews should be evacuated from Denmark or not.
>
> Q. Do you remember that you had to mediate between
> the military agencies who did not want to participate
> properly in this particular instance, in the West?
>
> A. I don't remember such a general activity of
> mediation but I remember one particular case . . . .
>
> Q. That is quite sufficient." (Trial Tr. p. 12466)

See also Prosecution Exhibit 1672, NG-4093, Doc. Bk. 60 B, p. 29, showing
the necessity of coordinating with the military authorities in these
deportations.

Again one year later, in the Spring of 1944, RITTER had to act
strongly in promoting and enforcing the annihilation program against

-6-

Jews; this time in Hungary.

In April 1944, RITTER was at the Foreign Office Headquarters at Salzburg and, in charge of supervising an coordinating the German extortionist policy against Hungary. The details of this action will be shown in a later chapter.

An important part of this policy was the pressure brought to bear on the Hungarian Government for the deportation of about eight to nine hundred thousand Jews in Hungary. At this late date, Jews still lived on there under the protection of the Hungarian Government in this remaining oasis in Nazi-controlled Europe. It was the defendant RITTER, who in this situation instructed the defendant Edmund Veesenmayer, the German Czar of Hungary, to make the necessary arrangements for the deportation of the Hungarian Jews. It was RITTER who ordered Veesenmayer:

> "In case of a further delay in the deportation,
> I suggest that you express clearly in your tele-
> graph report, that on your part everything
> possible and necessary had been done in order to
> carry out this operation as quickly as possible,
> (crossed out) that the deportation of the Jews
> who were ready for shipment was delayed by the
> fact that the authorities in charge of the de-
> portation and placement of the Jews did not make
> the necessary arrangements. signed RITTER."
> (Pros. Ex. 1812, NG-2196, Doc. Bk. 62 A, p. 94)

RITTER's order to Veesenmayer shows also his own cooperation with the RSHA (Reich Main Security Office, also known as Gestapo) in the whole scheme for the final solution. He himself refers in this cable to certain arrangements which were made with the Gestapo about putting the deportees into so-called "labor camps which are under the control of the Reichsfuehrer SS"---better known as extermination camps.

In country after country RITTER participated in the development of the anti-Jewish measures either by directing them, as in the above-mentioned instances, or by coordinatory and consenting activities. In order to keep au courant about the steps necessary to take, he also was constantly advised about the progress of the program. There is not one single instance where RITTER disagreed with the murderous policy, or refrained from concurring in the most brutal measures which were brought to his cognizance as background for whatever steps he might have to take.

251

The defendant RITTER took a consenting part in and was informed of the anti-Jewish measures in France, including the proposals of the German Ambassador in Paris, Otto Abetz, dated March 6, 1941, (Pros. Ex. 1694, NG-2432, Doc. Bk. 60 B, p. 142). The defendant RITTER received a copy of the report which informed the defendant Weizsaecker that the Military Commander of France was to arrest the Jews of various European nationalities living in France (Pros. Ex. 1695, NG-3264, Doc. Bk. 60 B, pp. 145-146). When so-called reprisal measures were undertaken against the Jews of France, including shooting of hostages, deportation and expropriation of Jews, the defendant RITTER received the proposals of the German Army in charge of some of these enterprises and passed the information on to the Reich Foreign Minister in Berlin in order to obtain the necessary authorization (Pros. Ex. 1696, NG-3571, Doc. Bk. 60 B, p. 115). When the foreign and stateless Jews were rounded up by the Germans in the newly occupied French territories, the defendant RITTER received the reports on these actions (Pros. Ex. 1797, NG-4959, Doc. Bk. 62 A, pp. 26-28).

The defendant RITTER also refrained from protesting against the "confiscation" of Jewish property in France (Pros. Ex. 1765, NG-3444, Doc. Bk. 64, p. 89). He knew also about the looting, with Foreign Office participation, of Jewish-owned art in Paris (Pros. Ex. 1766, NG-2970 B, Doc. Bk. 64, p. 91 et seq.).

When on the 18th of December 1941 certain "retaliations" were carried out it was the defendant RITTER who arranged with the defendant Weizsaecker that the German Ambassador in Paris was to take charge of the propaganda measures in connection with the shooting of hostages and other reprisals (Pros. Ex. 1471, NG-117, Doc. Bk. 60 B, p. 156-159).

When 50,000 Jews were called for, for deportation to Auschwitz, the telegram requesting the deportation of these Jews was distributed, among others, to the defendant RITTER for whatever action deemed necessary (Pros. Ex. 1705, NG-1967, Doc. Bk. 60 B, p. 190).

The defendant RITTER took a consenting part in the policy of the

Foreign Office which consisted of making "international Jewry responsible for German reversals", therefore inaugurating criminal actions against the Jewish population of the Occupied Territories cloaked as reprisals (Pros. Ex. 1775, NG-4882, Doc. Bk. 60 B, p. 195).

ITALY

When the German military and police authorities met with sharp Italian resistance to the German requests concerning the solution of the Jewish problem for the whole of Europe, the defendant RITTER informed the Foreign Office of German dissatisfaction with the obstructionist attitude of the Italian army and requested Foreign Office action in the matter (Pros. Ex. 1709, NG-2268, Doc. Bk. 60 B, p. 203).

ROUMANIA

No different from other Foreign Office defendants in this Case No. 11, the defendant RITTER, who was allegedly a friend of the Jews, did not consent to any mercy when such possibilities were raised for discussion. When the Roumanian Marshal Antonescu proposed the emigration of seventy-five to eighty thousand Jews from Roumania to Palestine and Syria, RITTER was informed about it on December 12, 1942 (Pros. Ex. 1784, 1785, NG-3986, NG-2200, pp. 22 and 25, Doc. Bk. 62 B). RITTER did not give any encouragement to this plan. In fact, it would have been easy for him as chief liaison man between the Foreign Office and the OKW to find a good military pretext favoring such action, especially in this winter of 1942/43 where it could be claimed that a large Jewish population might be hostile to the Axis countries, therefore would constitute a liability if kept in Roumania.

253

V. RITTER'S PERSONAL SUPERVISION OF THE EXECUTION
OF THE ANNIHILATION PROGRAM IN HUNGARY

On March 19, 1944 Hungary, partly as a consequence of its recalcitrance
in the Reich's Jewish Program, was robbed of its sovereignty completely.
The Third Reich, under a coordinated program of its diplomatic, military,
SS and civil branches, enthroned its proven activist Edmund Veesenmayer
with plenipotentiary powers in Budapest, Hungary. It was an enormous
and difficult assignment to disenthrone the aged Hungarian Regent, Admiral
Nicholas Horthy, and to place in his stead a young fiery-eyed SS
champion of the Nazi regime; difficult especially in March 1944 when the
Nazi battle fortunes were on the decline not far from the Hungarian
border.

Since diplomatic and military exigencies were involved, it was
deemed advisable by the leaders of Nazi strategy to place the defendant
RITTER, who was anyhow the liaison chief between the Foreign Office and
the military, in supervisory charge of this enterprise. Thus, over and
above the normal control and supervision exercised by the State Secretary
and the Foreign Office, this chapter of the persecution program was
placed under the personal control of the defendant RITTER.

It was the defendant RITTER who himself instructed the defendant
Veesenmayer in all details about the program he had to carry out.
RITTER advised him on March 19, 1944 as to the best procedure for forming
a new Hungarian government. It was also RITTER who advised Veesenmayer
which Hungarian dignitaries should be arrested and which not (Pros. Ex.
C-439, NG-5520, Doc. Bk. 207 A).

When Veesenmayer was installed in office on March 19, 1944, it was
RITTER who informed all Reich authorities including the Army, the Navy,
and the Airforce about the scope of the new Plenipotentiary's functions
(Pros. Ex. C-436, Doc. Bk. 27A). A Foreign Office memorandum of March
19, 1944 (Pros. Ex. C-437, NG-5525) shows on the second page that the
defendant RITTER made the decision as to how far the Roumanian, Croatian,
and Slovakian governments should be instructed on the various aspects
of the Hungarian undertaking.

One month later on April 16, 1944, RITTER gave Veesenmayer additional instructions about the policy which the new Hungarian government should follow as regards Slovakia (Pros. Ex. 442, Doc. Bk. 207 A).

About June 7, 1944 the defendant RITTER had a conference with General Keitel regarding the Hungarian situation. As a result of this conference RITTER had to coordinate important political and military measures in Hungary. RITTER himself set up the agreement about the measures which had to be coordinated, informed the defendant Steengracht, and instructed the defendant Veesenmayer accordingly (Pros. Ex. C-444, NG-5519, Doc. Bk. 207 A). This shows RITTER's continued activities in the supervision of the Hungarian situation, facts which can not be seriously contested by RITTER's defense claims.

It was RITTER who instructed Veesenmayer in March 1944 to send all reports about the Hungarian situation through his (RITTER's) hands to the Foreign Minister Ribbentrop (Pros. Ex. C-439, NG-5520, Doc. Bk. 207 A), an order which was carried out by Veesenmayer according to instructions.

Neither defense of RITTER nor defense of Veesenmayer have produced any evidence to show that both did not work together or did not cooperate in the fullest harmony throughout the entire year of 1944.

From surveying the evidence, it is clear that Veesenmayer sent inumerable reports from Budapest to RITTER himself, or via RITTER to the Foreign Minister von Ribbentrop and the Foreign Office. It is enough to refer to Prosecution Exhibits 3698 (NG-5582, Doc. Bk. 201, p. 2); Ex. 3713 (NG-5567, Doc. Bk. 201, p. 24); Ex. C-438 (NG-5522, Doc. Bk. 207 A, p. 54 et seq.); Ex. C-440 (NG-5526, Doc. Bk. 207 A, p. 59); Ex. C-441 (NG-5528, Doc. Bk. 207 A, p. 61).

The defendant RITTER was very well acquainted with the career of Veesenmayer, whose work he had to guide and supervise. They both had resided for a long time in the same town in Bavaria. Furthermore, the defendant RITTER knew from previous reports of Veesenmayer about the latter's experiences in various countries in anti-Jewish mopping-up operations.

RITTER knew, for instance, from Veesenmayer's reports from Serbia in September 1941 (Pros. Ex. 1741, NG-3354, Doc. Bk. 68, p. 3 et seq.) that Veesenmayer had been very efficient in removing the Jews from Serbia for final liquidation.

In Hungary in 1944, Veesenmayer's assignment, this time under the direction of the defendant RITTER, was on a larger scale. The number of his "final solution" victims was to be counted not in tens of thousands as in Serbia but this time in hundreds of thousands.

In Chapter IV of this trial brief, we have already discussed Exhibit 1812 (NG-2196, Doc. Bk. 62 A, p. 94) where RITTER gave Veesenmayer final directions for the execution of the anti-Jewish measures. Throughout the entire year 1944, the defendant RITTER received Veesenmayer's progress reports about the deportation and annihilation of the Hungarian Jews.

These reports were either sent to RITTER directly, or through RITTER to the Foreign Office, or RITTER was on the distribution list. Among the many exhibits covering this period, we find secret telegrams dated April 1944, May 1944, June 1944 and October 1944. Some of them should be cited specifically. On the third of April 1944, RITTER was on the distribution list of an urgent telegram sent to the defendant Steengracht (Pros. Ex. 1808, NG-1815, Doc. Bk. 62 A, p. 77; Ex. 1809. NG-2191, Doc. Bk. 62 A, p. 80; Ex. 1810, NG-2060, Doc. Bk. 62 A, p. 82).

On April 16, 1944 the defendant RITTER received specific information regarding the deportation of 150,000 Jews from the Carpathian area of Hungary and of a plan of further arrests for the deportation of approximately 300,000 Jews in that area (Ex. 1811, NG-2233, Doc. Bk. 62 A, p. 89).

On May 2, 1944 the defendant RITTER received information by a top secret telegram from the defendant Veesenmayer that 100 Jews should be killed for each Hungarian who had died in an allied air raid on Hungary (Pros. Ex. 1814, NG-2061, Doc. Bk. 62 A, p. 112). On the 4th of May 1944 the defendant RITTER and other officials of the Foreign Office were informed that 200,000 Jews in the Hungarian province of Transylvania had been arrested and that the arrest of several hundred thousand more Jews was being planned (Pros. Ex. 1815, NG-2262, Doc. Bk. 62 A, pp. 118-119). On the 31st of May 1944 RITTER learned from Veesenmayer that

256

204,312 Jews had already been deported and that two million pengoes were confiscated from the Jews (Pros. Ex. C-443, NG-5624, Doc. Bk. 207 A).

On June 5, 1944 the report of the Foreign Office official Thadden, who had visited Budapest on a duty trip for expediting the annihilation gave a detailed report on all criminal aspects of the German anti-Jewish program in Hungary, was submitted to the defendant RITTER (Pros. Ex. 1818, NG-2190, Doc. Bk. 62 A, p. 134). On June 8, 1944 RITTER learned from Veesenmayer that the deportation of the Jews in certain areas had been completed and that 289,357 Jews had been sent to the camps (Pros. Ex. C-445, NG-5620, Doc. Bk. 207A). On June 17, 1944 RITTER learned from Veesenmayer through a telegram directed to him personally, that 326,009 Jews had already been deported from Hungary (Pros. Ex. 3713, NG-5567, Doc. Bk. 201, p. 24) Pros. Ex. C-447, NG-5618, Doc. Bk. 207A).

On the 19th of October 1944 the defendant RITTER was again informed of a report by Veesenmayer which described the anti-Jewish policy in Hungary up to that date (Pros. Ex. 1828, NG-3157, Doc. Bk. 62 A, p. 179). During all these months the defendant RITTER, controller and supervisor, of the liquidation of the Hungarian Jews did not see any reason to object or offer demur to the excellent liquidation work Veesenmayer was doing. He was in complete concurrence with each step of the Reich Plenipotentiary in Hungary. He took care of coordinating matters between Keitel of the OKW and Veesenmayer (Pros. Ex. C-444, NG-5519, Doc. Bk. 207 A). He took care, as his own letter of August 16, 1944 shows, of the coordination of the work of the Reichsfuehrer-SS Himmler and Veesenmayer (Pros. Ex. C-450, NG-5592, Doc. Bk. 207A).

On July 7, 1944 the defendant RITTER learned from Veesenmayer that the American and British Ministers in Berne, Switzerland, had already learned that one and a half million Jews had already been liquidated and that the remaining, not as yet deported, Hungarian Jews would face the same fate. Through this cable he learned also that the Holy Father in Rome and the King of Sweden, the governments of Switzerland, prominent persons from Spain and Turkey had lodged protests in Budapest about these mass exterminations. RITTER was not moved to take any step to support such protests, despite the fact that the last-minute rescue of

-13-

Jews even performed sometimes by the SS would have redounded to Germany's credit in the future. But it seems that RITTER was of the same opinion as the Hungarian Prime Minister Stojay, expressed in Prosecution Exhibit C-449, NG-5523, Doc. Bk. 207 A. Stojay had declared that he did not feel himself threatened by the warning of the Allies that the persons responsible for these mass murders would later be called to an accounting for these deeds. He said:

> "In the event of a German victory such a warning would be of no interest. ... In the event of defeat one's life would be at an end anyway."

That this view coincided with RITTER's can be seen from the following:

In May 1944 the defendant Veesenmayer informed the defendant RITTER that the Hungarian Count Bethlen had openly stated that he as a local Hungarian official did not want to participate in the deportation of Jews and would rather resign than to become a mass murderer. About this report which was directed to the defendant RITTER, RITTER answered in cross-examination,

258

> "It shows that I read the telegram, but I do not know that any more today."

                         xxxxxx

> "Did you ever have an idea similar to Bethlen that you would rather resign than have to deal with such affairs in any form?

> A. I never had an idea that I was participating in this in any manner." (Trial Tr. p. 12468)

VI. CONCLUSION

RITTER, during his direct and cross-examination staggered up his defense as follows:

In his first line of defense he denied boldly that he had had anything to do with the murder of millions of Jews. But—realizing that it has been established through many documents that this line of defense is a complete deviation from the truth—he resorted to a second line of defense. This time he advanced the argument that he was "only" a liaison man who had no executive power. The documents cited above show very clearly that it was RITTER himself who supervised and controlled the annihilation of Hungarian Jewry. It does not matter whether he did this in his high rank as Ambassador for Special Assignments who—as RITTER himself stated (Tr. 12447)—had the rank of a State Secretary, or as a chief liaison man between the Foreign Office and the OKW, or in any other capacity. Murder remains murder whether performed officially or privately, during daytime or nighttime; and it remains murder also even when the murderer suggests that the victim would have been murdered anyhow by another murder gang or would die one day anyhow.

RITTER's participation in the liquidation of hundreds of thousands of Jews is established beyond a reasonable doubt through incontestable documents. RITTER is guilty of War Crimes and Crimes against Humanity as charged under Count V of the Indictment.

259